Irish Government Today

Sean Dooney and John O'Toole

6

Gill and Macmillan

...an Ltd
Goldenbridge
Dublin 8
with associated companies in
Auckland, Budapest, Gaborone, Harare, Hong Kong,
Kampala, Kuala Lumpur, Lagos, London, Madras,
Manzini, Melbourne, Mexico City, Nairobi,
New York, Singapore, Sydney, Tokyo, Windhoek
© Sean Dooney and John O'Toole 1992
Index compiled by Helen Litton
0 7171 1703 0
Print origination by
Seton Music Graphics Ltd, Bantry, Co. Cork
Printed by Colour Books Ltd, Dublin

A catalogue record is available for this book
from the British Library.

Contents

Preface

To put it succinctly, the task of the government is to run the country. The public service plays a central role alongside ministers in that task. This book provides comprehensive information, prepared by writers who know the system intimately from within, on the institutions of government, the central departments, the local authorities, state-sponsored bodies and health boards.

It describes the operation of government in practice and includes a great deal of information not hitherto published about cabinet procedures, the appointment and responsibilities of ministers, private offices, political advisers, the election and work of TDs, the whips' offices, the work of the Dáil and the changes on the way, what civil servants do, etc. . . . It outlines the provisions of the Constitution and discusses the functions of the President.

It goes on to describe the informal and formal means by which people may seek, and get, redress from the actions of public bodies, including valuable insights into the 'representations' system and the use of parliamentary questions. It discusses the ways in which the work of government and the public service has been influenced by membership of the EC and concludes by exploring a number of current issues including management practices and techniques as well as public service reform.

The book is aimed primarily at first- and second-year students in a number of faculties, particularly those studying politics, public administration and management, law, commerce, social science, journalism, marketing and business studies. It will, of course, be of interest, and useful also, to a wide variety of other readers, such as public servants and those considering a career in the public service; to trade union officials, politicians, journalists and other commentators on public affairs; to persons in agriculture, business and the professions who have dealings with the civil and public service; and to those working in international organisations who want reliable and up-to-date information on government in Ireland.

Irish Government Today is written by two experienced practitioners who draw widely on their knowledge of how the system actually works and on their experience as part-time lecturers on the degree courses at the Institute of Public Administration. Arising from the conventions relating to civil servants writing about government, it is considered appropriate to indicate that chapters 1, 2, 6, 7, 8 and 10 were written by Seán Dooney and chapters 4, 5, 9, 11 and 12 by John O'Toole. Chapter 3 was written jointly.

The views expressed by John O'Toole are personal and do not reflect the views of any organisation.

Because of the overriding constraints on size and price, the authors are aware that the book is not totally comprehensive and cannot provide all the answers to questions on the various subjects in the table of contents.

To avoid the continual use of awkward constructions such as 'his/her' or 'her/his' the words 'he', 'his' and 'him' are used throughout the book for both sexes whenever the sex of the person in question is of no consequence for the discussion.

Acknowledgments

The authors gratefully acknowledge the immense amount of encouragement, advice and information they got from many of their colleagues in the public service who, in accord with the best traditions of the service, wish to remain anonymous. Mary Prendergast, Librarian in the Institute of Public Administration, and her deputy, Renuka Page, were, as always, patient and pleasant in providing books, articles and references, often at short notice and at busy times. In particular, the authors want to express their thanks to the editor, Colm Croker, but for whose skill the book could not have been published.

Above all, we appreciate the tolerance and support of Clodagh and Patricia, who so agreeably accorded 'the book' the priority which we thought it warranted.

Sean Dooney
John O'Toole
January 1992

The Government and the Taoiseach

THE GOVERNMENT: STRUCTURE AND SCOPE

The Constitution provides that all power comes from the people, whose right it is to designate the rulers of the state; that the state is to be governed in accordance with the provisions of the Constitution; that the executive power of the state is exercised by or on the authority of the government; and that the government is responsible to the Dáil. The government consists of not less than seven and not more than fifteen members. It is frequently referred to as the cabinet, though this term does not appear in the Constitution. The members are selected by the Taoiseach (or in the case of a coalition by agreement between the leaders of the parties involved in government) and appointed by the President. No specific qualifications, beyond membership of the Oireachtas, are prescribed for membership of the government, but it is generally accepted that in the selection of ministers considerations of general ability, suitability for particular portfolios, personal popularity, service to or standing in the party and geographical location are matters taken into account. The Taoiseach may request a minister to resign, and if he refuses to do so, the President on the advice of the Taoiseach must terminate his appointment.

The government meets and acts as a collective authority and is collectively responsible for the departments of state. The Constitution contains no specification regarding the number of departments (this depends largely on the preferences of individual Taoisigh), and if there are more than fifteen at any time, individual ministers are assigned responsibility for more than one department. The Taoiseach and the Tánaiste, as well as the Minister for Finance, must be members of the Dáil; the other members of the government must be members of the Dáil or the Seanad, but not more than two may be members of the latter body. (Since the foundation of the state there have, in fact, been only three appointments of senators: Joseph Connolly in 1928, Seán Moylan in 1957 and James Dooge in 1981). Every member of the government has the right to attend and be heard in each House of the

Oireachtas. On the dissolution of the Dáil, ministers continue to carry on their duties and hold office until their successors are appointed.

In addition to the general provision in the Constitution that the government is the chief executive organ of the state, the Constitution also contains express provisions relating to the powers, duties and functions of the government in certain particular matters. For example, in relation to the public finances, presentation of the estimates to the Dáil by the Minister for Finance follows detailed consultation with his colleagues, and it is the government itself which has the final control over the form and amounts of the estimates, as well as the responsibility for them. The Dáil may not authorise the spending of money for any purpose unless such spending has first been authorised by the government and recommended to the Dáil by the Taoiseach.

The distribution of business between the government departments and the designation of members of the government to be the ministers in charge of particular departments are matters governed by law. The law is contained in the various Ministers and Secretaries Acts, the earliest of which was passed in 1924 and the most recent in 1983. The 1924 act designated the eleven departments then set up and indicated the work allocated to each. It provided that the minister in charge of each department would be a *corporation sole*, i.e. that in essence the minister would be the department and that the acts of the department would be the acts of its minister for which he would be responsible to the Dáil. That provision still obtains; its effect on the work of the civil service is described in Chapter 6. Subsequent acts provide for the setting up of new departments and for outlining their work.

THE WORK OF THE GOVERNMENT

In addition to the Ministers and Secretaries Acts there are various other acts which confer functions and powers on the government. For example, the government appoints the Civil Service and the Local Appointments Commissioners, the chairmen of some state-sponsored bodies, senior officers of the Garda Síochána and the Provost of Trinity College, Dublin; and it decides on applications by barristers to become members of the inner bar and to be designated senior counsel. As the chief executive organ of the state the government has, in addition, a considerable amount of work to do besides that which is specifically conferred on it by either the Constitution or by statute. This work is varied, including such diverse duties as considering applications for increases in air fares, allocating emergency aid to groups affected by natural disaster, appointing army officers, approving cultural agreements with countries abroad, refurbishing government buildings, and considering visits to Ireland by foreign heads of state.

A major task, which impinges on every citizen, is the consideration of the advice and recommendations of the officials in the Department of Finance and the Office of the Revenue Commissioners relating to the total tax revenue for the year ahead. Within this total, the government decides on the changes to be made in the rates and scope of individual taxes, including increases or decreases, and also on the introduction of new taxes or the abolition of existing ones.

Factors which the government takes into account include the estimated expenditure on what are called goods and services for the year ahead, the level of Exchequer borrowing and the desirability of reducing this, the estimates of tax revenue based on existing rates, the effects on the economy and the individual sectors thereof of increasing or decreasing individual rates, the need for equity between the various groups in the community, EC requirements in regard to reduction in rates of value added tax and of excise duties, and political commitments made by the parties in government before an election or as part of a post-election government programme in regard to taxation matters. Such matters are considered by the government over a number of meetings, and the final decisions are announced by the Minister for Finance in his budget speech.

The government is the centre of the administrative system in Ireland. In a sense it is the board of directors who formulate policies, promote legislation and direct the operations of the various departments of state. Farrell (1988:42) describes the cabinet as a 'closed group . . . bound together by shared experience . . . indisputably in charge of the executive organs of the state and usually able to push through its own legislative programme'.

The role of government was elaborated by the Public Services Organisation Review Group in its report published in 1969 (the Devlin Report):

> In addition to the basic functions of defence of the nation against outside aggression and maintenance of law and order, the role of government now embraces the provision of adequate health, education and welfare services. It also embraces the provision of environmental services and assistance of cultural activities. Government must exercise some regulatory function in regard to individual enterprise and ensure that the rights of the individual are exercised with due regard to the general good. It encourages economic activity in the private sector, and there are certain activities which it has undertaken itself.
>
> The government has two main tasks. First, it has to run the country, under the Constitution in accordance with the rules laid down by the Oireachtas and with the resources granted by, and accounted for to, the Oireachtas each year. Secondly, it deals in the Oireachtas with changes affecting the community . . . Through its legislative programme (including financial measures) the government exercises its main influence over the future development of the country; thereby it influences the economy and the structure of society. Acting collectively,

the ministers decide what is needed and how it should be achieved; their decisions depend on the quality of the information available to them and on their assessment of the requirements. They will, of course, become aware of these requirements in several ways—through their political machine, through the press and through the representations of the interests concerned—but, primarily, they will need to know the emerging needs of the community through the public service which operates existing programmes.

Legislation

Proposals by ministers which call for new or amending legislation must always be submitted to the government. If approval is given, the papers are sent to the Attorney General's office to have a bill drafted by the parliamentary draftsman. The bill is submitted (at this stage it is known as a 'white print') to the government to approve of the text and to authorise the minister concerned to present it to the Dáil (or Seanad) and have it circulated to members.

Before the government brings forward any legislation it may publish a green paper (a document setting out its proposals and inviting suggestions thereon) or a white paper (a statement of decisions taken). Any such papers are prepared in the promoting department.

Bills (other than those dealing with budgetary matters or estimates) are usually, when published, accompanied by an explanatory statement outlining the existing law and how the new bill proposes to change it.

Other Business

The government agenda also includes matters which ministers consider it advisable to bring to their colleagues' notice. The Minister for Foreign Affairs, for example, will communicate information on political developments abroad and their consequences; or the Minister for Justice on criminal matters. Among the many items regularly laid before the government for scrutiny are the annual reports and accounts of state sponsored bodies before their presentation to the Oireachtas.

Farrell (1988:76) comments that 'The available evidence . . . suggests a considerable degree of overload in the Irish cabinet system. The complex, the controversial and the insoluble compete with the current, the commonplace and the critical for scarce time and attention on the government agenda. The internal problems of Northern Ireland, the latest transport strike, the painful disciplines of controlling public expenditure, the dismissal of a postman, the effects of technical developments in the EC policies, the appointment of a Supreme Court judge, the timing of a by-election, the detailed discussion of major legislation and a myriad of other things crowd out considerations of longer-term strategic planning.'

There are also what are loosely termed 'twelve o'clock' or informal items. The origin of the phrase derives from an arrangement whereby the government sets aside time for consideration of matters not on the formal agenda which a minister wishes to raise informally and which may be dealt with quickly, for example any matters of current topical interest. Ministers also use this procedure to consult their colleagues informally as to the attitude they should take in relation to matters which come to them for decision on a day-to-day basis in the management of their departments but which might not be regarded as suitable for submission to government in the normal manner. Ministers may also wish to signal in advance problems which have arisen in their respective areas and in relation to which they may be submitting formal proposals at a later date. Matters thus mentioned might include strikes or pay disputes, petrol prices, proposals for visits abroad on St Patrick's Day, meetings with deputations, or the attitude to be taken on a private member's bill. Business initiated in this way is rarely the subject of formal government decision, but any informal decisions are conveyed by the government secretariat to the relevant ministerial offices, usually by telephone.

Government Meetings

The government normally meets twice a week, on Tuesday and Thursday, for about two and a half hours in Government Buildings, Upper Merrion Street, Dublin. Attendance is confined to the members of the government, the Government Chief Whip (see below), the Attorney General and the Secretary to the Government. On occasion, however, other persons such as ministers of state or civil servants may be called in to assist in the discussion of specific matters. There is no quorum for meetings. The government secretariat co-ordinates all the proposed business and prepares the agenda for each meeting. While meetings are in progress ministers and officials can avail of a fully equipped communication room which provides facilities for obtaining any up-to-date or additional information which they may need.

Because of the volume of business with which the government has to deal, the agenda for its meetings is always heavy. Sometimes there may be up to thirty items for consideration. In the light of this and to enable the members of the government to assimilate material quickly and thoroughly, a detailed procedure is laid down for the submission by departments of issues for decision. This procedure is set out in a booklet entitled *Government Procedure Instructions*, prepared in the Department of the Taoiseach.

Every item of business must be the subject of a memorandum from the minister concerned. Its format is rigidly prescribed. The first paragraph should outline what is being requested of the government. This may be the authority to initiate legislation, or to establish, modify or abolish some programme, or perhaps to bring forward for consideration an entirely new policy option; it may be to note developments in some area of national importance, or to make a statutory instrument. Then comes the background information, and, in cases requiring substantive action, an account of the problem, the solution being put forward, and the arguments for and against. The costs and staffing implications are then indicated, as well as the views of other ministers concerned, together with any counterviews of the promoting minister. The rule is that memoranda should be as brief as possible and not discursive, and that detailed material be supplied in appendices. The aim is that, ordinarily, memoranda should not exceed ten pages, and, where they do, they should be accompanied by a brief self-contained summary of the proposals, with the arguments for and against.

Thirty copies of each memorandum are sent by the private secretary of the promoting minister to the Secretary to the Government. These must reach the latter not less than three days before the meeting at which they are to be considered. At the same time, a copy is sent to the offices of the ministers consulted during the drafting.

On occasion, a minister may wish to have a matter considered at a particular government meeting but it may not be possible to have the memorandum finalised in time to meet the specified deadline. In such circumstances a certificate of urgency is signed by a senior official stating why the matter is urgent and why the memorandum could not be ready by the prescribed time. The reasons must be good if they are to result in such an item being accepted, ultimately by the Taoiseach, as urgent. If a minister is unable to attend a government meeting, his private secretary is obliged to inform the government secretariat as soon as possible and to state whether any other minister is to be briefed to deal with any item on the agenda which is of relevance to the absent minister's department.

Where there is disagreement on the merits of a proposal, the minister concerned is asked to consider its modification. Where ministers disagree, the matter may be referred to a sub-committee of the government to resolve. If disagreement persists, it may be necessary to have a decision reached by vote. No record of any such vote is kept other than its outcome. Cabinet proceedings are strictly confidential, and the principle of collective responsibility applies to decisions taken.

Immediately after meetings the Secretary to the Government transmits the decisions relating to particular departments to the private secretaries of the ministers concerned so that they may be acted on departmentally. It is the responsibility of individual ministers to ensure that such decisions are implemented at the earliest practicable date. In this connection, the government secretariat prepares at regular intervals a schedule of outstanding decisions, indicating the current position in each case. This schedule enables the Taoiseach to monitor progress and to raise with his colleagues any major deviations from targets.

As explained above, cabinet minutes record only the decisions taken. In 1976 the then Taoiseach, Mr Liam Cosgrave, instituted a policy of releasing, for inspection by the public, cabinet minutes and supporting records which were more than thirty years old. With the passing of the Archives Act, 1985, there is now a statutory obligation to make such minutes available for public inspection in the National Archives, the new body which has replaced the State Paper Office and Public Record Office. (A copy of the minutes of the meeting held on 9 December 1960 is reproduced in Appendix A.)

Incorporeal Meetings

Apart from the formal meetings, there are, on occasion, what are termed incorporeal meetings. These meetings relate to the conduct of unforeseen business which is so urgent as to require a decision before the next ordinary government meeting. It is business of a type that does not require substantive discussion and is extremely unlikely to provoke disagreement. An incorporeal meeting could be held, for example, if it were necessary to clear some routine report with a publication deadline, or if it were necessary to approve the urgent departure from the country of the President to attend, say, a funeral abroad.

The procedure in such cases is that the minister concerned prepares a brief note on the matter at issue which is circulated by the government secretariat to all ministers available, together with a notification that an incorporeal meeting will be held to discuss the matter at a specified time. In practice what then happens is that the Secretary to the Government telephones all the ministers available at that time to get their agreement to what is proposed. The meeting is formally recorded as having taken place under the chairmanship of the Taoiseach, Tánaiste or most senior government member available.

COLLECTIVE RESPONSIBILITY

Collective cabinet responsibility is a fundamental principle underlying the operation of Irish government. It results in all ministers being obliged to support government actions and policies publicly regardless of their personal opinions or private feelings. Thus the cabinet is collectively responsible for public policy, and the policy programmes of individual ministers must complement it. Once a cabinet decision is taken, it reflects the decision of all the ministers, and a minister who is fundamentally opposed to the decision should, in theory, resign.

In practice, however, a minister will, on occasion, be fundamentally opposed but may not wish to make his opposition public. Nevertheless, if he is unable to accept a decision or wishes to distance himself in public from a decision or feels he must explain his point of view in public, then the question of resignation must be seriously considered. Occasions have arisen when ministers have expressed fundamental opposition in public and have not resigned. Mr James Gibbons, Minister for Agriculture, made public his opposition to the Family Planning Bill, 1979, but did not resign. Nor did the then Taoiseach, Mr Liam Cosgrave, or his Minister for Education, Mr Richard Burke, resign after voting against the Control of Importation, Sale and Manufacture of Contraceptives Bill 1974, introduced in the Dáil by the Minister for Justice in the cabinet of which they were all members. On the other hand, Mr Frank Cluskey, Minister for Trade, Commerce and Tourism did resign in December 1983 when he found himself opposed to government proposals in regard to the Dublin Gas Company. Considerable efforts are made to achieve consensus. Mr Seán Lemass, a former Taoiseach, said it is 'the job of the Taoiseach to keep a team of ministers who are all individuals with their own personal characteristics working in harmony and ultimately emerging with agreement upon every matter put before them'. (Interview in the *Irish Press*, 3–4 Feb. 1960)

The Review Body on Higher Remuneration in the Public Sector (1972), in its consideration of the role and functions of various office holders, including the Taoiseach and other members of the government, commented:

> We regard as of paramount importance the collective responsibility of ministers, as members of the government, for the business of the government, i.e. the formulation of national policy and its execution subject to the approval of the Oireachtas. No greater or more complex task and no more important task for the well-being of the people faces any other body or group in the country.

MINISTERS' OBLIGATIONS

Should an occasion arise where a minister or his family has an interest in a matter before the government for decision, there is an obligation on him to bring this to notice before the matter comes up for discussion. Unless the government decides otherwise, the minister concerned may not take part in the discussion or vote on the issue, or seek to influence the attitude of his colleagues.

In so far as business interests or membership of other organisations is concerned, the basic rule is that a minister should not engage in any activity that could reasonably be regarded as interfering or being incompatible with the proper discharge of the duties of his office.

Ministers may not hold company directorships carrying remuneration. Even if remuneration is not paid, it is regarded as undesirable that a minister should hold a directorship. A resigning director may, however, enter an agreement with a company under which the company would agree his reappointment as director on the termination of public office. Similarly, ministers are not permitted to carry on a professional practice while holding office, but there is no objection to making arrangements for the maintenance of a practice during the period of tenure of office.

It was long regarded as undesirable that ministers should retain membership of subordinate public bodies, such as county councils or health boards, while in government. Nevertheless, this was a practice tolerated by successive governments. The Local Government Act 1991 now provides that ministers and ministers of state are excluded from election to or membership of local authorities.

Members of the government proposing visits or receiving invitations to travel which involve government-to-government contacts or public attendance abroad, as distinct from attendance at meetings of bodies such as the EC or the OECD, are obliged to consult the Minister for Foreign Affairs and the Taoiseach. They must have the approval of the latter before entering into commitments. Ministers who intend to visit Northern Ireland must advise the Minister for Foreign Affairs. In the case of private travel abroad by ministers, it is normal practice that Irish diplomatic missions and the authorities of the countries concerned are advised of the minister's travel plans.

Questions arise from time to time as to the proper attitudes to gifts. This is a subject on which there are no formal guidelines. The convention is for ministers to accept relatively inexpensive gifts to mark occasions such as official openings, and not to accept expensive gifts or, when presented, to return them. Any gift of national significance is regarded as the property of the nation and to be dealt with accordingly, for example by being displayed in a government building. Where doubts arise concerning the rules, guidelines and conventions set out above, the final decision rests with the Taoiseach.

THE TAOISEACH: OFFICE, DUTIES AND POWERS

The Taoiseach is appointed head of the government, or prime minister, by the President on the nomination of the Dáil. He may resign at any time by tendering his resignation to the President. If the Taoiseach resigns the other ministers are deemed to have resigned also.

In addition to being head of the government, and apart from the responsibilities which that role entails, the Taoiseach has, in himself, certain constitutional and statutory powers and duties. He may, in effect, compel any minister to resign for any reason which to him seems sufficient. He nominates the Attorney General for appointment by the President, and the ministers of state for appointment by the government. He appoints eleven members of the Seanad. He also appoints the clerks (chief officers) and clerks assistant of the Dáil and Seanad, as well as the Superintendent and Captain of the Guard in the Houses of the Oireachtas, after consultation with the chairmen of the Houses and the Minister for Finance. The Taoiseach initiates the process for the selection by interview board of candidates for the office of Director of

Public Prosecutions and proposes the candidate selected to the government for appointment. He is required to keep the President informed on matters of domestic and international policy and he is, besides, an *ex officio* member of the Council of State. He presents the bills passed by the Dáil and Seanad to the President for her signature into law. In the event of both Houses passing resolutions for the removal of the Comptroller and Auditor General, or of a judge, it would be the duty of the Taoiseach to notify the President.

On the advice of the Taoiseach, Dáil Eireann is summoned and dissolved by the President, but the President may, at her absolute discretion, refuse a dissolution to a Taoiseach who has ceased to retain the support of a majority in the Dáil. In fact no President has yet refused a dissolution. Thus in Ireland the practice differs from that in several European countries where the head of state frequently calls upon another member of the parliament to form a government in such a situation.

The Taoiseach must resign upon ceasing to retain the support of a majority in the Dáil, unless the President dissolves the Dáil on his advice and he secures the support of a majority in the new Dáil. A unique situation arising from these provisions occurred in 1989. The twenty-sixth Dáil, on convening after the general election in June, failed to elect the (outgoing) Taoiseach, Mr Charles Haughey. Relying on the constitutional provision just cited, the opposition parties pressed the view that the Taoiseach should resign. The Taoiseach did not accept the opposition view, on the basis of advice received by him from the Attorney General, and proposed instead that the Dáil adjourn to enable consultations between the parties with a view to forming a government. He acceded, however, to the political pressure and resigned, with his ministers. They remained in office, in an acting capacity, pending the outcome of the inter-party negotiations, which eventually led to Mr Haughey becoming Taoiseach of a coalition government. These events evoked considerable discussion on the interpretation of the provision in the Constitution.

Leadership: Style and Influence

In relation to the Taoiseach's position as head of the government, he has been described by a former Secretary to the Government as 'captain of the team'.

> In this capacity, he is the central co-ordinating figure, who takes an interest in the work of all departments, the figure to whom ministers naturally turn for advice and guidance when faced with problems involving large questions of policy or otherwise of special difficulty, whose leadership is essential to the successful working of the government as a collective authority, collectively responsible to Dáil Éireann, but acting through members each of whom is charged with specific departmental tasks. He may often have to inform himself in considerable detail of particular matters with which other members of

the government are primarily concerned. He may have to make public statements on such matters, as well as on general matters of broad policy, internal and external. (Ó Muimhneachain 1969).

The Taoiseach presides over all government meetings and has considerable influence in relation to the business transacted. In the first place, the agenda is prepared under his direction. If there are items of business which he wants taken at a particular meeting, this can usually be arranged. Secondly, in his capacity as chairman he can structure the discussion and so determine the manner in which the various items on the agenda, as well as other matters which ministers may wish to raise, are dealt with. Thirdly, and perhaps most importantly, the Taoiseach may put forward a proposal to government himself by way of memorandum or otherwise on any item of major policy. The length of meetings is influenced by the personal style of the Taoiseach; some, like Charles Haughey, prefer a brisk, businesslike pace, while others, like Garret FitzGerald, favour a more discursive approach that extends meetings.

Ultimately the Taoiseach carries the responsibility for the achievement or lack of achievement of the government. It is sometimes said that the office of Taoiseach is what the holder wishes to make of it. His authority has been described as 'a function not merely of the office but of the multiplicity of roles thrust upon him—simultaneously chief executive, government chairman, party leader, national spokesman, principal legislator, electoral, champion and media focus'. (Farrell 1988:44) In formulating public policy on all major issues, the Taoiseach plays a leading part in bringing together various strands of opinion around the cabinet table and in achieving consensus on the lines of major policy to be adopted. The Review Body on Higher Remuneration in the Public Sector has commented on the implications of the Taoiseach's overall authority:

> His is a special responsibility and a particularly onerous one. Apart from his constitutional position and responsibilities . . . he is in growing degree personally identified—and regarded by the public as answerable for—the totality of government policy. He must concern himself with all departments of state, in particular on all major matters. He must co-ordinate the efforts of his colleagues in the development and implementation of national policy. The achievement or lack of achievement of the government is laid primarily at his door.

Chubb (1982: 201) sees the pre-eminence of the Taoiseach among his colleagues as stemming from four facts. First, he is usually the party leader. Second, elections often take the form of gladiatorial contests between two designated party leaders, thus emphasising the personal leadership of the victor, and television and modern campaign practices have increased the propensity to focus on the leader. Third, except in the case of coalition governments, he chooses his colleagues. Fourth, by the nature of his position, he has a special responsibility to take the lead or speak when an authoritative intervention is needed.

The role of the Taoiseach has altered from being first among equals under the 1922 Constitution to one of effective authority under the 1937 Constitution. W. T. Cosgrave, President of the Executive Council from 1922 to 1932, reflecting the older approach, said that it was not open to the head of the government to ask for and to compel the resignation of a minister. (*Dáil Debates*, 14 June 1937, cols 347–8) Under the 1937 Constitution successive Taoisigh have moved ministers from department to department and dismissed them too. The power of the Taoiseach to rid himself of members of his government by requiring their resignation enables him to hold considerable dominance over his ministerial colleagues. Many commentators today speculate on a transition from cabinet to prime ministerial government.

Jack Lynch dismissed Charles Haughey and Neil Blaney in 1970 on the occasion of what was known as the 'arms crisis'. In 1986 the government, on the recommendation of Garret FitzGerald, dismissed four ministers of state, Joseph Bermingam, Donal Creed, Michael Darcy and Edward Collins, the latter for alleged conflict of interest and the others for differences over government policy. In 1990, Mr Haughey dismissed his Tánaiste and Minister for Defence, Brian Lenihan, because of conflicting statements made by Mr Lenihan about the making of telephone calls to the office of the President on the occasion of the defeat of the government on a vote in the Dáil in 1982. In November 1991, Mr Haughey dismissed the Ministers for Finance and for the Environment, Albert Reynolds and Pádraig Flynn, for publicly expressing lack of confidence in him as leader of the Fianna Fáil party.

In sum, it is difficult to define the office of the Taoiseach. It can only be described in terms of the use to which it is put by different individuals of varying personalities who face different problems and deal with different colleagues. A Taoiseach may, to quote Farrell again, see himself as either a chairman or a chief, encouraging, co-ordinating and monitoring the work of other ministers, or alternatively exercising a very positive leadership role and virtually dictating policy for the cabinet as a whole.

DEPARTMENT OF THE TAOISEACH: FUNCTIONS

The Department of the Taoiseach provides the assistance which the Taoiseach as head of the government and as a minister needs. It also provides the services which the government, acting as a collective authority, needs. It has a total staff of about 290 and is headed by a secretary, just as is every other department. The government has a separate secretary. These officials are on the same level. The tasks of the department include;

(1) the organisation, co-ordination, preparation and processing of government business in the Dáil and Seanad;

(2) formulation of policy and overseeing the implementation of settled policy in respect of matters of major national import in which the Taoiseach needs to involve himself from time to time, for example international and Northern Ireland affairs;

(3) the preparation of replies to parliamentary questions addressed to the Taoiseach;

(4) maintenance of liaison with the office of the President;

(5) major state protocol;

(6) the processing of correspondence addressed to the Taoiseach;

(7) government press relations and the government information services;

(8) provision of the secretariat to the government and to government committees;

(9) the administration of specific functions of government discharged from time to time under the aegis of the Taoiseach, for example arts and culture, the work of the Central Statistics Office and of the Local Appointments Commission.

The Department of the Taoiseach has responsibility for the National Economic and Social Council, the European Bureau, the Arts Council, the National Heritage Council, the National Archives, the National Concert Hall, the National Gallery of Ireland, the National Library, the National Museum, and the Royal Hospital, Kilmainham. There are at present two ministers of state at the Department of the Taoiseach: the Government Chief Whip who is also the Minister of State for Heritage Affairs (in charge of the Office of Public Works) and the Minister of State with special responsibility for the Co-ordination of Government Policy and European Community matters.

In recent years the Taoiseach has been increasingly active in the foreign relations of the state, mainly as a result of Ireland's membership of the EC. The focal point in the European context is the European Council which normally meets twice a year. Many of the major issues in the EC now come to this council for discussion, for guidance and for decisions. In between meetings of the European Council the Taoiseach is involved in correspondence and discussions with his counterparts, in discussions and meetings with his own ministers, and in taking decisions. While the Department of Foreign Affairs has overall responsibility for the co-ordination of European Community affairs, and while the Department of the Taoiseach relies heavily on the departments primarily concerned to keep it informed about important and sensitive issues in this and other international areas, each Taoiseach since Ireland's accession has found it desirable to maintain within his own department an advisory unit sensitive to his personal approach and preoccupations.

DEPARTMENT OF THE TAOISEACH AND DÁIL BUSINESS

Government Chief Whip

Every Taoiseach assigns a minister of state to his department to act as Chief Whip of the government party. His task relates essentially to (1) the business which is placed before the Dáil for discussion and determination, and (2) the attendance of deputies from the government side. The Chief Whip maintains close liaison with the whip of any other party in government and also with the whips of the opposition parties.

Before each Dáil session, through circulars addressed to all ministers, the Government Chief Whip finds out what legislation (or other business) their departments expect to place before the Dáil in the coming session and its state of preparation. During Dáil sessions he prepares weekly reports for the Taoiseach on the progress of legislation in the pipeline.

The officials in the Chief Whip's office keep in touch with ministers' private secretaries about business which ministers might wish to have dealt with in the week ahead, for example approval of a supplementary estimate or the introduction of a bill which has become urgent. Arising from these contacts, and having regard to the items which may be already on the order paper (agenda) of the Dáil—there being nearly always a backlog of items awaiting discussion—the Chief Whip prepares an agenda and a timetable for each sitting day of the following week. By convention, this is discussed with the opposition whips each Thursday morning. While the business to be dealt with is primarily a matter for the government, the opposition may on occasion seek to have time allocated by the government to discuss a matter which they consider to be of particular current importance. In such an event the Government Chief Whip will consult the minister responsible; sometimes it may be necessary to consult the Taoiseach or even the government. On these occasions the length of the debate as well as the length of the contributions to be made by the minister responsible, the opposition spokesman and other deputies are normally determined by precedent. The relationship between the whips of all parties is one of friendly trust. No minutes of whips' meetings are kept; a whip's word is his bond.

When agreement has been reached on the business for the week ahead, the Government Chief Whip sends to each deputy on the government side a notice which informs him of the times during which the Dáil will meet in that week, of the business to be transacted, of the times at which the various items will be taken and when voting is most likely to take place. The notice indicates the varying degrees of importance attached to the business and to deputies' attendance. Deputies are advised to be in the house at all times.

This weekly notice is commonly called the whip. If a deputy cannot be present, there is an obligation on him to notify his whip and explain his absence.

On each day when the Dáil is in session the Taoiseach announces the business for the day. Each item on the order paper (already circulated) is numbered, and the Taoiseach's announcement indicates the order of their discussion. Sometimes the order of business is disputed by the opposition parties, for example when it does not provide for discussion of some business considered urgent by them, when it provides for the taking of all stages of a bill on that day, or when no explanation is given as to why items are to be discussed in a particular order.

Deputies wishing to contribute to a debate normally notify their party whip. In general they determine the nature and length of their contributions themselves, that is to say no effort is made to prevent overlapping. This, of course, leads to considerable repetition.

The rule under which government deputies may not be absent save with the permission of the whip is necessary to ensure the carrying of any measure put forward by the government in the event of its being challenged to a vote by the opposition. If a member is unavoidably absent or (in the case of a minister) because of government business elsewhere, the government whip approaches the whip of the main opposition party for a pairing: he requests that in the event of a vote one opposition deputy abstains from voting for each government deputy absent. The practices in this regard are largely governed by convention. Informal arrangements between deputies of opposing parties are frowned upon by the whips on both sides; all pairing arrangements are expected to be made through the whips' offices. Sometimes the relationship becomes strained, as it did in May–June 1990 and in October 1991. These temporary breakdowns in the traditional arrangements led to considerable disruption in the normal business of the Dáil.

Parliamentary Questions to the Taoiseach

In practice, questions to the Taoiseach head the list on the order paper of the Dáil on each Tuesday and Wednesday. More questions are initially addressed to him then he actually answers. Some deputies prefer to address their questions to the Taoiseach if the subject is even remotely relevant to his department; some do so because of the possibility of misunderstanding. In the vast majority of such cases the question is transferred to the appropriate minister. This is a practice which frequently arouses the ire of the opposition, who accuse the Taoiseach of seeking to avoid responsibilities which they regard as proper to him. Examples of questions transferred are those asked about reviewing the electoral system and the appointment of a Minister for Dublin (transferred to the Minister for the Environment), about visits abroad by the President (Foreign Affairs), and about the commercial interests of members of the Oireachtas (Finance). Questions may not be asked about actions taken by the Taoiseach for which he is not responsible to the

Dáil, such as meetings with private individuals or visits to places within the country.

In general, the issues on which the Taoiseach answers questions are those relating directly to government policy and to the activities of his department, such as Northern Ireland, the President, the European Council, the Government Information Services, or the National Economic and Social Council. He also answers questions about statements made by him in the course of speeches outside the Dáil. Questions relating to the other matters for which he has responsibility, such as the Central Statistics Office, arts and culture, the National Archives and the National Heritage Council, are generally answered by one of the ministers of state at his department.

Parliamentary questions are not allowable about the discussions which take place at meetings of the government; nor are questions about government sub-committees, on the grounds that the work of such committees is a direct extension of the work of the government itself.

DEPARTMENT OF THE TAOISEACH: OTHER AREAS OF RESPONSIBILITY

Northern Ireland

The Taoiseach may assign another department to himself in addition to his own (for example, the Department of the Gaeltacht in 1987 and 1989). In addition, successive Taoisigh have reserved to themselves responsibility for Northern Ireland affairs. It is the Taoiseach who makes significant policy statements in this area and who answers parliamentary questions. It is the practice for the Taoiseach and the British Prime Minister to avail themselves of meetings of the European Council to discuss in the margins thereof matters of common concern. Over the past twenty years or so the records show that the two have met on about thirty-five occasions. After each meeting an official statement is issued.

The terms of the Anglo-Irish Agreement, 1985, were drawn up by officials from the Department of the Taoiseach with officials from the British Cabinet Office. The review of the working of the Anglo-Irish Interdepartmental Conference was carried out by these officials also.

However, in so far as Northern Ireland policy affects relations with the British government, such policy is also the concern of the Minister for Foreign Affairs. That minister is the permanent Irish ministerial representative to the Anglo-Irish Conference. The Department of Foreign Affairs has primary responsibility for the day-to-day operation of the Agreement and of Anglo-Irish relations generally.

Liaison with the President

The constitutional requirement that the Taoiseach keep the President informed on domestic and international policy is fulfilled by visits by the Taoiseach to Áras an Uachtaráin, or otherwise as suits both parties. There is regular contact between both offices at senior official level.

Practice in this respect varies: it is reported that Eamon de Valera when Taoiseach briefed the President monthly, while Liam Cosgrave did his briefing at irregular and less frequent intervals.

Apart from the constitutional requirement, there are a number of matters on which consultation between the Department of the Taoiseach and the Office of the President is necessary. These include the arrangements to be made for visits abroad by the President, including the drawing up of programmes and the preparation of speeches; the provision of advice on invitations received by the President to extend her patronage to events or to attend functions; messages to and from other heads of state; and matters relating directly to the work of other departments, including the presentation of credentials by incoming ambassadors, the signing of commissions for officers of the defence forces, and the appointment of judges.

Protocol

On the occasion of visits to Ireland by heads of state, prime ministers or other persons in high office (such as the President of the European Commission) the protocol arrangements are made in consultation with the Department of Foreign Affairs. Major state protocol is the responsibility of the Department of the Taoiseach, for example the ceremonial surrounding the inauguration of the President, the national day of remembrance and state funerals.

Correspondence

As might be expected, a large volume of representations, correspondence and requests for meetings is received by the Taoiseach. Almost all of the correspondence is about issues for which the Taoiseach has no direct responsibility. The procedure generally adopted in dealing with such correspondence is that material for reply thereto is sought from the department concerned, if not already available in the Department of the Taoiseach. The reply itself is signed either by the Taoiseach, by his private secretary or by one of his departmental officials. Alternatively, the correspondence is merely acknowledged and referred to the department responsible for direct reply. Replies to constituents are always signed by the Taoiseach himself.

Requests by individuals or groups for meetings are normally directed to the appropriate minister. In general the Taoiseach personally meets only those groups who are representative of what are loosely termed the social partners (representatives of employers, unions, churches, etc.) in connection with issues of major national policy.

Government Press and Information Services

The Government Information Service (GIS) is headed by the Government Press Secretary, who advises the Taoiseach and ministers on their dealings with the media and briefs political and specialist correspondents on the background to current political issues and government decisions. He does not attend government meetings, but is briefed after each meeting by a minister designated to do so. He normally accompanies the Taoiseach on official visits abroad and, in collaboration with the Irish ambassadorial staff in the country concerned, briefs the media from the Irish point of view.

The GIS supplies news and official documents to press, radio and television and provides them with information and facilities, arranges press conferences for ministers, briefs correspondents on the background to official statements, and interprets public feeling to departments. It advises on the co-ordination of departmental publicity and information and collaborates with the Department of Foreign Affairs in relation to the dissemination of information about Ireland abroad. Government Press Secretaries in recent years have been political appointments and remain in office only for the duration of a government's term of office. The GIS include a number of press officers, permanent civil servants, who deal with general media queries.

REFERENCES

Report of Public Services Organisation Review Group, 1966–69 [Devlin Report] (Dublin: Stationery Office, 1969)

Review Body on Higher Remuneration in the Public Sector (Dublin: Stationery Office, 1972)

Chubb, Basil, *The Government and Politics of Ireland*, 2nd ed. (London: Longman, 1982)

Farrell, Brian, *Chairman or Chief?: The Role of the Taoiseach in Irish Government* (Dublin: Gill & Macmillan, 1971)

Farrell, Brian, 'The Irish Cabinet System' in *Cabinets in Western Europe*, Jean Blondel and Ferdinand Müller Rommel eds. (Macmillan, 1988)

Ó Muimhneacháin, Muiris, *The Functions of the Department of the Taoiseach*, 2nd ed. (Dublin: Institute of Public Administration, 1969)

Appendix A

Meeting of the Cabinet
held in the Council Chamber
Friday, 9th December, 1960–11 a.m. to 12.15 p.m.

Ministers Present:

1.	Taoiseach	Mr Lemass
2.	Tánaiste, Minister for Health and Minister for Social Welfare	Mr MacEntee
3.	Minister for Finance	Dr Ryan
4.	Minister for Justice	Mr Traynor
5.	Minister for Industry and Commerce	Mr Lynch
6.	Minister for Defence	Mr Boland
7.	Minister for Lands	Mr Moran
8.	Minister for Posts and Telegraphs	Mr Hilliard
9.	Minister for Education	Dr Hillery
10.	Minister for the Gaeltacht	Mr Bartley

Ministers Absent:

Minister for External Affairs	Mr Aiken
Minister for Agriculture	Mr Smith
Minister for Transport and Power	Mr Childers
Minister for Local Government	Mr Blaney

Also in Attendance:

Parliamentary Secretary to the Taoiseach	Mr Ó Briain
Attorney General	Mr Ó Caoimh, S.C.
Secretary to the Government	Mr Moynihan

S. 16953
1. AGRICULTURAL CREDIT BILL, 1960.
Following consideration of a memorandum dated the 15th November, 1960, submitted by the Minister for Finance with the general scheme of the Agricultural Credit Bill, 1960, the Minister was authorised
(1) to have the Bill drafted on the lines of the general scheme accompanying the memorandum; and
(2) to move for leave to introduce the Bill in Dáil Éireann.
S. 16950
2. CENTRAL BANK BILL, 1960.
The Minister for Finance was authorised to move for leave to introduce the Central Bank Bill, 1960, in Dáil Éireann.
S. 13721 C
3. ROAD TRAFFIC BILL, 1960
Following consideration of a memorandum dated the 6th December 1960, submitted by the Minister for Local Government, the Minister was authorised to move for leave to introduce the Road Traffic Bill, 1960, in Dáil Éireann.

S. 16927

4. AGREEMENT OF INTERNATIONAL DEVELOPMENT ASSOCIATION, 1960: Signature and acceptance.

Following consideration of a memorandum dated the 8th December, 1960, submitted by the Minister for External Affairs,

(1)   it was decided that the Agreement of the International Development Association, as approved for submission to Government by the Executive Directors of the International Bank for Reconstruction and Development on the 26th January, 1960, should be signed and accepted on behalf of the Government; and

(2)   the Minister was authorised to arrange to have the necessary steps taken to that end.

S. 2850 H

5.   INDUSTRIAL GRANTS ACT, 1959: Approval of application for grant.

Following consideration of a memorandum dated the 8th December, 1960, submitted by the Minister for Industry and Commerce, approval was given for the making by An Foras Tiónscal of a grant of £550,000 towards the establishment at Limerick of a factory for the spinning of cotton yarn and the weaving of cotton grey cloth, entirely for export, on the basis indicated in paragraph 2 of the memorandum.

S. 16802

6.   INNER BAR: Admission.

Following consideration of a memorandum dated the 6th December, 1960, submitted by the Taoiseach, it was decided that a Patent of Precedence, entitling him to admission to the Inner Bar, should be granted to

Sir Paget J. Bourke

in February, 1961.

The meeting adjourned at 12.15 p.m.

(signed) Seán F. Lemass
13.12.'60

Ministers
and their Departments

SELECTION AND APPOINTMENT

Ministers do not attain their positions by accident. A mixture of personal ambition and public service reinforce each other in a TD's desire to be a minister. As membership of the Dáil is increasingly becoming a full-time career, more and more TDs are likely to aspire to ministerial status. To this end a TD must make considerable efforts to be well thought of in his party, in the Dáil, by the media, and above all, by his party leader. As already mentioned, it is the Taoiseach who at his absolute discretion, subject to the provisions of the Constitution, nominates ministers for appointment by the President (except in the circumstances where an inter-party arrangement to form a government has had to be worked out).

No formal selection criteria are prescribed, and Taoisigh do not indicate why they appoint a particular person to be a minister. At the same time, various 'qualifications' may be identified. These include such considerations as seniority, loyalty, popularity and length of service within the party. Ability to perform properly all of the tasks expected of a member of the government is not always seen as an overriding consideration, though occasionally a newly elected deputy of recognised exceptional talents has been appointed a minister on his first day in the Dáil (for example, Alan Dukes in 1981, and previously Noel Browne, Kevin Boland and Martin O'Donoghue).

Whether or not it is desirable that a minister should have detailed expert knowledge of his portfolio is a widely debated question, i.e. whether it is desirable that the Minister for Health should himself be a medical doctor, or the Minister for Education a teacher. On the one hand, there are those who argue that it is entirely logical that this should be the case. On the other hand, many say that the minister has sufficient advisers both within and without his department to provide him with all the expert information he needs. They say that what is required in a minister is that he be reasonably objective and be able to make decisions based on an intelligent appraisal of the advice proferred to him, in the light of his government's policy and of any other relevant political considerations.

On a more personal level, the Taoiseach is likely to take into account a prospective choice's compatibility both with himself as leader and with the rest of his ministerial team. On the other hand, he may possibly consider the inclusion in his cabinet of someone who might provide a focus for party disaffection if left on the back benches. This was said to be the case when Liam Cosgrave appointed Garret FitzGerald to Foreign Affairs in 1973, and when Jack Lynch appointed Charles Haughey to Health in 1977; also when Mr Haughey appointed Desmond O'Malley to Industry and Commerce in March 1982, and when Dr FitzGerald appointed Austin Deasy to Agriculture in December 1982.

Although constitutionally the selection of his ministers is a matter for the Taoiseach himself, there can be little doubt that he discusses the subject with his closest advisers in the party. Not in doubt either is that he informs those selected before he makes his formal announcement in the Dáil on his return from Áras an Uachtaráin following his own appointment by the President. At that stage he also announces the assignment of departments. A debate on the nominations for membership of the government follows, to which normally only the main spokespersons of the political parties contribute. When the Dáil approves of the names it adjourns for a few hours to enable the new ministers also to go to Áras an Uachtaráin and receive their seals of office from the President.

DISPOSITION OF PORTFOLIOS; INTERDEPARTMENTAL RELATIONS

The Taoiseach decides what the departmental structure of the government is going to be and assigns ministers to particular departments. The order in which ministers' names are presented to the Dáil for its approval is determined by the Taoiseach and becomes the order of precedence. Although the hierarchical principle has no basis in the Constitution, it is generally perceived by the electorate that some departments are of more importance than others. Some reasons for the perception would be the size of the department and its budget, its accepted importance in the life of the nation, its day-to-day impact on the ordinary citizen. It is obvious that the ministers in charge of the Departments of Finance, Foreign Affairs and Industry and Commerce have a higher political and public profile than, say, the Ministers for Defence or the Marine.

If a minister is absent or indisposed for a period of time, or is ill, his ministerial responsibilities are usually assigned to another minister, or indeed to the Taoiseach, during his absence. (The Finance and Justice portfolios are those generally assigned to the Taoiseach).

In recent years there have been several changes in the titles and in the functions assigned to the various departments. Changes of personnel, i.e. cabinet reshuffles, are rare, but do occasionally occur. Such changes may be made in order to improve the technical or administrative efficiency of a government, to signal a new priority or to change an existing priority, to give the impression of dynamism and reform or to alter the balance of power within a government.

Every minister, in addition to being a minister responsible to the Dáil, has two commitments. The first is as an individual heading a department; and the second is as a member of the government collectively responsible for what other ministers do. Because of the second of these, there is a need to resolve conflicts between individual ministers to the satisfaction of ministers collectively. Issues where individual departments and ministers do not see eye-to-eye arise all the time as the programmes of individual departments get entangled with one another. For example, in the international negotiations on the General Agreement on Tariffs and Trade, the Departments of Foreign Affairs, Agriculture and Food, and Industry and Commerce may not always adopt the same line (the latter two departments tend to see a continuing need to protect the interests of farming and industry, while the Department of Foreign Affairs is liable to take a broader view and see particular issues as part of global problems). Differences arise frequently between the Department of Finance and other departments in regard to various financial matters; for example, a dispute between the Department of Finance and the Department of Industry and Commerce in regard to the sale of Irish Steel Ltd was widely reported in the press in February and March 1990. There is no fixed procedure for dealing with such issues other than a spirit of give and take between officials in the first place and between ministers eventually. The ultimate arbiter is, of course, the government. However, the Taoiseach and ministers themselves do not take kindly to government business being clogged with issues that could (and should) be settled between the departments involved.

TAKING UP OFFICE

The new minister, having assembled with his colleagues in the cabinet room on his first full day in office, meets the secretary of his department and proceeds with him to the office in the department vacated by his predecessor. All documentary material has been removed from that office—emphasising that the new incumbent is starting from scratch. One of the minister's first tasks is, therefore, to discuss with the secretary the question of the staffing of his private office, who his private secretary is to be, and how many support staff he needs. The private secretary is generally in the grade of higher executive officer. This is the highest grade which ministers are, under Department of Finance regulations, permitted to have; only the Taoiseach may have a higher grade. His private secretary is an assistant principal. It is not unusual for a new minister to appoint the private secretary of his predecessor, thus displaying his confidence in the apolitical nature of the civil service. More often, however, he appoints a new officer to the post, and in such cases he is guided by the secretary in conjunction with the personnel section of the department. That section provides the names of four or five persons whom it considers suitable for the post, and those are normally interviewed by the minister before he makes his selection. The other staff assigned are usually those who have worked in the private office up to the date on which the previous minister left office.

On his first day in the office the new minister normally meets his senior officers—the assistant secretaries and the technical officers of equivalent rank, and perhaps principals and others as well. At this meeting the minister may outline his plans, priorities and aspirations for his period in office and seek the co-operation of all present in advancing these.

He then turns to his incoming correspondence, much of it from various pressure and interest groups seeking early meetings. His acknowledgments generally plead for time to familiarise himself with his portfolio and promise action as soon as possible.

In his early days in office the minister spends much of his time with the secretary of his department, upon whom he realises he must depend greatly. He seeks briefing on the major issues facing the department and on the time-scale for action on these. He will discuss, in particular, the matters relating to his department which were highlighted in the government's pre-election programme and will seek to implement them as a matter of priority. He seeks information on the various groups with which the department deals (Dooney (1989) describes 37 bodies which play a substantial part in the work of the Department of Agriculture and Food and lists 138 others which play a lesser part). He learns of the sensitive areas of the work and, in particular, of those where he may find himself engaged in public controversy. He finds out what legislation is pending and the background to this, as well as the attitude of the opposition parties and outside individuals or groups who are concerned. He inquires about the progress of any state-sponsored bodies under his aegis, the relationships between his department and them, and the appointments to the boards thereof which fall to be made during his period of office. He learns of the meetings abroad which he will have to attend, whether of the EC or of other international bodies or for the promotion of his department's work otherwise. He asks what money is available to carry out his plans. Above all, he is advised of any impending crisis and how best this might be dealt with.

INTERNAL DEPARTMENT WORK

A minister's route to office is always more political than administrative. He is not some kind of superior civil servant. In nearly all cases the responsibility which a minister assumes on taking office is one he is facing for the first time. The organisation and management of ministers' departments is an aspect of their work for which they have not been trained and for which they may have little experience. As it is one in which the officials have long experience, ministers are generally happy to leave the day-to-day running of the department to the secretary. As a general rule, ministers do not see their job as motivating their officials, improving the organisation of the department, or monitoring the performance of routine tasks. 'The skills needed to compete with other egoists in a parliamentary party are not the same as those required to provide executive leadership in a large bureaucratic organisation.' (Rose 1987:81) For his part, the secretary is happy to accept the responsibility, since not alone is he familiar with the ethos of the department and its needs, but he also knows the staff and their needs and is thus in a position to prevent any of the upheavals which might otherwise arise on changes of minister.

There is, however, one function where the minister must personally approve. That is the promotion of staff. As indicated in Chapter 6, the minister is the employer of all of the staff in his department; it follows that he is responsible for their promotion. In practice, however, ministers do not interfere in the actual promotion arrangements made by the Department of Finance for intra- or inter-departmental promotions but accept the recommendations in this respect submitted for their approval by the secretary. Nor, by convention, do ministers intervene in staff matters, unless they are absolutely forced to do so. They see no profit for themselves in interfering and are thus very willing for such matters to be dealt with by the personnel unit and the secretary.

The main task of a minister is to ensure that his department advances the national interest and, in particular, the interest of that sector of the community or of national life for which it was established. Success in this calls for the correct policies and for the effective implementation of these. Policies are in the main outlined in the pre-election programme. If the minister has ideas for a new policy, he simply sets out in broad terms what his wishes are and then leaves it to his officials to indicate what might be done. A former economic adviser to the British government noted that the tasks of the civil servant properly include 'beating the woolly vague impractical ideas that exist on any issue into some set of workable alternatives. Only then can a minister make any real choice.' (Opie 1968: 73)

Ministers and Civil Servants

During the course of their collaboration care is taken by both the minister and the departmental secretary to avoid any issues of a purely party political nature. In particular, neither touches on, even by inference, the personality or performance of the previous minister. For his part, the secretary maintains the traditional attitude of the civil service: that it is there to serve successive ministers with equal commitment and loyalty. Equally, the minister is conscious of the unwritten rules of the political club to which he belongs, one of which is that members do not criticise each other in front of officials. The official who might seek to ingratiate himself with his minister by passing a critical comment on the minister's predecessor can be assured of an icy response or none at all.

At the same time, neither minister nor civil servants allow themselves to forget the obligation of officials to involve themselves in, and be committed to, the policies and political preferences of the government of the day. Civil servants' tasks include support for ministers in promoting the interests of the government against those of the opposition. For example, in writing ministers' speeches for the Dáil, in preparing replies and accompanying notes for parliamentary questions and in assembling briefs for other occasions, civil servants present their minister's case in the best light possible without reference to the positive aspects of the opposition case. At all times the aim is not so much to denigrate the opposition as to enable the minister's light to shine as brightly as possible. This applies equally when the opposition is the former minister. Thus, in addition to technical or expert advice that is intellectually rigorous and does not avoid inconvenient questions, ministers get support of a positive nature. The roles of the minister and of his civil servants are complementary. The minister is the link between the department and the representative aspects of government and politics, and the deference that it is customary to pay to his office is, in a certain sense, a deference to the democratic process itself.

Civil servants like to see their minister display certain attributes. They want him to project what they regard, in almost a proprietary way, as their department in the best possible light, as a dynamic organisation manned by a competent and enthusiastic staff concerned at all times with the national interest. They want him to advance or defend, as occasion demands, the department at cabinet meetings, in the Dáil and elsewhere. This aspect of the relationship has been succintly and humorously described by a former British minister:

> The overriding duty of a departmental minister, in the eyes of his mandarins, however, is to defend and, where possible, to advance the territory of the kraal to which he happens to be assigned. For British civil servants are territorial animals, and nothing arouses such passion around the [Whitehall] village as trespass . . . for while departments expect their ministers to fight the good fight for departmental interests and departmental territory, to be seen off by a neighbouring predator is regarded as a badge of shame for which a minister will not lightly be forgiven by his mandarins; the whims of 10 Downing Street are accepted as blows of fate. (Bruce-Gardyne 1986: 62).

Civil servants greatly value decisiveness in their minister in dealing with the department's work, including knowing what he wants. Above all, when they put forward proposals to the minister for decision they want to have decisions taken. Indecisiveness in a minister is the characteristic which most frustrates them. Official proposals are never lightly put forward. They are always the outcome of intensive and extensive examination of the subject at issue and are presented in such a way as to lend themselves to decision taking. Civil servants do not generally mind what the nature of the decision is. What does upset them, though fully recognising the minister's prerogative and responsibilities, is the non-return of the papers because the minister is unable or unwilling to make up his mind. They do not want to be continuously approaching the private secretary to place the papers on the top of the minister's pile and otherwise to nudge him towards a decision. Equally upsetting are changes of mind on the part of the minister. It goes without saying that courtesy and appreciation are always valued by officials, especially a minister's willingness to back them when they are under attack by the media, by pressure groups or others.

Different ministers have different practices in dealing with their officials. Some discuss the work only with the secretary, the assistant secretaries and the heads of the technical branches. Some prefer to go deeper into the hierarchy and discuss issues with the officials actually dealing with them. The more restrictive style of consultation is undoubtedly more convenient for ministers, but it has two disadvantages. The first is that it cuts them off from those who are closest to the ground, so to speak. The second is the disadvantage noted in the Devlin Report and commented upon frequently by civil servants themselves. This is the forcing of unnecessary detail on senior officers at the expense of time which could be more usefully devoted to organisation, planning and more policy-orientated initiatives. Hence matters which in well-run business organisation would be dealt with at middle or lower level are in a government department dealt with at the top.

Discussions with his officials take up part of every day that a minister spends in his office. Even if he does not have matters which he wants to discuss with them, they will have matters which they want to discuss with him, so as to get a guideline or a decision, and will have apprised his private secretary accordingly. Nevertheless, the vast majority of officials, especially in larger departments, never meet their minister; indeed, a large number of them may never see him except on television.

Files

The work of officials is carried out on a file, the first page of which may be a note from the minister or from his private secretary or the secretary of the department saying that 'The minister wishes to have . . . examined'. The civil servants concerned take the matter on from there. In due course the file containing all the details of the examination, including accounts of the discussions carried out with concerned parties, is presented to the minister. He is not expected to read all of these details, but they are there for him if he wishes to do so. The last page on the file contains a very brief summary of what has gone before and a recommendation to the minister as to what action seems desirable. In the normal course the recommendation is that of the secretary, who may or may not concur in the recommendation made by the officials who have carried out the examination. For example, a Minister for Agriculture and Food under pressure from small farmers wanting to increase the size of their holdings or from landless people wishing to enter farming might ask his officials to examine how such people could be facilitated in achieving their aims. Policies might include controls on the sale of land, or the provision of low-interest loans, or grants. Any social and economic advantages of the course proposed would be pointed out, as would any likely objections from all possible quarters. When the matter has been examined the minister must decide whether or not to accept the recommendations arising from the examination, either fully or in part.

Ministers have different ways of dealing with files. Some read the file from cover to cover. This, however, is rare, since time does not normally permit such attention to detail. Most ministers read the final page only and draw up a mental or a written list of questions (usually the former) to ask the secretary. Others may not read any of the papers but may invite the secretary to tell them what they contain. Some ministers are more disposed to discussion than to reading. One way or the other, the minister arrives at some decision—even if it is a decision to put the file away among his papers for further consideration at a later date. When a positive decision is taken—and such a decision may be not to proceed further—this is communicated. Again, ministers differ in their manner of communication. Rarely does a minister write at length on a file. More generally, he merely writes 'I agree' or 'Go ahead' over his initials, or will communicate his wishes orally to his private secretary or to the secretary of the department, who will then briefly note the minister's decision on the file. The file is returned through the assistant secretary to the official directly concerned, who then arranges for whatever action is required, e. g. the putting in train of new legislation, the drafting of a scheme, or the writing of a letter. The minister does not normally bother himself with the details of the implementation of his decision, though this depends on the importance of the issue. If there is need for a publicity campaign, the minister will wish to be very much involved.

A wide variety of other files is also submitted to a minister. These include files on which his wishes are sought, on whom he wants to have appointed to a particular board or committee, or on whether he will attend a certain function or meet some deputation. It is not unusual that a recommendation is made to him in each of these situations. They include also files where his signature is required on statutory instruments or on warrants of appointment.

All files and all requests by officials to see the minister are channelled through the private secretary. The latter uses his discretion in presenting the files and requests, choosing the most opportune moment for doing so. On those occasions when it is vitally necessary to have some matter cleared quickly the private secretary can usually find a way to help his departmental colleagues, using his own experience of when and how it is best to get his minister's consent.

MEETINGS, COMMUNICATIONS AND PUBLIC RELATIONS

Meeting people is an essential part of a minister's daily work. The meetings he attends range from formal assemblies such as Dáil sessions and cabinet meetings to private interviews with individuals or small groups in his own office. The minister and his staff must make special preparations for each type of meeting. For many of these occasions he is provided with a brief which (in the case of meetings conducted by the minister himself) explains the background and purpose of the visit and suggests what action might be appropriate. In addition, the minister has contact with a much wider circle of people by means of correspondence; he also devotes considerable care to maintaining a high profile and projecting his image in the most favourable light among the public in general.

Dáil

Ministers must attend the Dáil for all business relating to their own departments. By convention, they also attend for the announcement of each day's business. They normally assemble for these occasions in the office of the Government Chief Whip in Leinster House and enter the chamber in file behind the Taoiseach, usually occupying the same seats each time. When presenting their own legislation ministers are accompanied in the chamber by the officials who have prepared it. Thorough briefing is provided, and ministers ensure that they are familiar with its every detail. The same level of briefing is not required when a minister is replying to a motion, whether one being debated in private members' time or on the adjournment of the Dáil, since on these occasions he delivers a prepared speech and the opposition has little opportunity to raise detailed questions of an *ad hoc* nature.

Government Meetings

Ministers are expected to attend all government meetings. The agenda always contains one or more items that have been placed there at ministers' requests, seeking authority to proceed with some piece of legislation, to introduce some new programme, or merely to bring to the notice of the government some matter such as the accounts of a state-sponsored body.

At meetings a minister argues forcibly for measures that he wants to introduce and must be in a position to counter arguments put forward by other ministers, particularly by the Minister for Finance, who is always fully briefed on every proposal. Ministers are often judged on their success in achieving what they seek at government meetings, where, however good their briefing, they must also exhibit considerable personal skills.

A second role which a minister has at government meetings is to contribute to the collective deliberations and decisions of the cabinet as a whole on matters which are intrinsically important or sensitive. His officials do not, because they are not so equipped, advise on matters which do not concern their own department, and for such briefing the minister relies greatly on the advice provided by his political adviser. The skills required by a minister in cabinet include succinctness and persuasiveness as well as analytic ability and a general understanding of issues not obviously interconnected. Also helpful is 'political weight' and a past record of good judgment.

Party Meetings

All the political parties hold weekly meetings of TDs, senators and members of the European Parliament in Leinster House when the Dáil is in session. Meetings of the party in office are attended by ministers, who advise the backbenchers of legislation and other projects under consideration in their departments. The ministers, for their part, receive grassroots views on how the public is reacting to the government's policies and on the issues which are of most immediate public concern. From these grassroots reactions the ministers quickly gauge how they themselves are performing.

Government Backbenchers

Government backbenchers may meet a minister individually or as a group. Individual interviews are much more frequent, because government parties have few backbench committees. The minister is not accompanied by officials when meeting backbenchers.

Ministers take particular care to be helpful to their backbenchers and many deputations are met at their request. Any information which is likely to be helpful to them in their constituencies is made available, and if a minister is going to visit a constituency, the first to know about the visit, and be invited to take part, are his local backbench colleagues.

Constituents

The needs of his constituents are very high on a minister's list of priorities, because ministers are keenly aware that without their constituents they would not be in office in the first place. In practice, however, constituents' needs do not generally take up much of a minister's personal time while in his office, since they are comprehensively dealt with by the staff in his private office.

Constituents do, however, take up a considerable amount of time at weekends. It is not unusual for a minister to spend Friday evening, all of Saturday and even part of Sunday in meeting his constituents. The latter, for their part, expect this attention. At these meetings, or 'clinics' as they are called, the minister listens, notes and promises to do all he can about the problems presented to him. It is then for the staff of his private office to follow up.

Deputations

In the case of deputations, who are usually seeking some specific action or favour, the minister is presented with a detailed brief informing him of all he should know about them, what further information he should seek from them, and how far he can accommodate their demands. Ministers generally have considerable skill in using their briefs at the actual meetings and in being able to send groups away impressed with their reception. Should unanticipated matters arise during the course of a meeting on which the minister does not consider himself adequately briefed he turns to the officials accompanying him for elaboration. Ministers are invariably accompanied by officials on these occasions. This is an arrangement which clearly suits the minister, but it is one which also suits the officials, since it keeps them in the picture. It has been cynically observed that the civil servants are there to ensure that the minister does not give anything away; civil servants might not altogether disagree with this, but are more likely to say they are there to ensure a productive outcome.

Members of the opposition parties normally visit a minister's office only as part of a joint deputation on some constituency issue. This applies even to former ministers or current shadow ministers.

Courtesy Visits

In the case of visitors who have no specific business and whose visits are more in the nature of a courtesy call (e. g. foreign dignitaries or ambassadors or the heads of international organisations) the minister's brief contains information about the caller personally, the current state of relations between his organisation and the department and suggestions as to matters which the minister might raise with him. Officials do not generally attend on these occasions.

Journeys Abroad

These journeys fall into four broad categories: to attend meetings of international bodies; to promote the image of Ireland abroad and to encourage investment both in Ireland and in Irish exports; to study particular developments that might be relevant to planned initiatives at home; and to support members of the defence forces engaged on foreign duty.

Meetings in the first category include those of the EC, mainly held in Brussels and Luxembourg, and of bodies such as the World Health Organisation, the International Labour Organisation, the General Agreement on Tariffs and Trade, the United Nations, the Organisation for European Co-operation and Development. The meetings of the Council of Ministers of the EC are the most numerous and regular. The ministers most in demand are those for Foreign Affairs, Agriculture and Food, and Finance, who have generally at least one meeting a month. Meetings demanding the attendance of other ministers, such as those for Energy, Labour, and Environment or Industry and Commerce, are held less frequently and at irregular intervals. The minister attending is provided with a brief on each item on the agenda and also with a speaking note (a short speech) on those items in which Ireland has a specific interest. Before each Council meeting the minister and his officials generally discuss the brief with Ireland's Permanent Representative to the EC and his staff to ensure that they have the latest information on the subject at issue, including the stances likely to be adopted by the other member states and that agreement is reached on the line to be taken at the Council.

Attendance at Council meetings generally involves bilateral contacts with other ministers or with members of the European Commission itself. These meetings, held on the margins of the Council meetings, are also attended by the officials, who are fluent in the EC languages and who are thus of considerable additional assistance to their ministers.

In addition to the formal Council meetings, it is sometimes necessary for a minister or even for a group of ministers to go specially to Brussels to make representations on behalf of Ireland or to explain more fully its position in certain cases, for example in the case of Ireland's application in 1989 for structural funds.

Meetings to promote investment at home or marketing abroad are generally arranged by the state-sponsored bodies concerned, such as the IDA (Industrial Development Authority), CBF (The Meat Export Board), Bord Fáilte (Tourist Board), or by the co-operative An Bord Bainne (Milk Board). Potential investors or purchasers are invited to meet the visiting minister while appearances on local television and at other social functions are also arranged. The detailed programme is put in place by the state-sponsored body concerned, some of whose officials accompany the minister, as does always one from his department. Sometimes the party is accompanied by exporters and by journalists.

Visits by the Minister for Defence to the forces on duty abroad under the auspices of the United Nations are largely for reasons of morale but also to see at first hand the situation in which they operate and to acquire information which may be of use in advising on government policy. On such occasions the minister is accompanied by the Chief of Staff and by one of his departmental officials.

Another regular occasion of visits abroad is the celebration, by parades, concerts and other social occasions, of St Patrick's Day, particularly in the USA and Australia. Irish ministers are the central figures in such celebrations, and it has frequently been commented upon that on St Patrick's Day there are very many more ministers abroad than there are at home.

Correspondence

All letters addressed to the minister are processed in the first instance by his private secretary, who reserves by far the greatest proportion to be dealt with by himself and the department's staff. The minister sees very little of the routine correspondence and is entirely dependent on the private secretary as to what he should see.

The private secretary is also responsible for determining which replies should be signed by the minister himself, and he carefully scrutinises each of these. The general guidelines are that ministers sign letters to other ministers, to government backbenchers, senators and local councillors, to previous ministers of any party, to shadow ministers, to people who are considered 'important' and, perhaps most frequent of all, to the minister's own constituents.

Public Relations

A development particularly noticeable in recent years is the constant and increasing search by ministers of all governments for publicity. All ministers are now very concerned with their public image and take considerable care to ensure that their activities are projected to the public as frequently and as favourably as possible. This projection is effected in a number of ways.

Nearly every department has an information section headed by a press or information officer, with whom the minister is in constant touch. This section is the point of contact for journalists and others seeking information about the department's activities. Civil servants do not speak to the press themselves, but are expected to supply promptly all requested material through the information section.

A significant part of the work of an information section is the issue of press releases through the Government Information Service (GIS) to the daily and provincial newspapers, to the radio and television stations and to relevant journals about departmental developments. These may be announcements about projects being introduced or being discontinued; exhortations to the public about health or safety measures; statements about moneys procured by the minister from the EC; or about his attendance at meetings at home or abroad.

The addresses given by ministers on purely party political occasions are not circulated by the GIS, even though they touch on the work of the minister's department. Instead they are circulated as appropriate by the minister's private office, with the phrase 'as requested' as a heading instead of the usual heading used by the GIS.

The same degree of propriety is exercised in regard to material sought by ministers for use either by themselves or by other ministers at national party conferences or during general election campaigns. This is a delicate area, and one in which each side appreciates the sensibilities of the other. It is generally dealt with by tactful requests on the part of the minister's private office and by the provision of purely factual information on the part of the civil service. The minister or his special adviser inject the desired political slant into the material provided. On major political occasions, however, such as regional party conferences or by-election conventions, the Government Press Secretary usually gives copies of the speeches to the political correspondents.

Ministers prepare carefully for their appearances on television and radio programmes or at press conferences. In recent years the preparation includes coaching by public relations and media consultants. It is sometimes rather cynically observed that ministers are inclined to decide in advance exactly what information they wish to impart in such interviews, and that they make sure they do so regardless of the questions that are actually put to them.

Most ministers and their information officers seek to establish a close relationship with the specialist journalists covering the work areas of their departments and, indeed, with journalists generally. Journalist contacts are used to get publicity for ministers' legislative and policy plans, for their stance in cabinet, for their victories over colleagues, or to publicise cuts by the Department of Finance affecting their projects. This publicity is achieved through phone calls from the minister himself, through interviews and press releases, through entertainment, and through invitations to accompany the minister on his official visits and other public appearances.

MINISTERS OF STATE

Ministers of state are commonly referred to as junior ministers. They are not members of the government and have no right of attendance at government meetings. They may attend when invited, to present information on subjects with which they are particularly familiar. Their responsibilities are assigned to them either by special orders (known as delegation of functions orders) made by the government and vesting ministerial powers in named ministers of state or by specific delegation by the minister in charge of the department.

It is the minister of state who initiates legislation in the areas of his responsibility, but he may not himself submit any proposals to government. Such proposals must first be approved by the minister in charge. If the minister does not approve of them, the proposals do not emerge publicly and must be abandoned by the minister of state. If they are approved by the minister and reach government, the minister of state may, depending on the attitude of the minister as noted above, present them there. In such a situation it is normally the minister of state who presents them to the Oireachtas subsequently and pilots them through the various stages there. Parliamentary questions in his area of work are also taken by the minister of state.

In general, the work of a minister of state is largely the same as that of a minister—in relation to his Dáil and constituency work, meeting deputations and attending to the needs of backbenchers and party members. In all of this work he has available to him the services of officials, including a private office almost identical in staffing and structure to that of the minister.

In 1987 special 'offices' within departments were created and placed in the charge of ministers of state, namely the offices of Trade and Marketing, Science and Technology, Food and Horticulture. In 1989 the Office of the Protection of the Environment was added. These offices are a new development, and there is no legislation to support them. The stated aim in creating them was to focus political attention on, and give greater impetus to, certain sectors where it was anticipated that wealth and employment could most readily be created. The powers delegated to these and other ministers of state are exercisable by them subject to the general superintendence and control of the member of the government who, under the Constitution, is in charge of the department. It seems clear that such offices are being used to accommodate ministers of state with talent above the ordinary but who cannot, for reasons such as age, seniority or geographical location, be accommodated in the cabinet, and/or to achieve greater publicity for certain aspects of government policy such as food or the environment.

A minister of state carries out his responsibilities under the watchful eye of his superior, who does not want to be up-staged and who wishes to be kept informed on everything that is going on. Indeed, it is not unusual to have a certain rivalry between minister and minister of state in the carrying out of the work of the department. Generally a minister retains all of the high-profile work such as that relating to the EC and the announcement of new projects likely to be well received publicly.

The role and status of a minister of state, therefore, to some extent depend on the attitude of the senior minister. Those to whom little of the department's work has been delegated must console themselves by devoting their time to their constituencies. Nevertheless, frustration occasionally leads them to approach the Taoiseach. Depending on the personality of the member of the government concerned, the complaint can sometimes be redressed. If it cannot, the Taoiseach can usually find a means of utilising the services of the minister of state by assigning him some work of benefit to the party, such as reviving party organisation in a constituency where it is flagging. In departments where rivalry exists between minister and minister of state the officials, by a judicious exercise of their traditional discretion, not to say caution, are generally able to maintain the balance to the satisfaction of all concerned.

THE MINISTER'S PRIVATE OFFICE

Guidelines as to the staffing of ministers' offices have been laid down by the Minister for Finance. The guidelines refer to the private and to the constituency offices, though in practice no such separate offices are discernible. The staff in the private office, headed by the private secretary, carry out whatever tasks the minister requires, making no distinction between departmental and constituency tasks. The guidelines provide that the number of staff in a private office should not exceed ten, that there should be not more than six in a constituency office, and that there should be not more than one personal secretary, one personal assistant and one special adviser per minister, i.e. a potential total of nineteen. Either the personal assistant or the personal adviser may be actually located in the ministers' constituency office. The tables in Appendix B show the numbers of staff in ministers' offices on 10 May 1989 as given in reply to parliamentary questions on that date. Up to the 1970s the number averaged about four. The embargo on the filling of vacancies in the civil service, operative from 1981 to 1989, did not apply to vacancies in ministers' offices. Such vacancies were always filled immediately by the withdrawal of staff from other sections of the department, leaving these other sections to carry the vacancy. This practice, needless to say, attracted some adverse comment from civil servants themselves.

The purpose of the private office is threefold: to provide a secretariat for the minister, to co-ordinate his activities, and to act as a liaision between him and his department. The office communicates ministerial instructions to the sections of the department and also acts as a filter between them and the minister. The private secretary must be prepared to work long and irregular hours. These arise particularly when the Dáil is in session. Ministers may be required to be in Leinster House until the Dáil adjourns at 8.30 or 10.30 p.m. and often some time after that. These late hours are a favourite time for backbenchers to seek out a minister. They are often accompanied by outsiders whom they want to introduce to the minister. The private secretary usually meets such persons in the first instance, advises them of the minister's availability, and notes their requirements for passing on, if necessary, to the department on the following day.

A major part of a private secretary's job is to get to know how his minister thinks so that he may confidently advise the departmental officials what view the minister would take in a particular situation or so that he may take decisions himself in the absence of the minister. He must know which letters should be seen by the minister personally and which he may himself sign on the minister's behalf, which telephone calls should or should not be put through, and what firm appointments can be made. Thus a new private secretary or a private secretary who gets a new minister requires some months before he is at ease in this aspect of his job.

The private secretary must normally deal with all of the correspondence addressed to the minister. A large proportion of this relates to constituency matters, from the minister's own constituents and from other ministers and backbenchers about their constituents' affairs. The balance is not of such an overtly political nature and deals, indirectly or directly, with the subject-matter of the minister's portfolio, making suggestions, drawing attention to developments and extending invitations. Nearly all of the correspondence is sent elsewhere for reply—to the heads of the various divisions. The replies fall into different categories. Some are for signature by the minister himself (a minister's signature always appears on letters to the constituents), some by the private secretary, and some (mainly those with no political element) by the officials as part of the normal departmental correspondence. The private secretary usually signs the letters to politicians not belonging to the government party and also such other letters as in his judgment the minister would be content to have him sign.

A certain amount of confidential or sensitive material is also received in a minister's office. This may relate to national security, political, financial or other such matters. This correspondence does not leave the minister's office. Examples are the reports from diplomatic missions or from the Anglo-Irish secretariat received in the Departments of Foreign Affairs and Justice, and the budgetary and financial data received in the Department of Finance.

A diary of all the minister's engagements for each week is circulated to the offices of the minister of state and of the secretary. Liaison is maintained with the Dáil staff, with the government secretariat, and with the Government Chief Whip's office in regard to the minister's attendance at government meetings and in the Dáil and Seanad. The private secretary is also responsible for ensuring that his minister has a firm 'pairing' arrangement if his official functions prevent him from being available for a critical vote in the Dáil. He also ensures that the minister has all the necessary papers for meetings of the government; that he has, in good time, the replies to his oral parliamentary questions; that he has, also in good time, copies of the speeches to be made on the various occasions; that he has the briefs for meetings well in advance, and generally that he is provided with whatever service he requires. If there is slippage, the minister complains to the secretary of the department, who then 'reminds' the entire staff through the issue of an appropriate notice over his own name of what is expected of them.

The private secretary presides over a busy suite of offices equipped with the most up-to-date devices such as word processors, telex, fax, photocopying machines and paper-shredders, as well as the most sophisticated telephone system available (including a special privacy set or 'scrambler' for the minister). The secretary's office is immediately adjacent to that of the minister, and the two are in constant liaison. The degree of formality between the minister and his private secretary varies greatly, and it is not unusual for those ministers with a less formal disposition to find time to chat with the staff in their office. All the staff in the private office develop a special loyalty to the minister of the day, different in some indefinable way from their loyalty to the department.

SPECIAL ADVISERS

The practice of appointing special advisers to ministers dates back to the inter-party government of 1954–57, when two appointments were made. The next appointment was not made until 1970, when Dr Martin O'Donoghue (on the staff of Trinity College, Dublin) became personal adviser to the Taoiseach, Mr Jack Lynch. The governments which took office in 1973 and 1977 had four and six advisers respectively. Since the early 1980s almost every minister has an adviser (variously designated as special, political, economic, social or policy adviser). The Taoiseach usually has more than one.

Advisers are not normally civil servants. The selection is made by the minister himself, but the appointment must be approved by the Taoiseach. The job is not advertised. Ministers appoint someone who is personally known to them, generally a party supporter in whom they have complete trust, with qualifications and contacts which the minister considers useful, and who will be totally committed to advancing the minister's policies and career. The qualifications need not necessarily be those of an expert. Advisers frequently accompany a minister from one portfolio to another.

In considering the role of advisers of this nature, it is necessary to bear in mind that while civil servants are conscious of political realities generally in furnishing advice to ministers and in recommending courses of action, they see their role as that of serving successive ministers and not as one of taking overtly political matters into account in framing policies, even if they were competent to do so. It is necessary to remember also that officials' experience is such as to enable them to provide information and advice only on the subject-matter of the minister's portfolio and not on the wider issues with which, as a politician and as a member of the government, a minister must concern himself.

The adviser, on the other hand, regards his employer as a politician, as a deputy, as a member of the government, and as a person. Thus the service which he provides for a minister is essentially different from that provided by officials. It includes the following elements:

(1) Discussing with the minister the political and electoral implications of the advice coming from the civil service, including its likely reception by the

media, especially in the case of delicate measures such as the withdrawal of a benefit or the imposition of a charge, for example a fee for a fishing licence.

(2) Discussing organisational changes suggested by the secretary of the department, or changes which the minister himself is thinking of proposing, for example in regard to the location of staff away from headquarters.

(3) Examining matters in breadth as well as in depth by consulting outside sources and taking soundings on (1) and (2) and drawing attention to aspects which the civil servants may not have referred to.

(4) Researching matters for discussion at government meetings and providing briefing for his own minister so that he can, if he wishes, take part in the discussion and put a point of view. As inferred earlier, this is a service which the minister's own officials cannot provide.

(5) Dealing with constituency matters in a broader framework than the normal constituency correspondence handled by the private secretary demands. This entails keeping in touch with government, local authority or other public service developments in the constituency and with commercial and business interests there.

(6) Examining formal speeches and informal addresses from a presentational point of view, having regard to the minister's personality and style of delivery, and thus turning information from within the department into politically usable material.

(7) Writing speeches of a specifically political nature for the minister.

(8) Acting as a replication of the minister in many respects, as an extension of his political personality, as an extra pair of eyes and ears, doing for him what the minister would do for himself if he had the time.

Advisers have access to departmental files and may see all submissions to the minister.

The arrangement bears some, though only a very limited, resemblance to the so-called 'cabinet' system which obtains in many European countries and in the EC. Under that system a minister (or a member of the European Commission) has a group of eight to ten people, known as a 'cabinet', whose work is broadly that described above, though on a more elaborate scale. There have been casual references from time to time to the establishment of a 'cabinet' system in Ireland, but the matter has not been considered in any detail. Its introduction would necessitate radical changes affecting the patterns, traditions and values of Ireland's political culture to an extent which would probably be unacceptable.

The current system of advisers has found general favour. In support, three broad arguments have been advanced. The first is that it prepares ministers for discussions at government level on areas outside their departments' responsibilities, thus enabling them to make a constructive contribution to the collective decision-making process of any government. The second is that it supplies specialised advice to ministers on certain policy areas, providing a different perspective (and thus a valuable alternative) to the expert advice available within the department. The third is that it gives advice on the political implications of policy or other measures, including the maintenance of a high public profile, thus enabling the civil service to keep out of party politics. Ministers and advisers often say that officials can be hidebound by their narrow specialist approach to issues and that they do not sense, and are not interested in, the political angle.

In general, civil servants live happily with advisers, especially now that their appointments terminate with the minister's leaving office. (Up to 1981 those advisers who wished to remain were often appointed established civil servants 'in the public interest', as provided for in the Civil Service Commissioners Act 1956. Needless to say, this practice did not find favour with existing civil servants, since it interfered with promotion arrangements.) Strains can arise, however, as when advisers reword letters, speeches or replies to parliamentary questions prepared by officials to make them overtly political or to include material discarded as unsuitable by the civil servants, or when advisers intrude into routine departmental work or departmental contacts, creating confusion as to who actually speaks for the minister. Nevertheless, a spirit of altruism generally prevails. Civil servants recognise that ministers and advisers tend to live for the present, whereas departments take the long-term view and have seen ministers come and go; they recognise the minister's prerogative in making such appointments and understand their political desirability. The advisers, for their part, though impatient at the outset at what they sometimes refer to scathingly as 'bureaucracy', come in time to see at least some of its advantages. Both sides know the rules of the game, and each is conscious of the need to keep off the other's territory.

REFERENCES

Bruce-Gardyne, Jock, *Inside the Whitehall Village* (London: Sidgwick & Jackson, 1986)

Opie, Roger, 'The Making of Economic Policy', Hugh Thomas ed., in *Crisis in the Civil Service* (London: Anthony Blond, 1968)

Dooney, Sean, *Irish Agriculture: An Organisational Profile* (Dublin: Institute of Public Administration, 1989)

Rose, Richard, *Ministers and Ministries* (Oxford: Clarendon Press, 1987)

Appendix B

Staff Employed in Ministers' Offices:
Numbers and Salaries

The figures given below were supplied by ministers in response to parliamentary questions in May 1989.

1. TAOISEACH

Private Office	£
4 Special Advisers	34,327
	22,352
	22,352
	£134 per diem subject to a maximum of £24,656 in any year
1 Personal Secretary	8,168
1 Assistant Principal (Private Secretary)	27,061
1 Higher Executive Officer (Asst. private Secretary)	21,632
2 Higher Executive Officers	15,629
	17,281
2 Clerical Officers	11,533
	9,733
1 Supervisor of Typists	11,533
4 Typists	9,020
	9,974
	9,974
	9,020

General and Constituency Office of the Taoiseach	£
1 Higher Executive Officer	15,224
1 Staff Officer	13,909
1 Clerical Officer	9,154
2 Clerical Assistants	9,953
	7,166
1 Typist	8,203
1 Personal Secretary	13,614

Minister of State and Government Chief Whip	
Private Office	£
1 Higher Executive Officer (Private Secretary)	19,167
1 Executive Officer	13,614
1 Staff Officer (Personal Assistant)	12,570
2 Typists	8,203
Constituency Office	9,974
1 Personal Secretary	14,816
2 Typists	9,167
	7,315

Minister of State, Deputy Máire Geoghegan-Quinn	
Private Office	
1 Administrative Officer (Private Secretary)	20,916
2 Typists	6,605
Constituency office	8,926
1 Higher Executive Officer	19,456
1 Executive Officer	11,766
1 Personal Secretary	13,614
1 Clerical Assistant	8,729
1 Typist	9,167

Minister of State for Heritage Affairs

No separate private office or constituency office is maintained in my Department by the Minister for Heritage Affairs.

2. GAELTACHT

Chomh fada is a bhaineann sé le Roinn na Gaeltachta is mar seo a leanas na sonraí:

1. Oifig Dháilcheantar
   1 Cúntóir Pearsanta —£11,290 sa bhliain

2. Oifig Príobháideach
   1 Ardoifigeach Feidh-miúcháin
   (Rúnaí Príobháid each) —£21,632 sa bhliain (liúntas mar Rúnaí Príobháideach san áireamh)

1 Oifigeach Cléir eachais —£9,154 sa bhliaín

1 Cúntóir Cléir eachais * —£9,202 sa bhliain

*Bíonn dualgais don Roinn le comhlíonadh ag an oifigeach seo freisin.

3. FOREIGN AFFAIRS

	Number	Salary
		£
A. Minister		
(a) Special Adviser	1	24,551
(b) Private Office		
Private Secretary (Third Secretary)	1	21,632
Executive Officer	2	14,408
Clerical Officer	1	11,553
Clerical Assistant	1	9,202
Shorthand Typist	1	9,202
(c) Constituency Office		
Personal Assistant	1	9,446
Personal Secretary	1	8,260
Clerical Officer	1	11,553
Clerical Assistant	1	7,765
Typist	2	9,202
B. Minister of State		
Private and Constituency Office		
Private Secretary (Higher Executive Officer)	1	21,632
Executive Officer	1	12,694
Personal Assistant	1	9,867
Personal Secretary	1	9,202
Clerical Assistant	1	6,876
Typist	2	1 @ 9,202
		1 @ 7,166
Civilian Driver	2	11,118

4. TOURISM AND TRANSPORT

Minister's Office	No. Employed	Rank	Salary
Constituency office	5	1 Adviser	£14,408.00 p.a.
		1 Executive Officer	£12,694.00 p.a.
		1 Clerical Officer	£175.44 p.w.
		1 Clerical Assistant	£158.09 p.w.
		1 Typist *	£137.34 + £8.39 allowance p.w.
Private Office	6	1 Private Secretary (Higher Executive Officer)	£17,281.00 plus £4,351 allowance p.a.
		1 Executive Officer	£14,408.00 p.a.
		1 Clerical Officer	£220.03 p.w.
		1 Clerical Assistant	£162.67 p.w.
		2 Typists *	£142.97 + £8.39 allowance p.w.
Constituency Office	5	1 Personal Secretary	£214.82 + £14.08 allowance p.w.
		1 Clerical Officer	£227.29 p.w.
		1 Typist	£176.36 + £6.40 allowance p.w.
		2 Civilian drivers	£213.08 p.w. £213.08 p.w.
Private Office	3	1 Private Secretary (Higher Executive Officer)	£17,281 + £4,351 allowance p.a.
		1 Clerical Officer	£175.44 p.w.
		1 Clerical Assistant	£176.36 p.w.

* Also work for the Department's Information Office.

5. SOCIAL WELFARE

Private Office		
1	Special Adviser	£20,905 p.a.
1	Higher Executive Officer	£19,575 p.a.
2	Executive Officers	£14,408 p.a.

Constituency Office		
1	Special Adviser	£26,605 p.a.
1	Executive Officer	£14,408 p.a.

Staff serving both Private and Constituency Offices

1	Staff Officer	£13,322 p.a.
3	Clerical Officers (average)	£9,697 p.a.
1	Clerical Assistant	£8,488 p.a.
5	Clerical Assistant (Typist)	£8,974 p.a. (average)
1	Personal Secretary (seconded from Personal Assistants, Houses of the Oireachtas)	£7,769 p.a.

6. JUSTICE

Persons employed in General Office

	£ p.w.
Personal Assistant to the Minister	214.82
plus secretarial assistant allowance	14.08

	£ p.a.
Executive Officer	14,408.00
Executive Officer	12,694.00
Executive Officer	9,643.00

	£ p.w.
Clerical Assistant	162.67
Clerical Assistant	131.79

Persons employed in the Private Office of the Minister

	£ p.a.
Assistant Principal Officer	22,352.00
plus allowance	1,305.00
Executive Officer	14,053.00
Executive Officer	12,694.00
Staff Officer	12,817.00

	£ p.w.
Clerical Assistant	162.67
Clerical Assistant	167.29

Minister's Typing Pool

	£ p.w.
1 Clerical Officer (Supervisor of Typists)	221.03
1 Clerical Assistant Typist	176.36
plus word processing allowance	12.58
plus confidential typing allowance	6.38
1 Clerical Assistant Typist	176.36
plus word processing allowance	12.58
plus confidential typing allowance	6.38
1 Clerical Assistant Typist	158.07
plus word processing allowance	12.58

7. AGRICULTURE AND FOOD

	Constituency office	Private office		Constituency	Private
Minister	5	6	Minister of State (Mr Walsh)	5	3
Minister of State (Mr Kirk)	4	5			

Rank	Minister of Office of the Minster	Office of Minister of State (Mr. Kirk)	Office of Minister of State (Mr. Walsh)	Salary
Principal Officer/ Personal Adviser	1	–	–	£24,628—£28,830 per annum
Special Adviser	–	1	–	£88 per day subject to a maximum of £14,800 per annum.
Private Secretary (Higher Executive Officer)	1	1	–	£14,408—£17,281 per annum plus allowance of £4,351 per annum.

Private Secretary (Executive Officer)	–	–	1	£7,346—£14,408 per annum plus allowance of £4,351 per annum
Executive Officer	2	1	1	£7,346—£14,408 per annum
Clerical Officer	2	1	1	£6,432—£11,533 per annum
Clerical Assistant/ Typist	4	4	3	£6,309—£9,302 per annum
Personal Secretary	1	1	1	(i) one at £11,049 per annum (ii) two on scale £6,333— £11,209 per annum plus allowance of £735 per annum
Personal Assistant (Clerical Duties)	–	–	1	£6,432—£11,533 per annum

8. FINANCE

Constituency Office of the Minister
  There are five people employed as follows:

Rank	Salary
Staff Officer	£13,322 per annum
Clerical Officer	£175.44 per week
Clerical Assistant	£162.67 per week
Personal Assistant	£228.90 per week
Personal Secretary	£228.98 per week

Constituency Office of the Minister of State
  There are four people employed as follows:

Rank	Salary
Personal Assistant	£155.33 per week
Personal Secretary	£169.32 per week
Civilian Drivers (2)	£213.09 per week

Private Office of the Minister
  There are eleven people employed as follows:

Rank	Salary
Higher Executive Officer (Private Secretary)	£20,391 per annum
Higher Executive Officer (Administrative Assistant)	£17,805 per annum
Staff Officers (3)	£13,322, £12,817 and £12,570 per annum
Clerical Officers (2)	£170.55 and £165.94 per annum
Clerical Assistants (4)	£195.35, £184.75, £171.06, £167.29 per week

Private Office of the Minister of State
  There are seven people employed as follows:

Rank	Salary
Executive Officer (Private Secretary)	£16,580 per annum
Executive Officer	£11,766 per annum
Clerical Officer	£165.94 per week
Clerical Assistants (4)	£184.74, £184.74, £176.35, £157.20 per week.

9. INDUSTRY AND COMMERCE

Private Office

	No.	Grade	Salary	Allowance
			£	£
Minister's Office	1	Private Secretary	14,408–17,281	4,351
	2	Executive Officer	7,346–14,408	–
	1	Clerical Officer	6,431–11,533	–
	2	Clerical Assistant	6,308–9,202	–
	3	Typists*	6,308–9,202	438

	No.	Grade	Salary	Allowance
Minister of State	1	Private Secretary	14,408–17,281	4,351
	1	Economic Adviser	27,160	–
	1	Clerical Officer	6,431–11,533	–
	2	Typists*	6,308–9,202	438
Minister of State	1	Private Secretary	14,408–17,281	4,351
	1	Staff Officer	11,535–13,322	–
	2	Typists*	6,308–9,202	438

Constituency Office

	No.	Grade	Salary	Allowance
			£	£
Minister's Office	1	Personal Assistant	17,281	–
	1	Personal Secretary	6,322–11,209	734
	1	Executive Officer-	7,346–14,408	–
	2	Clerical Officer	6,431–11,533	–
	1	Clerical Assistant	6,308–9,202	–
Minister of State	1	Personal Assistant	13,922	–
	1	Personal Secretary	6,332–11,209	734
	1	Clerical Officer	6,431-11,533	–
Minister of State	1	Personal Assistant	6,332-11,209	734
	1	Personal Secretary	6,322-11,209	734

*Shared with Constituency Office

10. COMMUNICATIONS

	No. Employed	Rank	Salary Paid
Minister's Private Office	1	Private Secretary (Higher Executive Officer)	£15,624 p.a. plus allowance of £4,351
	1	Clerical Assistant Typist	£176.35 p.w.

11. MARINE

	Private Office		Constituency Office	
Grade	No.	Salary	No.	Salary
		£		£
Minister's Office				
Private Secretary	1	21,632		
Executive Officer	1	14,053		
Staff Officer			1	12,570
Clerical Officer	1	11,533	1	9,733
Clerical Assistant	½	4,244	½	4,244
Clerical Assistant/	1	10,192		
Typist	½	4,601	½	4,601
Personal Secretary			1	8,120
Special Adviser	1	20 per hour		
Minister of State's Office				
Private Secretary	1	17,673		
Clerical Officer	1	9,154		
Clerical Assistant	1	9,202		
Clerical Assistant/	1	8,729		
Typist	1	8,006		
Personal Secretary			1	10,964

12. LABOUR

Private Office
1 Assistant Principal
1 Higher Executive Officer (Rúnaí Aire)
2 Executive Officers
1 Clerical Officer
2 Clerical Assistants
2 Clerical Assistants (typists)

Constituency Office
1 Personal Assistant
1 Executive Officer
1 Clerical Assistant
1 Clerical Assistant (Personal Secretary)
2 Clerical Assistants (typists)

The personal assistant and personal secretary in my constituency office are both employed on a contract basis.

The following are the salary scales for all of the grades listed above:

Assistant Principal:	£18,841–£22,352
Higher Executive Officer:	£14,408–£17,281 + allowance as Rúnaí Aire
Executive Officer and Personal Assistant:	£7,346–£14,408
Clerical Officer:	£6,431–£11,533
Clerical Assistant:	£6,308–£9,202

13. ENERGY

Minister's Private Office

No. of Staff Grade		Salary Scale
Higher Executive Officer (Private Secretary)	1	£14,408–£17,281 (plus an allowance of £4,351 per annum)
Executive Officer	2	£7,346–£14,408
Clerical Officer	1	£6,432–£11,533
Clerical Assistant (Typist)	3	£6,309–£9,202 (3 with allowances of £438 per annum for word-processing duties and 1 with an allowance of £334 per annum for confidential typing duties).
Total	7	

Minister's Constituency Office

Higher Executive Officer	1	£7,346–£14,408
Clerical Officer	3	£6,432–£11,533
Clerical Assistant	1	£6,309–£9,202
Personal Secretary	1	£6,333–£11,209 (plus an allowance of £735 per annum)
Total	6	

Minister of State's Private Office

Higher Executive Officer (Private Secretary)	1	£14,408–£17,281 (plus an allowance of £4,351 per annum)
Staff Officer	1	£11,535–£13,322
Clerical Assistant	1	£6,309–£9,202
Clerical Assistant (Typist)	1	£6,309–£9,202 (plus an allowance of £438 per annum for word-processing duties)
Total	4	

Minister of State's Constituency Office

Personal Assistant	1	£15,849
Personal Secretary	1	£6,333–£11,209 (plus an allowance of £735 per annum)
Clerical Assistant (Typist)	1	£6,309–£9,202 (plus an allowance of £438 per annum for word-processing duties)
Total	3	

14. HEALTH

Private Office:
  1 Assistant Principal (co-ordination of press
    and information services)
  1 Private Secretary (Higher Executive Officer)
  1 Executive Officer
  1 Clerical Officer
  4 Clerical Assistants

Constituency Office:
  1 Personal Secretary
  1 Clerical Officer
  2 Clerical Assistants

The number and rank of persons employed in the office of my Minister of State are:

  1 Private Secretary (Executive Officer)
  3 Clerical Assistants
  1 Personal Assistant

All of the above mentioned staff are paid in accordance with the salary levels determined for their grade by the Department of Finance.

15. EDUCATION

Minister's Office

Private Office		Constituency Office	Salary
Rank	Salary	Clerical Officer	£
Special Adviser to	£	Clerical Officer	221.03 per week
Minister	27,710 per annum	Clerical Assistant	162.67 per week
Higher Executive		Clerical Assistant	
Officer -Private		(Typist)	167.29
Secretary	18,978 per annum	Secretarial Assistant to	
Executive Officer	14,053 per annum	Minister	148.35 per week
Clerical Officer	200.82 per week	Minister of State's Office	
Clerical Assistant	176.36 per week	Private Office	
Clerical Assistant	176.36 per week	Special Adviser	20,463 per annum
Clerical Assistant	162.67 per week	Higher Executive Officer	
Clerical Assistant		—Private Secretary	18,759 per annum
(job - sharing)	88.18 per week	Executive Officer	14,053 per annum
Clerical Assistant		Clerical Officer	221.03 per annum
(job - sharing)	81.34 per week	Clerical Assistant	167.29 per week
Clerical Assistant		Clerical Assistant	167.29 per week
(Typist)	184.75 per week	Clerical Assistant	
Clerical Assistant		(Typist)	184.75 per week
(Typist)	184.75 per week	Total = 7	
Clerical Assistant			
(Typist)	182.74 per week	Constituency Office	
Clerical Assistant		Staff Officer	12,317 per annum
(Typist)	176.36 per week	Clerical Assistant	162.67 per week
Total = 12		Clerical Assistant	
(Job - sharers counted as 1)		(Typist)	148.82 per week
		Personal Secretary to	
		Minister of State	190.39 per week
		Personal Assistant to	
		Minister of State	14,408 per annum
		Total = 5	

16. DEFENCE

(1) Constituency Office

No.	Rank-Appointment	Salary
1	Personal Assistant	£17,281 per annum
1	Personal Secretary	£11,209 per annum plus allowance of £14.08 per week
1	Clerical Assistant	£7,765 per annum

(2) Private Office

1	Higher Executive Officer	£15,629 per annum plus allowance of £4,351 per annum
1	Staff Officer	£11,535 per annum
1	Clerical Assistant	£9,202 per annum
1	Clerical Assistant (Shorthand-Typist)	£9,202 per annum plus allowance of £8.40 per week for Word Processing duties and an allowance of £6.40 per week as confidential Shorthand-Typist

Minister of State
(1) Constituency Office
Nil
(2) Private Office

1	Executive Officer	£14,408 per annum plus an allowance of £4,351 per annum

17. ENVIRONMENT

Constituency Office		Minister for State at the Department of the Environment	
No.	Grade	Constituency Office	
2	Executive Officers	1	Executive Officer
1	Clerical Officer	1	Clerical Officer
1	Clerical Assistant	3	Clerical Assistants
Private Office		Private Office	
1	Higher Executive Officer	1	Higher Executive Officer
2	Executive Officers	1	Executive Officer
1	Clerical Officer	3	Clerical Assistants
3	Clerical Assistants	1	Personal Secretary

The Dáil
and the Seanad

The Constitution provides that the national parliament be known as the Oireachtas and it consists of the President and two Houses, namely Dáil Éireann and Seanad Éireann. The Oireachtas has the sole power of making laws, but any law repugnant to the Constitution may be annulled by the Supreme Court. It may not declare acts to be infringements of the law which were not so at the time of their commission. The Dáil and the Seanad must hold at least one session each year, and sittings must be public. In an emergency, however, either House may decide, with the agreement of two-thirds of the members present, to sit in private. Each House elects its own chairman, designated Ceann Comhairle in the case of the Dáil and Cathaoirleach in the case of the Seanad, and deputy chairman (Leas-Ceann Comhairle and Leas-Cathaoirleach) and determines its own rules and standing orders. Each House also determines its own quorum—20 for the Dáil and 12 for the Seanad. Members have the privilege of immunity from arrest in going to and coming from either House, and are not answerable to any court or authority other than the House itself for any remark made within either House. No person may be at the same time a member of both Houses.

THE DÁIL

MEMBERSHIP
Membership of the Dáil is open to citizens over the age of twenty-one. Members of the judiciary, civil service, defence forces and the Garda Síochána are ineligible, as are persons undergoing prison sentences and undischarged bankrupts.

The total number of deputies is fixed by law, though the Constitution specifies that this number may not be less than one for every 30,000 of the population or more than one for 20,000. The Twenty-sixth Dáil has 166 members.

Deputies represent constituencies also fixed by law, and the constituencies must be revised at least every twelve years in the light of population changes. The Constitution provides that the ratio between the numbers to be elected for each constituency and the population of each constituency is to be as far practicable the same throughout the country. In practice, constituencies are revised on the publication of the results of each census of population (normally every fifth year). The practice is for the government to set up an independent commission, presided over by a judge of the High Court, to recommend a revised scheme of constituencies which may or may not be accepted by the Dáil when submitted to it.

The Ceann Comhairle of the previous Dáil is returned automatically as a member.

ELECTIONS AND CONVENING

Members are elected under a system of proportional representation (P.R.) by means of single transferable vote, and no constituency may have less than three members. (An extract from a government publication describing the system is given in Appendix C).

The Constitution provides that no Dáil may continue for more than seven years and that a shorter period may be fixed by law. Such shorter period has, in fact, been fixed and is five years. The Minister for the Environment determines the date of the poll when the President has dissolved the Dáil. A general election must take place not later than thirty days after a dissolution, and the new Dáil must meet within thirty days of polling day. An example of the P.R. system in operation in a representative constituency is given in the official return reproduced in Appendix D).

When the votes have been counted at a general election, the person responsible for the conduct of the election in each constituency (who is called the Returning Officer and is normally the County Registrar) notifies the Clerk of the Dáil of those who have been elected. The Clerk then notifies each member to attend at Leinster House to sign the Roll of Members, in his presence. A member is not entitled to take his seat nor to be paid any allowance until he has signed the Roll.

The first business at the first meeting of the Dáil after the election is the reading by the Clerk of the proclamations of dissolution and of convening, and then the names and constituencies of all the members elected. The Clerk acts as chairman until the Ceann Comhairle is elected.

PROCEDURES

The Ceann Comhairle

The duties of the Ceann Comhairle are set out in elaborate detail in the standing orders of the Dáil. Broadly speaking, these are to preside over the sittings, to keep order, to call members to speak, to put questions to a vote if called for at the end of the debate, to enforce the rules of the debate, and generally to exercise supervision over the conduct of business. The Ceann Comhairle appoints a number of deputies who may preside when either he or the Leas-Ceann Comhairle is unable to do so. These are called panel chairmen; they receive no extra remuneration.

The Ceann Comhairle, or the presiding chairman, has no vote except where there is equality of voting. He has then a casting vote, which he must exercise. The basis on which the casting vote is given is the usual one, namely maintenance of the status quo, thus providing an opportunity for review of the question at issue. In effect, this involves the Ceann Comhairle voting with the government of the day.

Standing Orders and Conventions

In the conduct of the day-to-day business the Ceann Comhairle relies greatly on the standing orders. These provide for the conduct of proceedings, the passage of bills, the rules of debate, the rules of financial procedures, the preservation of order, and the operation of committees. The Ceann Comhairle's rulings on the interpretation and application of these orders may not be questioned in the house, though members may bring complaints to the attention of the Committee on Procedure and Privileges (see p. 66). To ensure consistency in interpretation a book containing rulings of the chair, i.e. a book of precedents, is kept, showing all rulings made by chairmen since the foundation of the state.

A member who behaves in a disorderly fashion may be ordered by the Ceann Comhairle to withdraw from the chamber for the remainder of that day's sitting. If the deputy refuses, the Ceann Comhairle may have him 'named', i.e. may call on the Dáil, by vote if necessary, to have him suspended. The duration of the suspension is determined by the frequency of the offence—a first offence entails three days' suspension.

The standing orders are supplemented by conventions and practices. Many of these relate to the behaviour of members. For example, when the Ceann Comhairle rises to speak, any member then speaking must sit down; members must bow to the chair when passing to or from their seats in the chamber; they must address the chair; they are called on to speak at the discretion of the Ceann Comhairle; it is the practice that members are called upon alternately by party, with a preference for ministers and for leaders of the opposition parties. In general, members may speak once only in debate, and words which may be deemed offensive or disorderly may not be used; imputations of improper motives and personal reflections on members are regarded as disorderly. Members who persist in irrelevance or repetition may be ordered by the chair to stop speaking, though ruling deputies out of order is extremely rare. Other conventions are that matters considered *sub judice* are not discussed, and that a member making a maiden speech is heard without interruption.

Debates

The Dáil has three sessions a year, from mid-October to Christmas, from about the third week in January to Easter and from after Easter to about the end of June. In the years 1980–90 it met for an average of 84 days a year. A meeting of the Dáil cannot begin until the quorum of twenty is present and the Ceann Comhairle has entered the chamber in his robes and taken his place. Attendance at debates is not compulsory, and no record is kept of the members attending.

By convention, a minister or minister of state (not necessarily the minister whose business is being discussed) is present in the chamber throughout each debate. He is accompanied by officials whose task it is to assist him with matters that arise during the debate and to take notes of points raised by speakers for the use of the minister in the course of his reply. The disposition of members and officials is shown in the diagram opposite. The press gallery is situated behind the Ceann Comhairle, and the public galleries are behind the members. The business under discussion is shown on the indicator board in the chamber by reference to the number of the item on the order paper, and on closed circuit television in all the principal areas of Leinster House, with the name of the member speaking and, in the case of a bill, the stage it has reached.

In certain circumstances, debate may be limited by what is known as the *guillotine*. Under this procedure, the government seeks the approval of the Dáil for limiting to a specific number of hours the debate on particular stages of a bill.

As a result of a procedural reform introduced in April 1991, the last fifty minutes of each day's sitting may be devoted to (a) short debates, and (b) short statements. Under (a) the Ceann Comhairle selects three items from amongst those which members wish to have discussed. Each of the three members may make a five-minute speech to which the minister has five minutes to reply. Under (b) five members may make take a two-minute statement to which the minister may make a two-minute statement in reply. The matters selected must, of course, relate to public affairs connected with government departments or to matters of administration for which a minister is responsible. Ministers are in attendance on a rota basis.

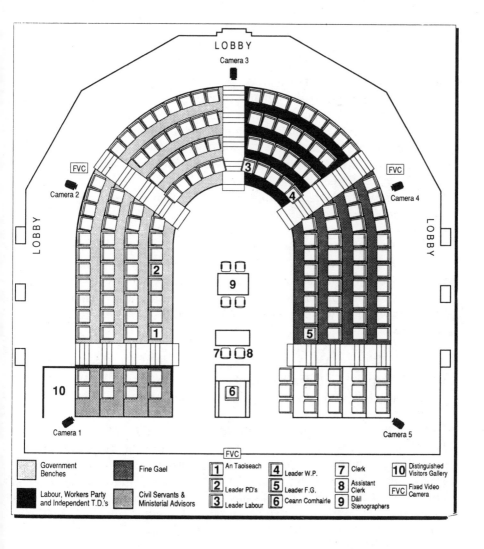

The Dáil Chamber
(January 1991)
Reproduced by courtesy of The Irish Times

When a vote is to take place, electric bells are rung for three minutes in Leinster House and also in the offices of those ministers in the immediate vicinity, e. g. in Merrion Street and Kildare Street. The doors to the chamber are locked after three minutes and only those actually present may vote. Having gone up the steps facing camera 3, those voting for the government turn left and those opposing turn right into what are usually referred to as the Tá and Níl lobbies. Tellers are appointed by the government side and by the opposition, two for each, and they count the numbers entering each lobby. The result of the vote is brought to the Ceann Comhairle by the tellers for the lobby in which there was a higher vote. The Ceann Comhairle formally announces the result and then proceeds to the next business.

An official report of the debates of each House is published under the supervision of the Ceann Comhairle. They are periodically revised, collated, indexed, bound and published in volumes and are on sale at the Government Publications Sale Office. Minutes of the daily proceedings of each House are made by the Clerk. These include times of sittings, business transacted and related matters. Signed by the Ceann Comhairle and published daily, they are the permanent official record of the work of the Dáil and are referred to as the *journal of proceedings*.

WORK OF THE DÁIL
The work of the Dáil falls into four broad categories. The Dáil considers proposals for legislation initiated by ministers or by private members; it considers expenditure proposals presented by ministers; it debates motions; and it is a forum in which questions may be addressed to ministers.

Legislation
Proposals for legislation are initiated as bills. Bills fall into various categories: public bills (including private member's bills), private bills, consolidation bills, money bills and bills to amend the constitution.

Public Bills. By far the largest number of bills are public bills, i.e. bills for the benefit of the public as a whole, such as a bill to deal with broadcasting. Nearly all public bills are put forward by ministers. Each such bill has five stages, or readings, in the House in which it was introduced, i.e. it is considered on five separate occasions. (Bills, other than money bills or bills to amend the Constitution, can be introduced in either house.) The first of these stages is when the House is made aware that the bill is on the way. The title of the bill and a short description of its purpose appears on the order paper. This stage is normally a formality and evokes no debate. It leads to the fixing of a date for the second reading, when the minister deals with the general principles of the bill. He indicates why it is necessary and explains the reasons for each of its provisions. These explanations lead to a debate on what is proposed, including suggestions for improved or alternative means of achieving the ends sought. (Those seeking to know the background to any act should study the minister's speech introducing the second reading.) Opposition to the proposals in a bill is expressed by voting against it. Amendments are not permitted at this stage. They must be reserved for the next stage, which is known as the committee stage.

At the third (committee) stage the bill is considered in detail—section by section, even word by word—by a committee which, in practice, consists of all members of the House. This stage is one of relative informality where members may speak more than once on the same aspect. Amendments may be made, to add, delete or substitute words, but these may not be in conflict with the principle of the bill as approved at the previous stage. Amendments to government bills are rarely accepted by ministers. Ministers like to think that they have considered every aspect of a subject before introducing a bill and are reluctant to bear the adverse impression which acceptance of an amendment might imply. If a bill is going to result in increased public expenditure, a special money resolution authorising such expenditure must be put forward and passed before committee stage. This may be put forward only by a minister or a minister of state, the purpose being to demonstrate that the proposed expenditure has the authority of the government as provided for in the Constitution.

The bill is then 'reported' to the House as its fourth stage. Further amendments may be made provided they do not conflict with any amendments rejected at committee stage. Normally any such amendments deal only with minor matters, such as drafting. If no amendments are offered, there is no debate on the report stage.

The fifth stage is usually a formality, unless a bill is contentious. In that event there may be a debate similar to that which took place on the second reading. The stage is normally taken immediately after the report stage, and the question put to the Dáil is 'that the bill do now pass'. This means that in the case of a bill which has originated in the Dáil it goes to the Seanad for its consideration, or in the case of a bill which has originated in the Seanad it goes to the Dáil.

Another form of public bill is a *private member's bill*, which is a bill initiated by a member who is not a minister, usually a member of an opposition party, with the approval of his party. The party must have at least seven members. The title of the bill, and its purpose, appears on the order paper in the same way as a government bill, as its first stage. If introduction is opposed (in practice this would be by the government), the member moving the bill has five minutes in which to explain its purpose and the member designated to oppose has five minutes in which to outline objections to it.

After that there is a vote which determines whether the bill goes on to a second reading. If a bill is not opposed, the second reading is taken in private members' time, i.e. in the time set aside for business other than government-initiated business. Private members' business is usually dealt with between 7 p.m. and 8.30 p.m. on Tuesdays and Wednesdays. The time normally allowed for debate on the second reading is six hours. If it passes this reading, it is referred for its third reading to a special committee of the House in which it has been introduced. As mentioned earlier, a bill involving expenditure (as most bills do) cannot proceed beyond this stage without a positive money resolution from the government, that is a resolution to provide the public funds, e. g. salaries or cost of equipment needed to give effect to whatever the bill provides for. Thus, if such a resolution is not put forward, a bill can, in effect, be made to lapse at this stage. If, however, the bill proceeds, the fourth and fifth stages are also taken in private members' time.

Very few private members bills are passed, because even if the government accepts the principle of the bill, it usually asks the member to withdraw it on an assurance that the government will itself introduce a measure, officially drafted, to meet the situation. The Judicial Separation and Family Law Reform Act, passed in December 1989, was the first successful private member's bill for thirty years.

When a public bill has been passed in the Dáil, it is sent to the Seanad, where it is regarded as having passed its first stage but is debated at the other stages in the same way as in the Dáil. If the Seanad makes amendments, or recommendations in the case of money bills, these are considered by the Dáil. If the Dáil does not agree with the amendments, the matter is reconsidered by the Seanad, which may decide whether or not to insist on them. If it decides to insist, the Dáil may after a period of ninety days pass a resolution deeming the bill to have been passed.

Private Bills. These are bills dealing with special interests, such as those of a particular body or locality as distinct form the public interest as a whole. An example of a private bill is the Limerick Marts Bill 1989, which was deposited in the Private Bill Office in December 1989 and subsequently referred to a select committee of the Dáil and Seanad. (The main purpose of this bill is to increase the number of commodities which may be sold in the Limerick market place and to give the trustees certain powers in relation to tolls, rents and disposal of premises.) The persons who wish to have a private bill passed, known as the promoters of the bill, engage a parliamentary agent (a practising solicitor) to undertake on their behalf the formalities prescribed under standing orders relating to the presentation of such a bill. These include the extensive advertising of its contents, as well as the notification of parties likely to be interested. The bill is introduced in the Seanad at second stage, after which it is referred to a committee of both Houses, consisting of three deputies and three senators, none of whom may have a personal interest in the bill and, in the case of the deputies, none of whose constituents has a personal interest. The committee consults government departments, takes evidence from interested parties, and hears counsel on behalf of the promoters and any objectors. The committee makes a report on the bill to both Houses and then sends it to the Seanad for consideration at fourth and fifth stages. After that it goes to the Dáil, also for fourth and fifth stages. It is then enacted in the same way as a public bill, i.e. it is signed by the President and becomes law. Fees must be paid to the state by both promoters and opponents of private bills.

Consolidation Bills. These are bills to tidy up the law. Where, for example, there have been a number of acts passed through the years, each amending and/or adding something to the law relating to a particular subject, it may be considered desirable, for ease of reference, to repeal obsolete parts and to get all of the up-to-date provisions into one act. A consolidation bill does not contain any substantive amendment of the law and is almost invariably introduced in the Seanad. After its second reading it is referred for examination to a joint committee of both Houses. The bill is then considered on fourth and fifth stages in the initiating House, after which it is sent to the other House, where the first, second and third stages are waived and it is considered on fourth and fifth stages only. Such bills are rare because neither ministers nor officials are enthusiastic about devoting scarce time to them unless there is a very obvious need and supporting pressure. The most recent consolidation act was the Social Welfare Act 1981.

Money Bills. These may be initiated in the Dáil only. They are bills which deal with taxation, public debt, loans and such matters. When they go to the Seanad for consideration, that body has only twenty-one days to consider them, and it may make recommendations only; it cannot amend them. If a money bill is not returned within twenty-one days, or is returned with recommendations which the Dáil does not accept, it is deemed to have been passed by the Dáil at the end of that time.

Bills to amend the Constitution. Any proposal to amend the Constitution must first be passed in the form of a bill, which may not contain any other proposal. Such a bill may be initiated in the Dáil only. When passed there, it is considered in the Seanad in the same way as a public bill.

Financial Procedures

Article 28.4.3 of the Constitution obliges the government to prepare estimates of receipts and of expenditure for each year and to present these to the Dáil.

They are presented by the Minister for Finance in his budget statement, normally in January. In this statement he outlines, among other things, his taxation proposals for the years ahead. As it is desirable that some of these, such as excise duties on petrol or tobacco, come into operation on the day they are made public, the proposals are voted upon on budget day. They are put forward in the form of budget resolutions which, under the Provisional Collection of Taxes Act 1927, have immediate effect and continue in operation for up to four months from the date of passing. The main debate on the budget proposals continues over a number of weeks. When it is concluded, the Finance Bill is introduced by the Minister for Finance. Its enactment gives final legislative effect to the taxation measures in the budget.

The Dáil then considers the estimate for each individual department, which is presented by its minister. In his speech the minister reviews the work of his department in the previous year, outlines his programme for the year ahead, and explains the need for the money he is seeking. The estimates are presented in the form of a number of spending items called subheads, which enumerate clearly the various items of expenditure. Thus in all departments, subhead A represents the amount sought for pay, subhead B for travelling expenses, and subhead C for equipment. The other letters of the alphabet are used for the specific needs of individual departments. When the Dáil has approved the expenditure of the total sum, the estimate then becomes known as the vote for the relevant department. (See Appendix E for estimate of Department of Industry and Commerce for 1991).

Under the terms of the Central Fund (Permanent Provisions) Act 1965, the Minister for Finance is empowered to make available to a department four-fifths of the sum which it had in the year before, to enable it carry out its work, i.e. to enable public services to be carried on during that part of the year when the estimates for these services are being considered. When the estimates for all departments have been agreed by the Dáil, normally by May or June of each year, the Minister for Finance introduces the Appropriation Bill to transfer to departments the moneys voted for them.

If in the course of a year a minister finds that for some unforeseen reason he needs more money to run his department than the Dáil has allowed under the procedures described above, he must seek the Dáil's approval of a supplementary estimate. The debate on this occasion is confined to discussion of the particular items for which the extra money is being sought.

Motions
A motion is a proposal made by a member (a minister or an ordinary TD) to do something, order something to be done, or express an opinion with regard to some matter. It must be phrased in such a way that, if passed, it will be seen to express the judgment or will of the House. Motions may be conveniently

classified into (a) *substantive motions*, which are self-contained proposals drafted in such a way as to be capable of expressing the will of the house, for example the motion 'that Dáil Éireann approve the terms of the Convention on the Physical Protection of Nuclear Material done at Vienna on 26 October 1979, copies of which were laid before Dáil Éireann on 27 March 1990' (proposal of the Minister for Energy), and (b) *subsidiary motions*, which are largely procedural in character, such as 'that the debate be adjourned'.

Parliamentary Questions

Deputies may address questions to a minister about matters connected with his department or about public affairs for which he is officially responsible. There is no formal obligation on ministers to answer such questions, but in practice, they do so. One hour and a quarter is set aside each sitting day for parliamentary questions.

The procedure is that a deputy submits his question in writing to the general office in the Dáil before 11 a.m. on the fourth preceding day for questions seeking an oral reply and on the third preceding day for questions nominated for priority and for written replies. The question is examined in the office (and ultimately by the Ceann Comhairle should the need arise) to ensure that its purpose is genuinely to seek information or clarification on matters of fact or policy; that such information has not been provided within the preceding four months; that it contains no argument or personal imputation; that it does not deal with a matter which is *sub judice*; and that it does not seek to anticipate a matter of which the Dáil has been give notice and on which the Ceann Comhairle is satisfied a debate will take place within a reasonable time.

Questions for oral reply are divided into two categories: questions nominated for priority, and questions not so nominated. In the case of the latter a lottery is held on the fourth day preceding that on which the questions are to be answered. Deputies can enter two questions for each lottery. The questions appear on the order paper in the sequence in which they have been drawn from the lottery.

The priority questions are confined to groups in opposition (parties of not less than seven members), and no more than five such questions may be answered in any one day. The party decides what questions are to be designated as priority and the members in whose names they are to be asked. Only the members named may ask supplementary questions seeking elaboration of the information provided in the answer to the question. The sequence in which priority questions are listed on the order paper is determined by lot. Questions not answered on the day on which they appear on the order paper, because of time constraints, receive written answers unless the deputies concerned wish them to be again nominated as priority questions or re-entered in the lottery.

Oral questions are answered by ministers on a rota system. Under this system ministers present themselves in the Dáil in sequence to answer the questions addressed to them. This means that each minister answers oral questions about once in every five weeks. Where a question put down for oral answer is of such a nature as to require a lengthy reply, or a reply in the form of a tabular statement, the minister may not wish to answer it orally. In such a situation the Ceann Comhairle must accept a request from the minister that the answer be provided in the official report for that day. The deputy gets a copy of the reply in advance of publication.

In addition to the questions to which deputies seek an oral reply (so that they may ask what is known as a *supplementary question* to press for additional information if not satisfied with the reply), deputies also ask questions for written reply. The vast majority of these written questions relate to constituents' problems, such as when payments are expected to be made under social welfare and grant schemes of various kinds.

Presentation of Documents

Many kinds of documents are presented to the Dáil under the provisions of legislation, for example, the annual reports and accounts of state-sponsored bodies and statutory regulations made by ministers. Rarely are these documents debated. Statutory regulations may, however, be revoked by the passage of a resolution to that effect, but such a resolution is also rare. The purpose of presenting these documents is to make their existence known and to make them available in the library for interested members of the Oireachtas.

DÁIL REFORM

Procedural Aspects

In recent years there has been considerable criticism from academics, other interested observers and from politicians themselves about the procedures and practices under which the Dáil conducts its business. These are generally regarded as belonging to another more leisurely age, having been largely adopted from those obtaining in the British parliament at the time of the foundation of the Irish state. The accepted view is that there has been a failure to adapt and develop the system so that it reflects adequately the changes that have taken place over the past few decades. C. H. Murray, a former Secretary of the Department of Finance, writes: 'It is doubtful whether a parliamentary Rip Van Winkle who was familiar with the Dáil procedures on 1922 would discern any major changes in the Dáil procedures of 1989.'(Murray 1990:149).

In considering what changes should be made, all commentators are conscious of individual deputies' perception of their role. In general, the latter do not see this as helping to formulate policy by contributing to debates on legislation, as monitoring the performance of ministers and public bodies, and as giving leadership to the community. They regard themselves mainly as welfare officers for their constituents, and as having a need to preserve their image with a view to protecting their seats. They are forced into this situation largely because of the multi-seat proportional representation system which generates competition not only between deputies of different parties but also between deputies of the same party. The system places a premium on welfare politics as each candidate seeks to woo the constituent. Gemma Hussey, a former Minister for Education and for Social Welfare notes: 'Dáil sittings merely interrupt the business of the TDs in looking after their constituents rather than being the central part of their political lives.' (*The Irish Times*, 16 August 1989). A backbench TD is recorded as acknowledging that the existing electoral system leads to mediocrity which inevitably affects the quality of debate in the Dáil chamber. What we need, he said, 'in order to free TDs to carry out more work at parliamentary level is a different electoral system'. (*Irish Independent*, 15 December 1989). On the other hand, Pádraig Flynn, Minister for the Environment, in response to Mrs Hussey's comments, said: 'I am wary of calls for reform which would depersonalise the process of political representation so that our TDs and ministers were dealing only with issues and concepts and large umbrella groups.'

Proposals for Reform

In 1971 an informal committee of Dáil members recommended modest changes in regard to such matters as parliamentary questions, adjournment debates and legislative procedures. The changes were evolutionary rather than revolutionary and served merely to bring some standing orders into line with current practices. The committee avoided any thorny issues. In regard to Dáil sittings, for example, it recommended that the house should meet on church holidays, but avoided questions such as five-day sittings and shorter recess periods. Some four or five years afterwards the sitting times, on the three days a week the Dáil meets, were revised to bring them more into line with normal business hours.

In 1980 the Fine Gael party published a policy document entitled *Reform of the Dáil*, which became part of the policy of the Fine Gael/Labour government during its period of office in 1982–87. However, as reform measures need consensus, it was necessary that the proposals be acceptable to the Committee on Procedure and Privileges, representative of all parties. As a result, some were dropped and others were modified. The most significant of the changes made in that period were (1) the broadcasting of proceedings; (2) new procedures for parliamentary questions (described earlier) and for debating departmental estimates; (3) an increase in the number of committees.

The government which came into office in 1987 took the view that Dáil reform was not a matter for the government but for the Dáil as a whole, and so the initiative in this respect reverted to the Committee on Procedure and Privileges. In May 1988 a resolution was passed in the Dáil requesting that committee to make proposals for televising proceedings and for a general reform of procedures. These proposals had not been finalised before that government left office in May 1989.

The government which took office in 1989 outlined the following topics for the attention of the Committee on Procedure and Privileges: the procedures for the passage of legislation through the Dáil and Seanad, the committee system, question time, the *sub judice* rule, and the proposal that MEPs qualify for membership of the Oireachtas committees relevant to EC affairs. The committee reported in March 1990. Following debate, the Dáil decided that televised broadcasting would commence with the budget of 1991 and that broadcasting of proceedings of committees meeting in public and not hearing evidence would commence as soon as possible thereafter.

It is expected that the other issues to which the committee will address itself will include the following:

(1) *Length of Dáil recesses*. Each year the Dáil resumes after the summer recess towards the end of October, at about the time that schools are having their mid-term break. Furthermore, most people find it difficult to understand why it meets on three days a week only. If its committees were to meet all year round (except for Christmas, Easter and August), the working time of the Dáil would correspond more closely to that of other outside activities.

(2) *Parliamentary committees*. Greater use of such committees would, in addition to the advantages noted later in this chapter, have the merit of speeding up the passage of legislation, of providing a form of access to the legislative process by interested groups, of enabling a wider range of subjects of public interest to be discussed in the Dáil, and of affording more time for the discussion of the annual estimates, which are at present frequently passed without any examination by the Dáil.

(3) *Parliamentary questions*. The arrangements for these are always regarded as inadequate by the opposition parties. Their criticisms derive in the main from the provisions in standing orders which make it difficult for deputies to raise at short notice matters which they consider urgent. They also complain about the propensity of ministers to avoid awkward questions, for example, in relation to state-sponsored bodies. It has to be said, however, that the same desire for reform is noticeably less obvious when opposition parties themselves become the government parties.

(4) *Order of business*. Opposition parties also complain that the ordering of the business to be discussed lies too much in the hands of the government and that more time for private members' business should be provided.

(5) *Speaking time*. The fixing of reasonable limits is suggested. At present members have, generally, unlimited speaking time, and it is not unknown for speakers to expatiate at inordinate length on a particular issue. The rules about repetition in individual speeches are loosely observed, and there is no provision stipulating that speakers do not repeat each other.

(6) *Calling speakers*. At present a member who wishes to speak 'catches the Ceann Comhairle's eye'. Even though the Ceann Comhairle generally calls on speakers in party rotation, a more efficient way would be to draw up a list of speakers in advance who would have allocated speaking time.

(6) *Voting*. At present a call for members to vote on an issue may be made more or less at random, thus effectively necessitating members' presence in Leinster House during the whole of each sitting day. To have votes taken at a fixed time would avoid the undignified sight of ministers and deputies rushing from their offices and other places to reach the chamber within the three-minute deadline. It would, in addition, be more efficient to have the actual voting take place by roll-call or by some electronic means.

The October 1991 Review of the Programme of Government 1989/93 contains a list of proposed reforms of the Oireachtas, including extended sitting hours and sessions, the feasibility of an electronic voting system and the establishment of a register of interests.

THE SEANAD

The theoretical case for having a bi-cameral legislature is that the upper House (Seanad Éireann) provides (1) a check on the main legislative chamber; (2) representation for particular areas or interest groups; (3) an additional input of expertise into policy formation and legislation. The Constitution of 1937 introduced a new concept, that of a vocational Seanad, to draw on the knowledge of persons from a wide range of vocations. The concept has remained merely a concept since, in practice, the emphasis in the election of members is on political affiliation rather than on professional knowledge.

The Seanad has no independent life. An election for the Seanad must take place not later than ninety days after dissolution of the Dáil, and the first meeting of the new Seanad takes place on a day fixed by the President on the advice of the Taoiseach. Outgoing senators hold their seats until the day before polling day for the new Seanad.

MEMBERSHIP

The Seanad is provided for in Articles 18 and 19 of the Constitution. The same conditions apply in relation to eligibility for membership as in the case of the Dáil. The Seanad consists of sixty members, of whom forty-nine are elected and eleven are nominated by the Taoiseach. Of the forty-nine elected members, forty-three are selected from vocational panels of candidates. Of the remaining six, three represent the National University of Ireland, and three the University of Dublin.

The five vocational panels contain the names of persons having knowledge and practical experience of:

(1) the national language and culture, literature, art, education, law and medicine;

(2) agriculture and allied interests;

(3) labour matters;

(4) industry and commerce;

(5) public administration and social services.

Each panel is divided into two sub-panels. One of these (Oireachtas sub-panel) contains the names of candidates nominated by not less than four members of the Houses of the Oireachtas. The other (nominating bodies' sub-panel) contains the names of those nominated by bodies on the register of nominating bodies. The method of compilation and revision of the register, and the provisions relating to eligibility, are laid down in the Seanad Electoral (Panel Members) Acts 1947 to 1960. The register is the responsibility of the Clerk of the Seanad.

The electorate for the forty-three members from the panels consists of the members of the Dáil, Seanad, county and borough councils, a total of about 960, all of whom are practising politicians. Election is by proportional representation and by secret ballot. Appendix F reproduces an extract from *Seanad General Election, 1987* which shows the voting for candidates on the labour panel in that year.

The six university representatives are elected by the graduates of the two universities indicated. This provision has frequently been criticised as being curiously out of date in the present day. Apart from its overtones of elitism, there is a considerable imbalance in the two electorates. The National University, with four constituent colleges, had in 1990 an electorate of about 76,000, while the University of Dublin has one constituent college only (Trinity College) and an electorate of 19,500. Furthermore, the two new universities established in 1989, Dublin City University and the University of Limerick, do not have representation in the Seanad.

The nomination of eleven members by the Taoiseach under Article 18.3 of the Constitution enables persons of special calibre to reach parliament without going through the electoral process. The Taoiseach also tends to nominate party candidates who failed to get elected in the preceding Dáil election, those who seem to stand a good chance of being elected at the next Dáil election, or persons who have worked well for the party over the years. As well as rewarding the worthy, this also helps to strengthen the voting power of the government party (or parties) in the Seanad.

Functions

While the Seanad does have a role in initiating legislation, the number of bills which begin their life in the upper House is small. Traditionally, the main function of the Seanad has been to review legislation passed by the Dáil. In practice, however, the Seanad exerts no significant control on the business of the Dáil. Bills passed by the Dáil are almost invariably passed by the Seanad, and it is only rarely that it suggests any significant amendment. This is because the manner of electing senators results in the Seanad having the same political complexion as the Dáil. While those elected by the Universities are seldom members of any political party, and therefore independent, the vast majority of the remainder are, inevitably, members of one or other of the political parties.

The low level of Seanad activity has sometimes been adversely commented upon. The number of days on which the Seanad was in session in each of the years 1980–90 is as follows: 28 in 1980; 32 in 1981; 22 in 1982; 34 in 1983; 52 in 1984; 56 in 1985; 78 in 1986; 47 in 1987; 63 in 1988; 42 in 1989; 61 in 1990. Clearly this is a body which is neither overused nor overworked, and this has led to a questioning of the need for such a body, almost since the beginning of the state. Speaking in the Dáil in 1928, Seán Lemass expressed his party's belief that the Seanad should be abolished, and declared that, failing this, it should be 'a group of individuals who dare not let a squeak out of them except when we [the Dáil] lift our fingers to give them the breath to do it'; he also concurred with the description of the ideal Seanad as 'a penny-in-the-slot machine'. (*Dáil Debates*, 14 June 1928, col. 614). Subsequently in the 1930s there was a long-drawn-out feud between Eamon de Valera's government and the Seanad, culminating in its abolition in 1936. It is clear that in the formulation of the 1937 Constitution Mr de Valera had serious doubts about the desirability of having an upper House at all, or at least of giving it any effective role in legislation.

In 1966 a committee of nine TDs and three senators was set up to review the constitutional, legislative and institutional bases of government which reported in 1967. In regard to the Seanad, it recommended, in essence, no change in the status quo.

In more recent years there have been calls to make changes in the manner of electing the Seanad and to find ways to make it more effective. Indeed, one of the parties in the government formed in 1989, the Progressive Democrats, openly supports the abolition of the Seanad. These calls, however, receive very little support from politicians generally.

THE INFRASTRUCTURE

Oireachtas Committees
The Oireachtas has established a number of committees to deal with aspects of its work. Some of these are joint committees; others contain members of the Dáil only. Party representation on committees is determined by reference to their relative strengths in the Houses. Generally committees are set up to do work for which either House, as a large assembly, would not be suited, for example, detailed inquiry or the examination of witnesses. They may engage any legal, economic or financial consultants they require to assist them in their work. Committees have not the power to make decisions in their own

right. They prepare reports on the matters they have examined for presentation to the Oireachtas and for publication. These reports are only rarely debated in either House.

The committees in the Twenty-sixth Dáil can be broadly divided into four kinds. These are (a) the housekeeping committees concerned with Oireachtas affairs; (b) those set up to consider a single issue and which lapse once they have reported back to the Oireachtas; (c) those established to review administrative performance; and (d) in a category of its own, the permanent Joint Committee on Secondary Legislation of the European Communities, whose task is to examine the regulations, directives and decisions made by the European Commission and to report on their relevance to Ireland.

Examples of (a) are the Committee on Selection and the Committee on Procedure and Privileges. The former is the first committee set up at the commencement of every new Dáil and Seanad; its task is to nominate the members to serve on the various other committees. The latter, as its title suggests, deals with matters such as changes in standing orders, and the facilities for members to carry out their work.

Examples of (b) are the committee on Administrative Justice in 1977, which led to the appointment of the Ombudsman, and, more recently in 1988, the Committee on Marital Breakdown, which led to the enactment of the Judicial Separation and Family Law Reform Act 1989.

Examples of (c) are the Public Accounts Committee and the Joint Committee on Commercial State-Sponsored Bodies. The former is perhaps the most important committee of all. It comprises members of the Dáil only and is formed at the beginning of each new Dáil. It reports on the accounts prepared by the Comptroller and Auditor General on the manner in which the moneys granted by the Dáil to meet public expenditure have been spent. It also suggests such alterations as it considers desirable in the format of the annual estimates submitted to the Dáil. Traditionally the chairman is a member of the main opposition party. The committee questions the Comptroller and Auditor General, the accounting officers and the officials of the Department of Finance about the financial (as distinct from the policy) aspects of matters under review. The committee's reports are not debated in the Dáil, but the recommendations contained in them are implemented under the direction of the Department of Finance.

The Joint Committee on Commercial State-Sponsored Bodies considers all aspects of the work of these bodies. It also examines and reports on matters common to a number of bodies, such as structure and organisation, the responsibility of the board, accountability and financing, as well as the relationship with central government and the Oireachtas. (See also p. 162).

The committee system is a feature of parliamentary life in many countries, including the USA and several member states of the European Community.

The system has, however, come late to Ireland, and it is not clear that members of the Oireachtas yet view participation in the work of parliamentary committees as an integral part of their work. Owing to the priority given by TDs to constituency work with a view to re-election, little importance is attached to service on parliamentary committees, which is of little help in that connection; and this attitude may be responsible for the low numbers of deputies interested in such work, and for the small amount of time they are prepared to devote to it. This apparent lack of interest may be reflected in the fact that neither House has yet organised a standing procedure to discuss committee reports on a regular basis.

No formal evaluation of the cost or worth of the committee system has yet been made public. Advantages generally put forward are that it provides a more relaxed atmosphere with more give and take than obtains in the House itself, where contributions are largely adversarial in nature, and that it enables members to acquire a detailed knowledge of the subject at issue and to discuss it in a minute way. Disadvantages are that privilege does not attach to witnesses before committees meeting in public, and that witnesses may not, in any event, be compelled to attend. To provide accordingly would require legislation.

REMUNERATION; EXPENSES; PENSIONS

The remuneration paid to each deputy, senator and office-holder is referred to in the relevant legislation—the Oireachtas (Allowances to Members) and the Ministerial and Parliamentary Offices Acts—as an 'allowance'. The allowances are subject to review from time to time by the Review Body on Higher Remuneration in the Public Sector, which makes recommendations to the government about their appropriate level. The pay rounds, applied on a general basis to the civil service, are normally applied to members of the Oireachtas. On 1 January 1991, the allowance for deputies was £28,894. In addition to the allowance, the following additional sums were payable: Taoiseach, £46,354; Tánaiste, £35,137; ministers and the Ceann Comhairle, £30,903; ministers of state and the Leas-Ceann Comhairle, £16,555. On the dissolution of the Dáil, the allowance for ordinary deputies (including office-holders), ceases, but each deputy on the dissolution receives one-eighteenth of the allowance as a once-off payment. The allowance for senators is £16,754. Additional sums of £12,140 and £6,622 are paid to the Cathaoirleach and Leas-Cathaoirleach respectively.

Members of the Dáil and Seanad receive supplementary payments to cover the costs of travel on official business (e.g. to and from meetings of the Houses or committee meetings). These payments are normally by way of mileage allowance for car transport at the rates prevailing for civil servants. However, members who live within ten miles of Leinster House are paid a flat rate travel allowance (currently £26.40 a day) in lieu of mileage payments. An overnight allowance (£45.10 in January 1991) is payable to members who live more than twenty miles from Dublin.

Official cars with drivers (members of the Garda Síochána) are supplied to the Taoiseach, ministers, the Attorney General and the Ceann Comhairle. The cars are available for private use as if they were the office-holders' own cars, but may be used only with their official drivers. The benefit deriving from the private use of these cars is taken in account by the Review Body in determining remuneration. The same arrangements applied to ministers of state, to the Leas-Ceann Comhairle and the Cathaoirleach up to 1984. Since then, they provide their own cars and are paid mileage allowances for official travel in these cars. In these cases, civilian drivers are engaged by the office-holders themselves; the drivers are paid by the state.

There are separate pension schemes for ordinary members and for office - holders of the Dáil and Seanad. Under their scheme the members contribute 6 per cent of their parliamentary allowance. In return, those with not less than eight years' service are entitled to one-fortieth of the allowance for each year of service. Under the scheme for office-holders, the minimum qualification period for a pension is three years, and contributions are not required. The amount payable is 28 per cent of salary (defined as that part of total remuneration exceeding a deputy's allowance), increasing to 51 per cent after eight years' service. The   'iemes also provide for death gratuities (for members who die in service) and widows' and children's pensions.

In 1988 the government announced its acceptance of recommendations made by the Review Body under which

(a) the allowances of TDs and senators would be reconstructed as salaries and become subject to taxation in the normal way;

(b) TDs and senators would no longer claim tax deductions from their salaries for job related expenses, and would instead be paid separate, flat rate expense allowances which would be non-taxable and non-pensionable;

(c) office-holders' pension arrangements would be revised, so that these pensions would not normally become payable before age 55, and would be abated so long as a recipient remained as a TD or senator;

(d) new schemes of severance payments for TDs, senators and office-holders would be introduced.

The legislation to give effect to these recommendations was introduced towards the end of 1991.

ALLOWANCES TO PARTIES

Under the Ministerial and Parliamentary Offices Act 1938 and the Oireachtas (Allowances to Members) Act 1960, allowances for party expenses are paid to the leaders of political parties which contested the previous general election as organised political parties and had not less than seven members elected.

The allowances payable on 1 January 1991 were: Fianna Fáil, £123,159; Fine Gael, £176,203; Labour £99,250; Workers' Party, £99,250.

SECRETARIAL ASSISTANCE

Ministers have offices in their departments and in Leinster House. They are assisted in all of their work—parliamentary, departmental, constituency and social—by the civil service. Each deputy has, since 1981, one secretarial assistant whose salary is paid by the state. Some deputies choose to have their secretaries located in Oireachtas premises, while others prefer to locate them in their constituency offices. Secretarial assistance for senators is on the basis of one secretary for every three senators.

Since the secretaries of deputies devote most, if not all, of their time to constituency work, it follows that any research has to be carried out by the deputies themselves, with voluntary assistance from party supporters. Apart from the library, there is a marked absence of research facilities available to members.

Each deputy and senator is allowed 1,250 ordinary pre-paid envelopes each month which they may post in Leinster House. They also enjoy free telephone facilities for all local calls and trunk calls of unlimited duration to one designated number (usually a deputy's constituency office) and trunk calls within the state, limited to six minutes.

STAFF

The staff in the Houses of the Oireachtas are civil servants, but with a legal distinction from the civil servants who serve ministers in government departments. Because they are under the control of the chairmen of the Dáil and Seanad, rather than under that of ministers as other civil servants are, they are properly referred to as *civil servants of the state* under the Staff of the Houses of the Oireachtas Act 1959. The total number of staff is about 190.

The most senior official in each house is called the Clerk of that House, and his deputy is called the Clerk Assistant. These officials are appointed by the Taoiseach on the nomination of the appropriate chairman and the Minister for Finance. The other senior staff are also designated clerks, e. g. principal clerk, committee clerk, etc. The latter officials are interchangeable and are generally referred to as the joint staff of the Houses of the Oireachtas.

The staff includes a Superintendent of the Houses and a Captain of the Guard. Their duties are not prescribed, but, broadly speaking, the former is responsible for members' accommodation and security. The latter is a uniformed officer who can remove disorderly members at the request of the Ceann Comhairle or Cathaoirleach. It rarely comes to this, however, since such offenders usually leave voluntarily when called upon to do so.

Also on the staff is an editor of debates and a number of reporters. As it is stipulated that all acts of the Oireachtas, the daily order paper, the journal of proceedings and other official documents must be published in both Irish and English, the staff also includes several translators.

ACCOMMODATION

Most of the business of the Oireachtas is carried out in Leinster House. In recent years, however, because of the increased use of committees, and the increase in the numbers of secretarial staff, some of the work is now done in buildings adjacent—in the former College of Science in Merrion Street and in the former College of Art in Kildare Street. Other offices are located in Molesworth Street and in Merrion Square.

Members of the public may gain access to Leinster House only on introduction by a member of either House. This necessitates contacting a member and asking him to make arrangements for access. This having been done, the person may enter in the company of the member, or, more frequently, the member authorises the issue of an admission ticket to the public gallery which is available from the ushers' office. A special gallery is reserved for the press, and another for distinguished visitors (indicated in the diagram on p. 53).

REFERENCES

Hussey, Gemma, *At the Cutting Edge: Cabinet Diaries, 1982–87* (Dublin: Gill & Macmillan, 1990)

Murray, C.H., *The Civil Service Observed* (Dublin: Institute of Public Administration, 1990)

Appendix C
Election to the Dáil

(1) Electorate

Every Irish citizen and British citizen (as defined by the British Nationality Act 1981), over 18 years who is ordinarily resident in a constituency and whose name appears on the register of electors is entitled to vote at a Dáil election in that constituency. Each elector has one vote only. A new register of electors is compiled by the local county council and county borough corporation and comes into force on 15th April each year. A draft register is published on the 1st December each year and is displayed for public inspection in post offices, libraries and other public buildings. Claims for corrections in the register may be made up to the following 15th January. Claims are adjudicated on by the county registrar who is a legally qualified court officer. There are 2,445,515 electors on the register for the year 1986/87.

Members of the Garda Síochána and the Defence Forces are entitled to vote by post only. As from April 1987, civil servants (and their spouses) attached to Irish missions abroad are deemed to satisfy the residence requirement for registration as electors and may also vote by post.

Electors who are disabled may apply to have their names entered on the special voters' list and may vote at home. A ballot paper is delivered to them at their residence by a special presiding officer accompanied by a member of the Garda Síochána.

(2) General Elections

A general election must be held within thirty days after the dissolution of the Dáil. The Clerk of the Dáil issues a writ to the returning officer in each constituency instructing him to hold an election of the prescribed numbers of members. The returning officer is the county registrar except in the county and county boroughs of Dublin and Cork, where the Sheriff is the returning officer. The Ceann Comhairle (chairman of the Dáil) is automatically returned without an election unless he signifies that he does not wish to continue as a member. The latest time for nominating a person as a candidate is 12 noon on the ninth day after the issue of the writs.

The Minister for the Environment fixes the date of the poll, which must be not earlier than the eighth or later than the sixteenth day after the last day for receipt of nominations (Sundays, bank and public holidays are not reckoned). He also fixes the hours of polling, which must be for a period of not less than 12 hours between 8.30 a.m. and 10.30 p. m.

(3) Nomination of Candidates

A candidate may nominate himself or be nominated by a Dáil elector for the constituency. A deposit of IR £100 must be lodged in respect of each candidate. The deposit is refunded if the candidate withdraws, or is elected, or if the greatest number of votes credited to him exceeds one-third of the quota (see section 6 for explanation of the 'quota'). A candidate may include his party affiliation in his nomination paper, if he represents a registered political party. The party affiliation will appear opposite his name on the ballot paper. If he has no party affiliation, he may describe himself as 'non-party' or leave the appropriate space blank.

A register of political parties is maintained by the Clerk of the Dáil. In it he registers particulars of each party which applies to him for registration and which satisfies him that it is a genuine political party and is organised to contest elections.

The returning officer must rule on the validity of a nomination paper within one hour of its presentation to him. He is required to object to the name of a candidate if such name: is not the name by which the candidate is commonly known; is misleading and likely to cause confusion; is unnecessarily long or contains a political reference. He is also required to object to the description of a candidate which is, in his opinion, incorrect; or insufficient to identify the candidate; or unnecessarily long. The candidate may amend the particulars shown on the nomination paper, or the returning officer may do so.

The returning officer may rule a nomination paper invalid only if it is not properly made out or subscribed.

(4) The Poll

Polling places are appointed by county councils or county borough corporations, subject to the approval of the Minister for the Environment. The returning officer provides polling stations at each polling place. Usually schools or other public buildings are used. The returning officer is responsible for the organisation of the poll, printing of ballot papers and counting of votes in each constituency. He must send a polling card to each voter, except a postal voter or special voter, informing him of his number on the register of electors and the polling station at which he may vote. He sends ballot papers to the postal voters by post and encloses special envelopes for the return of their votes to him. He arranges to have ballot papers delivered at their homes to disabled electors registered on the special voters' list. The postal and special ballot paper envelopes are placed unopened in a special ballot box when returned to the returning officer. Each polling station is supervised by a presiding officer assisted by a polling clerk. A candidate may be represented at a polling station by an agent who assists in the prevention of electoral offences. Before being given a ballot paper, an elector may be asked to produce evidence of identity.

(5) Voting

Voting is by secret ballot and on the system of proportional representation, each elector having one transferable vote. The names of the candidates appear in alphabetical order on the ballot paper. The voter indicates the order of his choice by writing 1 opposite the name of his first choice and, if he so wishes, 2 opposite the name of his second choice, 3 opposite the name of his third choice, and so on. He then places the ballot paper in a sealed ballot box. In this way the voter gives instructions to the returning officer to transfer his vote to the candidate of his second choice if the candidate of his first choice receives more than the quota of votes necessary for election or if his first choice is eliminated (through receiving so few votes as to have no chance of election). If the same applies to his second choice, the vote may be transferred to his third choice, and so on.

(6) Counting the Votes

Before the counting of votes begins, the envelopes containing the postal and special voters' ballot papers are opened in the presence of the agents of the candidates and the ballot papers are placed in an ordinary ballot box which is taken with all the other ballot boxes to a central counting place for each constituency. Agents of the candidates are permitted to attend at the counting place to satisfy themselves that the ballot papers are correctly sorted and counted.

The count commences at 9 a.m. on the day after polling day. Each ballot box is opened and the number of ballot papers checked against a return furnished by each presiding officer. They are then thoroughly mixed and sorted according to the first preferences recorded for each candidate, invalid papers being rejected. The *quota* of votes, which is the minimum necessary to guarantee the election of a candidate, is ascertained by dividing the total number of valid papers by the number of seats plus one and adding one to the result; e. g. if there were 40,000 valid papers and four seats to be filled, the quota would be 8,001, i.e. $\frac{40,000+1}{(4+1)}$. It will be seen that in this example only four candidates could possibly reach the quota.

At the end of the first count any candidate who has received a number of votes equal to or greater than the quota is deemed to be elected. If a candidate receives more the quota, his surplus votes are transferred proportionately to the remaining candidates in the following way. If the candidate's votes are all first preference votes, all his ballot papers are sorted into separate parcels according to the next preference shown on them. A separate parcel is made of his non-transferable papers (papers on which a subsequent preference is not shown). Each remaining candidate then receives from the top of the appropriate parcel of transferable papers a number of votes calculated as follows:

$$\frac{\text{surplus}}{\text{total number of transferable papers}} \quad \text{x number of papers in parcel}$$

If the surplus is equal to or greater than the number of transferable votes, each candidate will receive all the votes from the appropriate parcel of transferable papers.

If the surplus arises out of transferred papers, only the papers in the parcel last transferred to that candidate are examined, and this parcel is then treated in the same way as a surplus consisting of first-preference votes. If two candidates exceed the quota, the larger surplus is distributed first.

If no candidate has a surplus, or the surplus is insufficient to elect one of the remaining candidates or to affect the order of these candidates, the lowest of the remaining candidates is eliminated and his papers transferred to the other remaining candidates according to the next preference indicated on them. If a ballot paper is to be transferred and the second preference shown on it is for a candidate already elected or eliminated, the vote passes to the third choice, and so on.

Counting continues until all the seats have been filled. If the position is reached where the number of seats left to be filled is equal to the number of candidates still in the running, these candidates are declared elected without having obtained the quota.

A returning officer may re-count all or any of the papers at any stage of the count. A candidate or his agent is entitled to ask for a re-count of the papers dealt with at a particular count or to ask for one complete re-count of all parcels of ballot papers. When re-counting, the order of the papers must not be disturbed. When a significant error is discovered, the papers must be counted afresh from the point at which the error occurred.

(7) Results

Having publicly announced the results of the election, the returning officer endorses the names of the elected members on the writ issued to him by the Clerk of the Dáil. He then returns the writ to the Clerk of the Dáil.

(8) By-elections

Casual vacancies in the membership of the Dáil are filled by by-elections. On the instructions of the Dáil the Clerk issues a writ to the returning officer for the constituency concerned directing him to hold a by-election to fill the vacancy. Procedure at a by-election is the same as at a general election.

Department of the Environment
February 1987

Appendix D

Dáil General Election Return: Dublin South, 1989

Total electorate 82,936. Valid poll 54,162. Number of seats 5. Quota 9,028

Names of Candidates	First Count Votes	Second Count Transfer of Brennan's Surplus	Result	Third Count Transfer of Kitt's Surplus	Result	Fourth Count Transfer of Ó Liatháin's Votes	Result	Fifth Count Transfer of Mitchell's Votes	Result	Sixth Count Transfer of Ormonde's Votes	Result	Seventh Count Transfer of Shatter's Surplus	Result	Eighth Count Transfer of FitzGerald's Votes	Result
*Brennan, Séamus (F.F.)	13,927	− 4,899	9,028	−	9,028	−	9,028	−	9,028	−	9,028	−	9,028	−	9,028
*Colley, Anne (P.D.)	4,607	+ 207	4,814	+ 32	4,846	+ 60	4,906	+ 286	5,192	+ 528	5,720	− 56	5,776	+ 941	6,717
Fennell, Nuala (F.G.)	4,983	+ 105	5,088	+ 17	5,105	+ 48	5,153	+ 1,187	6,340	+ 439	6,779	− 266	7,045	+ 1,292	8,337
FitzGerald, Eithne (Lab.)	4,134	+ 99	4,233	+ 25	4,258	+ 669	4,927	+ 99	5,026	+ 435	5,461	− 17	5,478	− 5,478	–
Garland, Roger (G.P.)	4,771	+ 129	4,900	+ 39	4,939	+ 433	5,372	+ 79	5,451	+ 1,034	6,485	− 15	6,500	+ 2,332	8,832
*Kitt, Tom (F.F.)	7,217	+ 3,452	10,669	− 1,641	9,028	–	9,028	–	9,028	–	9,028	–	9,028	–	9,028
Mitchell, Olivia (F.G.)	2,786	+ 36	2,822	+ 12	2,834	+ 26	2,860	− 2,860	–	–	–	–	–	–	–
Ó Liatháin, Eamonn (W.P.)	1,440	+ 22	1,462	+ 11	1,473	− 1,473	–	–	–	–	–	–	–	–	–
Ormonde, Ann (F.F.)	2,328	+ 675	3,003	+ 1,443	4,446	+ 72	4,518	+ 63	4,581	− 4,581	–	–	–	–	–
*Shatter, Alan (F.G.)	7,969	+ 174	8,143	+ 62	8,205	+ 70	8,275	+ 1,107	9,382	–	9,382	− 354	9,028	–	9,028
Non-Transferable Papers Non Effective						+ 95	95	+ 39	134	+ 2,145	2,279		2,279	+ 913	3,192
Total	54,162	–	54,162	–	54,162	–	54,162	–	54,162	–	54,162	–	54,162	–	54,162

Names of Candidates Elected:— Brennan, Séamus (F.F.) Kitt, Tom (F.F.) Shatter, Alan (F.G.) Garland, Roger (G.P.) Fennell, Nuala (F.G.)

Source: *Election Results and Transfer of Votes in General Election for Twenty-sixth Dáil* (Dublin: Stationery Office, 1989)

*Outgoing member

Appendix E
Estimate of the Department of Industry and Commerce for 1991

1.   Estimate of the amount required in the year ending 31 December 1991 for the salaries and expenses of the Office of the Minister for Industry and Commerce, including certain services administered by that Office, and for payment of certain loans, subsidies, grants and grants-in-aid.

Two hundred and forty million and one thousand pounds.
(£240,001,000)

II.   Subheads under which this Vote will be accounted for by the Office of the Minister for Industry and Commerce.

	1990 Estimate	1991 Estimate	Change 1991 over 1990
	£000	£000	%
A.1.—Salaries, Wages and allowances	8,220	8,572	+4%
A.2.—Consultancy Services	608	740	+22%
B.1.—Travelling and incidental expenses	1,576	1,347	−15%
B.2.—Office machinery and other office supplies (a)	1,074	1,200	+12%
B.3—Office premises expenses	365	500	+37%
C.1.—Postal and Telecommunications services	370	400	+8%
C.2.—Advertising and publicity	90	86	−4%
D.—Subscriptions to international organisations etc.	3,196	3,885	+22%
E.1.—Shannon Free Airport Development Company Limited—Administration and General Expenses (Industrial Development) (grant-in-aid) (b)	1,800	1,700	−6%
E.2.—Shannon Free Airport Development Company Limited—grants to industry (grant-in-aid) (b) (c) (d)	6,812	11,000	+61%
F.—Currency Exchange Loss on Certain Industrial Credit Corporation plc Foreign Borrowing for Industrial Development	7,900	3,750	−53%
G.1.—Córas Tráchtála—administration and general expenses (grant-in-aid) (b) (e)	24,637	32,500	+32%
G.2.—Córas Tráchtála—Market Entry and Development Scheme (grant-in-aid) (b) (e)	520	386	−26%
H.1.—Eolas—Administration and General Expenses (grant-in-aid) (b)	10,800	11,200	+4%
H.2.—Eolas—capital expenditure (grant-in-aid) (b) (d)	2,700	2,700	—
I.1.—Industrial Development Authority Administration and general expenses (grant-in-aid) (b)	15,600	16,700	+7%
I.2.—Industrial Development Authority Building Operations (grant-in-aid) (b) (d)	107,850	106,00	−2%
I.3.—Industrial Development Authority Building Operations (grant-in-aid) (b) (d)	11,500	11,950	+4%
J.—Irish Productivity Centre—Administration and General Expenses (grant-in-aid) (f)	600	625	+4%
K.—Irish Goods Council—Administration and general expenses (grant-in-aid) (b)	1,800	2,065	+15%
L.—National Development Corporation Limited—Administration and General expenses (grant-in-id) (f) (g)	300	100	−67%

	1990 Estimate	1991 Estimate	Change 1991 over 1990
M.1.—National Micro-electronics Research Centre, University College, Cork—Administration and General Expenses (grant-in-aid) (*h*)	400	416	+4%
M.2.—National Micro-electronics Research Centre, University College, Cork—Capital expenditure (grant-in -aid) (*d*) (*h*)	400	416	+4%
N.1.—Export Guarantee arrangements under the Insurance Act, 1953 (as amended)	2,274	2,854	+26%
N.2.—Credit Financing of Certain Capital goods exports	125	200	+60%
O.—Commissions, committees and special inquiries	45	43	−4%
P.—Miscellaneous payments	143	168	+17%
Q.—Science and technology development programme (*i*)	15,350	26,882	+75%
R.—Kilkenny Design Workshops Limited— Administration and general expenses (grant-in-aid) (*b*)	1	1	—
Gross total	227,056	248,386	+9%
Deduct:—			
S.—Appropriations in aid (*j*)	8,036	8,385	+4%
Net total	219,020	240,001	+10%
Net increase (000) + 20,981			

(*a*) Includes capital service 1990, £663,000; 1991 £700,000.

(*b*) Issues from the grant-in-aid will be made by the Minister for Industry and Commerce with the consent of the Minister for Finance. The Accounts will be audited by the Comptroller and Auditor General, and, together with his report thereon, will be laid before each House of the Oireachtas by the Minister for Industry and Commerce.

(*c*) Non-voted capital expenditure on industrial promotion by the Company, estimated at £3,780,000 in 1991, will be met by way of advances from the Central Fund.

(*d*) Capital Service.

(*e*) Amending legislation will be required to enable the total amount to be issued.

(*f*) Issues from the grant-in-aid will be made by the Minister for Industry and Commerce with the consent of the Minister for Finance. The audited Accounts will be laid before each House of the Oireachtas by the Minister for Industry and Commerce. In addition, the accounts will be made available, if required, for examination by the Comptroller and Auditor General.

(*g*) Non-voted capital expenditure by the Corporation, estimated at £3,500,000 in 1991, will be met by way of advances from the Central Fund.

(*h*) Issues from the grant-in-aid will be made by the Minister for Industry and Commerce with the consent of the Minister for Finance. The Accounts will be audited by the Comptroller and the Auditor General.

(*i*) Includes capital service 1990, £7,700; 1991 £11,282,000.

(*j*) Includes capital service receipts 1990, £185,000; 1991, 185,000.

Appendix F

Seanad General Election, 1987: An rolla oibreachais, Labour Panel

Number of Valid Votes 948. Value of Valid Votes 948,000. Quota (Value of Votes sufficient to secure the election of a candidate) 79,001.

In the result sheet as printed below the italicised type refers to the Nominating Bodies Sub-Panel and the roman type to the Oireachtas Sub-Panel

Names of Candidates (and placing in Order of Preferences)	First Count		Second Count		Third Count		Fourth Count		Fifth Count		Sixth Count		Seventh Count		Eighth Count		Ninth Count	
	Number of Votes	Value	Transfer of Cassidy's Surplus	Result	Transfer of Hanafin's Surplus	Result	Transfer of Mullooly's Surplus	Result	Transfer of Kiely's Surplus	Result	Transfer of Merrigan's Votes	Result	Transfer of Harte's Surplus	Result	Transfer of Greene's Votes	Result	Transfer of Brennan's Votes	Result
Brennan, Michael (18)	5	5,000	–	5,000	–	5,000	–	5,000	–	5,000	+2,000	7,000	–	7,000	–	7,000	–7,000	–
*Browne, John (12)	49	49,000	–	49,000	+ 282	49,282	–	49,282	–	49,282	–	49,282	–	49,282	–	49,282	–	49,282
*Cassidy, Donie (1)	95	95,000	–15,999	79,001	–	79,001	–	79,001	–	79,001	–	79,001	–	79,001	–	79,001	–	79,001
*Cregan, Denis (6)	75	75,000	–	75,000	+ 282	75,282	–	75,282	–	75,282	–	75,282	–	75,282	–	75,282	–	75,282
*Fennell, Nuala (9)	53	53,000	–	53,000	+ 141	53,141	–	53,141	–	53,141	–	53,141	–	53,141	–	53,141	–	53,141
Greene, Noirin (19)	5	5,000	+ 340	5,340	–	5,340	+ 36	5,376	–	5,376	+1,170	6,546	–	6,546	–6,546	–		
*Hanafin, Des (2)	92	92,000	–	92,000	–12,999	79,001	–	79,001	–	79,001	–	79,001	–	79,001	–	79,001	–	79,001
Harte, John (5)	77	77,000	+ 850	77,850	+ 282	78,132	+36	78,168	+ 130	78,298	+1,000	79,298	–297	79,001	–	79,001	–	79,001
Herbert, Tony (13)	48	48,000	+ 4,420	52,420	+ 4,089	56,509	+1,152	57,661	+1,040	58,701	–	58,701	–	58,701	+ 1,036	59,737	–	59,737
*Hillery, Brian (7)	55	55,000	+ 2,550	57,550	+ 4,512	62,062	+864	62,926	+ 910	63,836	+ 141	63,977	–	63,977	–	63,977	–	63,977
*Kelleher, Peter (14)	34	34,000	–	34,000	–	34,000	–	34,000	–	34,000	–	34,000	–	34,000	–	34,000	–	34,000
Kiely, Dan (4)	78	78,000	+ 3,740	81,740	–	81,740	–	81,740	–2,739	79,001	–	79,001	–	79,001	–	79,001	–	79,001
Kirwan, Chris (16)	17	17,000	–	17,000	–	17,000	–	17,000	–	17,000	–	17,000	–	17,000	–	17,000	–	17,000
Lydon, Donal (10)	50	50,000	+ 3,910	53,910	+ 2,961	56,871	+ 756	57,627	+ 650	58,277	–	58,277	–	58,277	+ 1,340	59,617	–	59,617
*McMahon, Larry (11)	49	49,000	–	49,000	+ 282	49,282	+ 72	49,354	–	49,354	–	49,354	–	49,354	–	49,354	–	49,354
Merrigan, Matt (20)	4	4,000	+ 170	4,170	+ 141	4,311	–	4,311	–	4,311	–4,311	–						
*Mullooly, Brian (3)	82	82,000	–	82,000	–	82,000	–2,999	79,001	–	79,001	–	79,001	–	79,001	–	79,001	–	79,001
O'Connell, Maurice (15)	18	18,000	–	18,000	–	18,000	–	18,000	–	18,000	–	18,000	–	18,000	+ 1,000	19,000	–	19,000
*O'Toole, Paddy (8)	55	55,000	–	55,000	–	55,000	+ 36	55,036	–	55,036	–	55,036	–	55,036	–	55,036	–	55,036
Rice, Robert Patrick (17)	7	7,000	–	7,000	–	7,000	–	7,000	–	7,000	–	7,000	+ 297	7,297	+ 1,000	8,297	+7,000	15,297
Non-transferable value not effective			+ 19	19	+ 27	46	+ 47	93	+ 9	102	–	102	–	102	+ 2,170	2,170	–	2,170
Loss of value owing to disregard of fractions			–		–		–		–		–		–		–		–	
Total	948.000			948,000		948,000		948,000		948,000		948,000		948,000		948,000		948,000

Names of Candidates Elected: Donie Cassidy, Des Hanafin, Brian Mullooly, Dan Kiely, John Harte, Denis Cregan, Nuala Fennell, Brian Hillery, Donal Lydon, Larry McMahon, Peter Kelleher.

*Candidate was an outgoing senator.

Number of members to be elected 11. Minimum number of members to be elected from each sub-panel 4.

	Tenth Count		Eleventh Count		Twelfth Count		Thirteenth Count		Fourteenth Count		Fifteenth Count		Sixteenth Count		Seventeenth Count		Eighteenth Count		Nineteenth Count		Twentieth Count	
	Transfer of Rice's Votes	Result	Transfer of O'Connell's Votes	Result	Transfer of Cregan's Surplus	Result	Transfer of Kirwan's Votes	Result	Transfer of Browne's Votes	Result	Transfer of Fennell's Surplus	Result	Transfer of Herbert's Votes	Result	Transfer of Hillery's Surplus	Result	Transfer of Lydon's Surplus	Result	Transfer of McMahon's Surplus	Result	Transfer of O'Toole's Votes	Result
	—	—	—	—	—	—	—	—	—	—	—	—	—	—	—	—	—	—	—	—	—	—
	—	49,282	+2,000	51,282	+640	51,922	+1,000	52,922	-52,922	—	—	—	—	—	—	—	—	—	—	—	—	—
	—	79,001	—	79,001	—	79,001	—	79,001	—	79,001	—	79,001	—	79,001	—	79,001	—	79,001	—	79,001	—	79,001
	+1,000	76,282	+4,000	80,282	-1,281	79,001	—	79,001	—	79,001	—	79,001	—	79,001	—	79,001	—	79,001	—	79,001	—	79,001
	—	53,141	+5,000	58,141	—	58,141	+5,000	63,141	+16,000	79,141	-140	79,001	—	79,001	—	79,001	—	79,001	—	79,001	—	79,001
	—	—	—	—	—	—	—	—	—	—	—	—	—	—	—	—	—	—	—	—	—	—
	—	79,001	—	79,001	—	79,001	—	79,001	—	79,001	—	79,001	—	79,001	—	79,001	—	79,001	—	79,001	—	79,001
	—	79,001	—	79,001	—	79,001	—	79,001	—	79,001	—	79,001	—	79,001	—	79,001	—	79,001	—	79,001	—	79,001
	—	59,737	—	59,737	—	59,737	—	59,737	—	59,737	—	59,737	-59,737	—	—	—	—	—	—	—	—	—
	—	63,977	—	63,977	—	63,977	+3,000	66,977	+1,000	67,977	—	67,977	+20,000	87,977	-8,976	79,001	—	79,001	—	79,001	—	79,001
	—	34,000	—	34,000	+320	34,320	+2,000	36,320	+14,000	50,320	—	50,320	+1,300	51,620	+2,000	53,620	+969	54,589	—	54,589	+49,000	103,589
	—	79,001	—	79,001	—	79,001	—	79,001	—	79,001	—	79,001	—	79,001	—	79,001	—	79,001	—	79,001	—	79,001
	+11,297	28,297	—	28,297	—	28,297	-28,297	—	—	—	—	—	—	—	—	—	—	—	—	—	—	—
	—	59,617	—	59,617	—	59,617	+1,000	60,617	—	60,617	+140	60,757	+26,000	86,757	—	86,757	-7,756	79,001	—	79,001	—	79,001
	+1,000	50,354	+5,000	55,354	+320	55,674	+4,297	59,971	+16,922	76,893	—	76,893	+1,488	78,381	—	78,381	+3,876	82,357	-3,256	79,001	—	79,001
	—	—	—	—	—	—	—	—	—	—	—	—	—	—	—	—	—	—	—	—	—	—
	—	79,001	—	79,001	—	79,001	—	79,001	—	79,001	—	79,001	—	79,001	—	79,001	—	79,001	—	79,001	—	79,001
	+1,000	20,000	-20,000	20,000	—	—	—	—	—	—	—	—	—	—	—	—	—	—	—	—	—	—
	—	55,036	+4,000	59,036	—	59,036	+2,000	61,036	5,000	66,036	—	66,036	+1,914	67,950	—	67,950	+2,907	70,857	+969	71,826	-71,826	—
	-15,297	—	—	—	—	—	—	—	—	—	—	—	—	—	—	—	—	—	—	—	—	—
	+1,000	3,170	—	3,170	—	3,170	+10,000	13,170	—	13,170	—	13,170	+9,035	22,205	+6,976	29,181	—	29,181	+2,287	31,468	+22,826	54,294
	—	102	—	102	+1	103	—	103	—	103	—	103	—	103	—	103	+4	107	—	107	—	107
	—	948,000	—	948,000	—	948,000	—	948,000	—	948,000	—	948,000	—	948,000	—	948,000	—	948,000	—	948,000	—	948,000

4

The Constitution of Ireland

The Constitution of Ireland (Bunreacht na hÉireann) is a fundamental document which establishes the state; it not only expresses legal norms but also reflects the aspirations, aims and political theories of the people. It is necessarily concerned with guiding principles and guarantees certain basic rights of the people in general terms and imposes limitations on those rights in almost equally general terms.

The Constitution regulates the government and the distribution of the powers of government and, more importantly, limits the power of government and imposes obligations upon those exercising that power; as such, it has been defined as 'a selection of the legal rules which govern the government and which have been embodied in a document' (Wheare 1966: 000). It has a higher legal status and authority than other laws and cannot be changed in the manner of ordinary legislation. In combination with an independent judiciary which has the power to review, it comprises an essential framework to protect the welfare of a liberal democratic country.

The Constitution was adopted by referendum in 1937. Its preamble envisages a system of fundamental law which can absorb or be adapted to changes as society changes and develops. It can therefore only be fully appreciated in conjunction with the legal traditions and precedents and the body of constitutional cases which have evolved since 1937. It should also be considered against the background of the two constitutions which preceded it in 1919 and 1922.

The Constitution of Dáil Éireann, 1919

This was the first Irish Constitution. The definitive text is in Irish and is published in the minutes of the first Dáil. It is a short document with five articles, covering the appointment of a chairman, the competence of the Dáil, the appointment of a Prime Minister and a government and their powers, the provision of funds, the audit of expenditure and provision for amendment. It is written in a clear straightforward manner.

The system of government adopted by this Irish constitution was parliamentary democracy based on the Westminster model then in operation in Britain. 'The founders of the new state were constitutionalists within a strongly developed parliamentary tradition'. (Farrell 1969:135). The Sinn Féin candidates elected at the general election of December 1918 were in rebellion against British rule in Ireland. They had neither the means, the time nor the inclination to draw up a detailed constitution. The members of the first Dáil saw themselves as completing the work of 1916 by ratifying and establishing the Republic of the 1916 Proclamation. By drawing up a constitution which set out the machinery of government, together with an economic and social programme, the Dáil sought to give practical effect to the declaration of independence and establish the legitimacy of the independence movement.

The Constitution of the Irish Free State, 1922

The Constitution of the new Irish Free State (Saorstát Éireann) was enacted by Dáil Éireann sitting as a constituent (i.e. constitution-making) assembly in the autumn of 1922 and was included as the first schedule to the Constitution of the Irish Free State Act 1922. The Treaty (Articles of Agreement) signed at London on 6 December 1921 between the United Kingdom and the Irish delegation was included as a second schedule to this Constitution. Section 2 of the act stated that 'If any provision of the said Constitution or any amendment thereof or of any law made thereunder is in any respect repugnant to any of the provisions of the Scheduled Treaty, it shall to the extent only of such repugnancy, be made absolutely void and inoperative.'

The Constitution acknowledged in its preamble that all lawful authority 'comes from God'. Article 1 declared that 'The Irish Free State is a co-equal member of the Community of Nations forming the British Commonwealth of Nations.' Article 2 declared that 'All powers of government and all authority, legislative, executive and judicial, in Ireland, are derived from the people of Ireland, and the same shall be exercised in the Irish Free State through the organisations established by or under, and in accord with, this Constitution.' The Constitution guaranteed the liberty of the person, the inviolability of the dwelling of each citizen, freedom of conscience and the free profession and practice of religion, and the right of free expression of opinion, as well as the right to assemble peaceably and the right to free elementary education.

The legislature of the new state was the Oireachtas, which was to consist of the king and two houses, the Dáil and the Seanad. The sole and exclusive power of making laws for the Irish Free State was vested in the Oireachtas, with the Dáil as the dominant partner. It was to be elected by all adult citizens voting by proportional representation. Each of the two universities was to elect two members, and there was to be one Teachta Dála for every 20,000 people. The Dáil was empowered to elect the President of the Executive

Council (which was replaced by the office of Taoiseach in the 1937 Constitution) and to approve his ministers; it could also, in theory, dismiss him, and select his successor.

The Seanad had sixty members of whom one-quarter were to be elected every three years by popular vote. It could delay bills for 270 days, but could not stop them. Membership of the Seanad was 'composed of citizens who shall be proposed on the grounds that they have done honour to the Nation by reason of useful public service or that, because of special qualifications or attainments, they represent important aspects of the Nation's life' (Article 30). As a result of the very active part played by the Seanad which frequently brought it into conflict with the government, especially after 1932, when the first Fianna Fáil government came into office, it was abolished in May 1936.

The 1922 Constitution could be amended by referendum and also by the Oireachtas without reference to the people, so it imposed no effective limitations on the power of the legislature. Article 47 did, however, provide for the reference of bills to the people, but this article was removed by the Constitution (Amendment No. 10) Act 1928 when the Fianna Fáil party sought to have a referendum on the oath of allegiance to the king, provided for in the Constitution. Article 50 provided for a referendum on amendments to the Constitution, but no referendum was held under the 1922 Constitution. Article 50 provided that the Constitution could be amended by simple act of the Oireachtas. Initially it was intended that all amendments would require a referendum. During the Dáil debate this was changed to allow for parliamentary amendment of defects that might become obvious during its first eight years. Subsequently this period of flexible amendment was extended to sixteen years. 'So, during the whole of its life, the Irish Free State Constitution could be changed as easily as any other law, without direct reference to the people. Both the Cosgrave and de Valera governments took full advantage of the latitude, and between 1923 and 1936 twenty-five bills were passed amending many provisions of the original text.' (Farrell 1988: 29).

The Free State Constitution reflected some of the major features of the unwritten British Constitution, such as the institution of cabinet government led by a prime minister, accountable to and ultimately controlled by the legislature, and an independent judiciary. It formally defined the separation of legislative, executive and judicial powers. It also sought to qualify the doctrine of ministerial responsibility by creating an additional tier of 'extern ministers' outside the Executive Council. These ministers were placed in charge of departments of a technical or non-controversial nature (e. g. Agriculture, Fisheries, Post and Telegraphs). This interesting constitutional experiment in enhancing individual responsibility at the expense of collective cabinet responsibility failed and was abandoned in 1927, when the Constitution was amended in such a way that no extern ministers were ever appointed again.

The Constitution contained an inherent conflict within itself between the British monarchical system and Irish republicanism which caused Mansergh (1952: 296) to describe it as 'an essay in frustration'. Examples of the influence of the British monarchy were the oath of allegiance to the British crown to be taken by members of the Oireachtas under Article 17. The king's assent to legislation was necessitated, and there was provision for appeal to the British Privy Council which was a usual feature of Commonwealth constitutions. Ó Briain (1929: 71) described the 1922 Constitution as 'monarchical in external form, republican in substance and, withal, essentially democratic'.

MAIN PROVISIONS

The basic elements of the 1937 Constitution can be broadly stated as follows. All powers derive, under God, from the people. For the purpose of enacting laws and taking other major decisions the people periodically elect representatives to sit in the principal house of the Oireachtas, the Dáil, which is free to take whatever decisions it thinks proper within the limits set by the Constitution. Every person over eighteen years has the right to vote in these elections, and every person over twenty-one to seek a seat in the Dáil. In addition to the Dáil, the Oireachtas consists of a President elected directly by the people and an indirectly elected Seanad. The President, who is the head of state, has prescribed functions in relation to the protection of the Constitution. The day-to-day administration of the nation's affairs is entrusted to the executive body known as the Government which is chosen by the Dáil and is responsible to that House only; the government goes out of office on losing support in the Dáil. The interpretation and application of the laws is entrusted to the courts, which are independent and subject only to the Constitution and the laws; these courts also have the function of determining whether any law is repugnant to the Constitution; and trial by jury for ordinary offences is guaranteed.

Certain fundamental rights of the individual are guaranteed, such as personal liberty, equality before the law, freedom of expression (including criticism of the government), freedom of assembly and association, rights relating to the family, education, dwelling and property, and religious freedom. Retrospective legislation may not declare any action to be an offence. Broad principles of social policy are set out for the guidance of the Oireachtas. Certain provisions of the Constitution may be suspended in times of emergency, in accordance with procedures set out in the Constitution; but actual amendments to the Constitution may be effected only by vote of the people in a referendum. As Mr de Valera put it during the Dáil debate on the draft Constitution, 'If there is one thing more than another that is clear and shining through this whole Constitution, it is the fact that the people are the masters.'

Article 1 refers to the nation's 'sovereign right . . . to determine its relations with other small nations'. While Article 2 states that the national territory consists of the whole island of Ireland, its islands and territorial seas,

Article 3 confers reality on the situation by providing that, 'pending the re-integration of the national territory', the laws enacted by the Irish Parliament 'shall have the like area and extent of application as the laws of Saorstát Éireann and the like extra-territorial effect'. Article 4 provides that the name of the State is Éire, or in the English language, Ireland. Article 5 declares that Ireland is a sovereign, independent, democratic state.

Article 6 specifies three powers of government, legislative, executive and judicial which is the cornerstone of the Irish system of government. This Article acknowledges that these powers derive, under God, from the people. The President acts as head of state and the guardian of the people's rights under the Constitution.

The national parliament is referred to as the Oireachtas and consists, as already indicated, of the President, together with the Dáil and Seanad, with the Dáil holding the dominant position. Article 15.2.1 vests the exclusive power of making laws for the state in the Oireachtas. The same article forbids the Oireachtas from enacting any law repugnant to the Constitution.

The status and powers of the government and the Taoiseach (see Chapter 1) are defined in Article 28; and other articles set out procedures for the passage of legislation, e. g. presentation to Dáil and Seanad, signing and promulgation, and reference to the Supreme Court.

Article 27 provides that a bill, other than a bill to amend the Constitution, may be recommended to the President for referral to the people by a majority of the Seanad and not less than one-third of the members of the Dáil. This article has never been invoked.

Article 28.4.2 states that the government shall meet and act as a collective responsibility, and shall be collectively responsible for the departments of state administered by the members of the government.

The Constitution provides for the offices of Attorney General, who advises the government on legal matters, and Comptroller and Auditor General, who audits all moneys administered by the Oireachtas. Under the Constitution, the financial powers of the Dáil are limited. It may not pass any vote or resolution, or enact any law for the spending of public moneys, unless it has been recommended to the Dáil by a message from the government, signed by the Taoiseach.

Under Article 34, justice is to be administered in courts established by law by judges appointed under the Constitution. The courts comprise courts of first instance, i.e. including courts of local and limited jurisdiction and the High Court, as well as a court of final appeal, the Supreme Court. Judges of the High Court and Supreme Court are appointed by the President on the recommendation of the government. All other judges are appointed by the government. The independence of the judiciary in the exercise of their judicial functions is provided for.

Article 50.1 carries into force laws enacted before the Constitution came into operation, provided that they are not inconsistent with it.

FUNDAMENTAL RIGHTS

The Constitution firmly establishes the natural law as the basis of many of the rights guaranteed as fundamental rights. It puts outside the reach of the executive or of the legislature the power to act contrary to these rights or to endeavour to suppress them or deny them. One of the most fundamental political rights which the citizen has guaranteed is the right of access to the courts. Another essential civil liberty is the right to vote and to have an electoral system, and 'no voter may exercise more than one vote at an election for Dáil Éireann'(Article 16.1.4).

Under the heading 'Personal Rights' it is declared that 'All citizens shall, as human persons, be held equal before the law.' This is qualified by the statement that 'This shall not be held to mean that the State shall not in its enactments have due regard to differences of capacity, physical and moral, and of social function.' Persons may not be deprived of rights to their liberty save in accordance with law, of the right to express convictions and opinions, to associate with fellow-citizens and to assemble. The right of association, the right of assembly, and the right of freedom of speech are all subject to the overriding consideration of public order and public morality.

Under Article 40, the state also guarantees in its laws to respect and, as far as practicable, to defend and vindicate the personal rights of the citizen. It guarantees that the state shall, in particular, by its laws protect the citizen as best it may from unjust attack and, in the case of injustice done, vindicate the life, person, good name, and property rights of every citizen. Article 40.3 has emerged as the 'due process' clause of the Irish Constitution. Ó Dálaigh C.J. said *In re Haughey* (1971 IR 217, p. 263) that:

> Article 40.3 of the Constitution is a guarantee to the citizen of basic fairness of procedures. The Constitution guarantees such fairness, and it is the duty of the Court to underline that the words of Article 40.3 are not political shibboleths but provide a positive protection for the citizen and his good name.

Article 41 recognises the family as the natural, primary and fundamental unit group of society and as a moral institution possessing inalienable and imprescriptible rights. *Inalienable* means that which cannot be transferred or given away, while *imprescriptible* means that which cannot be lost by the passage of time or abandoned by non-exercise.

The family is also dealt with in Article 42, where it is recognised as the primary and natural educator of the child. That article guarantees to protect the right and the duty of parents to provide, according to their means, for the education of their children. In this context, education is referred to as including religious and moral, intellectual, physical and social training. In the provision dealing with the state's right, as guardian of the common good, to require certain minimum education for all children, the reference is to the moral, intellectual and social elements of education.

Article 43 declares the right to the private ownership of external goods. The state accordingly guarantees to pass no law attempting to abolish the right to private ownership or the general right to transfer, bequeath and inherit property. It goes on to recognise that in civil society the exercise of these rights should be regulated by the principles of social justice, and that the state accordingly, as the occasion requires, may delimit by law the exercise of these rights with a view to reconciling their exercise with the exigencies of the common good.

The guarantee of freedom of conscience and the free profession and practice of religion is made subject to public order and public morality. This consideration is not referred to in Articles 41, 42 or 43.

THE SUPREMACY OF THE CONSTITUTION

The supreme status of the Constitution is reflected in its adoption by the people; in the declaration of its own supremacy in Article 15.4, which states that any laws which are repugnant to its provisions are null and void; in the process of judicial review, which makes independent adjudication possible; and in the process of amendment under Article 46, which states that a proposal to amend must be passed by both Houses of the Oireachtas and then submitted to the people in a referendum.

Constitutional supremacy is, however, qualified in two ways. Firstly, under Article 28.3.3, nothing may invalidate any law enacted by the Oireachtas which is expressed to be for the purpose of securing the public safety and the preservation of the state in time of war or armed rebellion. Secondly, following a referendum in 1972, membership of the EC imposes limitations which provide that laws enacted or measures adopted by the state which are necessitated by membership of the European Communities may not be invalidated by the Constitution.

The Constitution is rigid but can be amended. Since coming into operation it has been amended ten times; these amendments are briefly outlined below.

Constitutional Amendments

Article 51 of the 'Transitory Provisions' of the original Constitution permitted amendments to be made by the Oireachtas without reference to the people. The first two amendments to the 1937 Constitution were made by this method. These transitional arrangements were superseded in 1941, and all subsequent amendments have required the approval of the people in a referendum.

(1) and (2) took place in 1939 and 1941. Both made changes in Article 28.3.3 to take account of the emergency created by the outbreak of war in Europe.

(3) took place in May 1972 and allowed Ireland's entry to the European Community (Article 29.4.3).

(4) lowered the voting age from twenty-one to eighteen (December 1972).

(5) removed the reference to the 'special position' of the Roman Catholic Church and the recognition of other churches and religious denominations in Ireland (December 1972).

(6) rendered adoption orders made by the Adoption Board immune from the requirement that justice must be administered by a court (1979).

(7) allowed the redistribution of university seats in the Seanad (1979).

(8) added the right to life of the unborn to the Constitution (1983).

(9) extended the franchise in Dáil elections to non-citizens (1984).

(10) enabled the state to ratify the Single European Act 1986 (1987).

There have been three unsuccessful attempts to amend the Constitution. Proposals for electoral reform in 1959 and 1968, both including the replacement of proportional representation by the 'straight vote' system, were defeated; and a proposal to legalise divorce was defeated in 1986.

DIRECTIVE PRINCIPLES OF SOCIAL POLICY

Article 45 consists of a number of principles 'for the general guidance of the Oireachtas', presenting a comprehensive vision of society and social policy founded on Catholic social teaching. In the early years this article was largely ignored by the courts, as exemplified by the judgement of Kingsmill Moore J. in the case of *Comyn v. Attorney General* (1959 IR 142), when he said that Article 45 'puts the state under certain duties, but they are duties of imperfect obligation since they cannot be enforced or regarded by any court of law, and are only direction for the guidance of the Oireachtas'.

In more recent years Article 45 has become an increasingly important influence, as exemplified by the decision of Finlay J. in *Landers v. Attorney General* (109 ILTR 1), in which he held that he was entitled to be guided by these directive principles of social policy which impose upon the state the obligation of endeavouring to meet the common good.

However, Henchy J. in the Supreme Court in *The People (Director of Public Prosecutions) v. O'Shea* (1982 IR 384) stated that 'If any person were to institute proceedings in the High Court seeking to compel the state to give effect to any of the specified directives, the High Court would be bound to strike out those proceedings for want of jurisdiction.'

JUDICIAL REVIEW

Judicial review includes the power to invalidate on constitutional grounds acts of any administrative agency and to decide whether any law is in keeping with the provisions of the Constitution. It is an important aspect of the organic process of review and interpretation of the Constitution and ensures that constitutional provisions are observed and that the various political institutions act within their proper sphere of authority. This power is conferred on the High Court and Supreme Court (under Articles 26, 34.3 and 34.4). The process can be used before a bill becomes law if the President, using his powers under Article 26, decides to refer it to the Supreme Court for a decision. The more common practice, however, is to have laws tested in the High Court or Supreme Court in the course of ordinary litigation.

The Irish judiciary have since the mid-1960s become increasingly innovative in their interpretations of the Constitution. This approach included, for example, considerations relating to the Preamble, Article 45 on the directive principles of social policy, the nature of Irish society, and 'concepts of prudence, justice and charity which gradually change or develop as society changes and develops and which fall to be interpreted from time to time in accordance with prevailing ideas' (O'Higgins C.J. in *The State (Healy) v. Donoghue* (1976) IR 325, p. 347). In *Tormey v. Ireland* (1985 IR 289) Henchy J. said that

> The Constitution must be read as a whole, and its several provisions must not be looked at in isolation, but be treated as interlocking parts of the general constitutional scheme.

The entire body of judicial decisions on constitutional law is regarded as part of the living aspect of the Constitution. The courts are the ultimate guardians of the Constitution, but they cannot move until their powers are invoked. The Attorney General, by virtue of his constitutional office, has also cast upon him, in the appropriate case, the duty of defending the Constitution.

In a wide range of cases the courts have made explicit certain rights and entitlements of citizens that they have found to be implicit in the 1937 Constitution. For example, in the case of *Ryan v. Attorney General* (1965 IR 294), which is related to the fluoridation of water, the court held that there are many personal rights of the citizen which follow from the Christian and democratic nature of the state which are not mentioned in Article 40 at all. It instanced as examples of such personal rights, the right to bodily integrity, the right to free movement within the state, and the right to marry. Speaking fifteen years after his Ryan judgment, Mr Justice Kenny acknowledged in the course of a lecture the significance of the epoch which he inaugurated, when he said, in connection with Article 40.3: 'Judges have become legislators, and have the advantage that they do not have to face an opposition.' (1979 NILQ 189, p. 196).

Ó Dálaigh C.J. said in delivering the Supreme Court's judgement in this case, that

> The Court agrees with Mr Justice Kenny that 'personal rights' mentioned in section 3.1 are not exhausted by the enumeration of 'life,

person, good name, and property rights' in section 3.2 as is shown by the use of the words 'in particular', nor by the more detached treatment of specific rights in the subsequent sections of the article. (pp. 344–5)

In a further case, relating to a law prohibiting the importation or sale of contraceptives, Walsh J. stated in *McGee v. Attorney General* (1974 IR 284):

Articles 41, 42 and 43 emphatically reject the theory that there are no rights without laws, no rights contrary to the law and no rights anterior to the law. They indicate that justice is placed above the law and acknowledge that natural rights, or human rights, are not created by law but that the Constitution confirms their existence and gives them protection.

Since the decision in the Ryan case the courts have defined many other rights which the state is pledged to defend and vindicate even though they are not specifically enumerated in the Constitution. These include the right not to be unconstitutionally restrained from earning one's livelihood (*Murtagh Properties v. Cleary* (1972 IR 330)); the right to litigate claims, found to be a personal right of the citizen within Article 40 in *O'Brien v. Keogh* (1972 IR 144); the right to work (*Murphy v. Stewart* (1973 IR 117)); the right to marital privacy (*McGee v. Attorney General* (1974 IR 284)); the right of access to the courts (*McAuley v. Minister for Posts and Telegraphs* (1966 IR 345)); the right to avail of such facilities as the state has obtained for its citizens to travel abroad (*The State (M) v. Attorney General* (1979 IR 73)); the right to fair procedures (*The State (Healy) v. Donoghue* (1976 IR 325)); and the right to privacy in one's communications with others (*Kennedy v. Ireland* (unreported, 12 Jan. 1987)).

THE REPUBLIC OF IRELAND

The Constitution provides (Article 4) that the name of the state is Éire, or in the English language, Ireland. The normal practice is to use the name 'Éire' in texts in the Irish language and to use 'Ireland' in all English-language texts, with corresponding translations for texts in other languages. The Republic of Ireland Act 1948 provides for the description of the state as 'the Republic of Ireland', but this provision has not changed the usage 'Ireland' as the name of the state in the English language.

Article 5 of the Constitution declares that Ireland is a sovereign, independent, democratic state. It does not, however, proclaim that Ireland is a Republic, nor does any other Article of the Constitution, despite the fact that many of its provisions have a distinctly republican stamp. The omission of this proclamation of a republic in the Constitution of 1937 was deliberate. Mr de Valera stated in the Dáil of 14 June 1937 that if the Northern problem was not there 'in all probability, there would be a flat, downright proclamation of the Republic'.

In 1948 the Republic of Ireland Act was passed, repealing the Executive Authority (External Relations) Act 1936 (which had retained the crown for purposes of diplomatic representation and international agreements, in the hope that such an arrangement might, as Mr de Valera put it, facilitate the construction of a bridge 'over which the Northern Unionists might walk') and providing instead for the declaration of a republic. In accordance with this act, on Easter Day 1949 Ireland became a republic.

CONCLUSION

'Nowhere in the world is the right to personal liberty more fully protected than under the Irish Constitution': so wrote Mr Justice Brian Walsh of the Supreme Court in *The Irish Times* on 29 December 1987 on the occasion of the fiftieth anniversary of the Constitution. He continued:

> The Constitution is a living law. As a document it dates from 1937, as a law from today. It is written in the present tense. It has always been interpreted in the light of the circumstances of the contemporary epoch. Therefore it is designed in general principles to look after the future as well as the present. In practice the Constitution of Ireland has worked very well. In many ways the civil service has shown a greater awareness and appreciation of its provisions than has been the case among many politicians. In particular it can be said that the Department of Justice, often the subject of unjust criticism, has in the last twenty years shown great sensitivity to the provisions of the Constitution.

Dr Tom Garvin noted in his contribution to the same edition of *The Irish Times*:

> The great achievement of 1937 was that an arena was established in which the issues of individual *versus* collective interest could be contested. This was the first time such an arena or basic framework had ever been provided in Irish history and was a major step forward in the provision of political order in Ireland. We have come to take that political order so much for granted that we sometimes forget what a formidable achievement it was.

The Constitution gives an incomplete picture of the mechanics of Irish government. What a Constitution says is one thing and what actually happens in practice may be quite another. While the sole power of making laws is vested in the Oireachtas, in practice it is actually the government that makes the laws, which are then passed by the Oireachtas. Farrell (1987:162) notes that

> The Constitution provides not merely an incomplete, but in a number of important respects a misleading, account of the nature, functions and operations of basic political institutions. It enshrines mythologies that

bear little relation to the actualities of power. It ignores some real sources of influence, elevates some marginal authorities, distances some relationships and misrepresents the balance of forces that maintain the Irish political system. Political parties are not even mentioned. The role of both Dáil and Seanad in the actual making of legislation is exaggerated. The real dominance of the government is obscured by a pedantic emphasis on parliamentary accountability. The Constitution is a rulebook that has only a tangential connection with the Irish political and governmental game.

Ireland is not unique in having a gap between political practice and constitutional theory. The most important aspect of this is the decline in the power of the legislature. Farrell (1987: 163) notes that the government controls the Dáil rather than the declaration in Article 15.2.1 that 'The sole and exclusive power of making laws for the State is hereby vested in the Oireachtas.' The reasons for this, he suggests, include party politics, the clientist role of deputies, the electoral system of multi-seat proportional representation constituencies, and the government's control over public expenditure.

Article 28.3.3 gives wide powers to the Oireachtas to pass legislation to deal with emergency situations. This power to secure the public safety and to preserve the state in times of war or armed rebellion is often referred to as the 'suspension of the Constitution', as no right to life, liberty or property is protected in any way against such legislation. Under the Emergency Powers Act 1939, the Oireachtas can enact any law, however repugnant to the provisions of the Constitution it may be, for the purpose of securing public safety under the provisions of Article 28.3.3. In 1976 the Oireachtas declared that the 1939 emergency had ended and that another existed; fresh emergency resolutions were passed by both houses and were cleared for constitutionality by the Supreme Court after referral there by the President (see p. 103).

The desirability of revising the Constitution has been discussed from time to time. It is recorded that as early as 1947 Mr de Valera expressed a wish to change the provisions relating to proportional representation, Seanad representation and property rights (Rau 1960: 310). In 1966 an informal all-party committee of TDs and senators was set up to consider possible changes in the Constitution. Its report (December 1967) discussed twenty-seven aspects of the Constitution, leaving it to the government of the day to decide the items which should be selected for inclusion in any legislative proposals that might emerge. It made the unanimous recommendation that Article 44.1.2–3 (on the special position of the Roman Catholic Church and recognition of the other churches) should be deleted; this was given effect to by the Fifth Amendment in 1972. It also made recommendations for the rewording of Article 3 (on the extent of the application of the laws of the state) and of Article 41 (on marriage). The report commented that the all-party committee was not aware of any public demand for a change in the basic structure of the Constitution and concluded that 'As a general proposition, therefore, it might be said that our inclination was to adhere to the constitutional provisions which have worked so well in practice, and to consider changes only in the case of those provisions which, from experience, might be regarded as not adequately fulfilling their purpose.'

In his foreword to O'Reilly and Redmond (1980) Mr Justice Brian Walsh observed: 'For so long as the Constitution reflects the politics and social culture of the majority of the people, and there is little real evidence that it does not, it is difficult to justify claims that a drastic overhaul is needed.' In this connection, the Taoiseach stated in the Dáil on 23 October 1991, in reply to a parliamentary question on the matter, that he had no proposals at that time to reform the Constitution.

REFERENCES

Farrell, Brian, 'A Note on the Dáil Constitution, 1919' in *Irish Jurist*, iv (1969), 127–38

Farrell, Brian, 'The Constitution and the Institutions of Government: Constitutional Theory and Political Practice', in *The Constitution of Ireland 1937–87,* F. Litton ed. (Special issue of *Administration*, Vol 35, No. 4 , 1987)

Farrell, Brian ed., *De Valera's Constitution and Ours* (Dublin: Gill & Macmillan for RTE, 1988)

Mansergh, Nicholas, *Survey of British Commonwealth Affairs: Problem of External Policy, 1931–39* (London: Oxford University Press 1952)

Ó Briain, Barra, *The Irish Constitution* (Dublin/Cork: Talbot Press, 1929)

O'Reilly, James, and Redmond, Mary, *Cases and Materials on the Irish Constitution* (Dublin: Incorporated Law Society, 1980)

Rau, Benegal N., *India's Constitution in the Making*, B. Shira Rau ed. (Bombay: Orient Longmans, 1960)

Wheare, Kenneth C., *Modern Constitutions* (London: Oxford University Press, 1966)

5

The President of
Ireland

The President of Ireland (Uachtarán na hÉireann) is the only officer of state who can be directly elected by all the citizens of the country. She is elected for a period of seven years and can only be re-elected once. Her main functions include acting as ceremonial head of state; formalising a number of appointments; summoning and dissolving Dáil Éireann in certain circumstances; signing into law and promulgating bills which have been passed by the Dáil and Seanad; and operating as a check but not as a veto on legislation.

Every citizen over thirty-five years of age is eligible for the office, but a candidate must be nominated by at least twenty members of the Dáil or Seanad or by four county councils. (During the presidential campaign of 1990 this system was criticised, and it was suggested that there should be wider democratic procedures for nominating candidates.) A former or retiring President may become a candidate on her own nomination. A President may not be a member of either House of the Oireachtas or hold any other office or position for which she receives payment; on election to office she must vacate any seat or position.

The electorate is the same as that for Dáil elections. If only one candidate is put forward, there is no election and the candidate becomes President on the declaration of the returning officer. Elections have in fact been avoided by the nomination of a single agreed candidate on five out of ten occasions since the office was first filled in 1938.

The role of the President is defined in the Constitution of 1937, and the limitations on that role have been determined not only by the articles of the Constitution but more emphatically by convention. Among the relevant provisions of the Constitution are Article 12.1, which provides for the office of the President of Ireland, 'who shall take precedence over all other persons in the State', and Article 15.1.2, which provides that the Oireachtas shall consist of the President and two Houses. The President is the head of state, and although she is formally a part of the Oireachtas, her primary function is to act as a check on the Houses of parliament. Under Article 13.8.1, the President is not 'answerable to either House of the Oireachtas or to any Court for the exercise and performance of the powers and functions of his office'. She is expected to be above and apart from politics, although under Article 28.5.2 the Taoiseach is obliged to keep her generally informed on matters of domestic and international policy.

The emoluments of the President are fixed by statute from the Central Fund and cannot be reduced during her term of office. The total amount required for the salaries and expenses of the presidential establishment for the year 1991 is £384,000 (an increase of 43 per cent over the 1990 figure). The President is provided with an official residence, Áras an Uachtaráin, in the Phoenix Park, Dublin which is maintained by the Office of Public Works. The President has the assistance of a number of staff in her duties, including the Secretary to the President. This officer is a civil servant of the state (see p. 107), who is appointed by the government following consultation with the President and does not retire from office with the President. The Secretary to the President is Clerk to the Council of State and *ex officio* Secretary to the Presidential Commission. The President also has the assistance of an aide-de-camp, who is normally a colonel in the army.

The President has a seal of office, which is referred to in Articles 27, 31, 33 and 35 of the Constitution. The Presidential Seal Act 1937 provides that the President shall have custody and control of this seal, which is affixed to documents issued by her and which must be authenticated by her signature.

The first President of Ireland was Douglas Hyde, a Gaelic scholar who was appointed in 1938 following all-party agreement; Sean T. O'Ceallaigh became President in 1945 after an election and served a second term after nominating himself in 1952; Eamon de Valera served two terms following election, in 1959 and in 1966; Erskine Childers was elected to the Office in 1973; Cearbhall O' Dalaigh was appointed in 1974 following all-party agreement; as was Patrick Hillery in 1976 and 1983. Mary Robinson became the seventh President in 1990 and is both the first woman and the youngest person to hold the office.

FUNCTIONS AND LIMITATIONS OF THE PRESIDENT

The President normally acts on the advice and authority of the government. The Constitution emphasises in several places that the President requires the approval of the government before taking action. Article 13.9 declares that the powers and functions conferred on the President by the Constitution are exercisable and performable by her only on the advice of the government, except where it is provided by the Constitution that she acts in her absolute discretion or after consultation with or in relation to the Council of State, or on the advice of any other person or body. In addition, Article 13.11 provides that

'No power or function conferred on the President by law shall be exercisable or performable by him save only on the advice of the Government.' A private member's motion brought before the Dáil in October 1990, during the presidential election campaign, to extend the powers of the President by law within the limits set out in the Constitution was defeated by 125 votes to 24.

In the case of appointments and decisions, the President acts only on the binding advice of the government. For example, members of the judiciary cannot be appointed except on that advice. There are also important provisions in the Constitution which specifically require the initiative of some other person or body before action can be taken by the President. For example, the Attorney General is appointed by the President on the nomination of the Taoiseach (Article 30), and the Comptroller and Auditor General is appointed by the President on the nomination of the Dáil (Article 33). In the case of the removal of persons from these offices, the Constitution obliges the President to act as requested by the appropriate authorities. She must terminate the appointment of the Attorney General and of ministers on the advice of the Taoiseach, and the Comptroller and Auditor General, and judges, on a resolution of the Dáil and Seanad.

The primacy of the government is manifest from the provision of Article 12.9, under which the President cannot leave the state during her term of office without the consent of the government. Under Article 13.1, the President appoints the Taoiseach on the nomination of the Dáil and other members of the government 'on the nomination of the Taoiseach with the previous approval of the Dáil' (Article 13.1.2), while she is required to terminate ministerial appointments on the advice of the Taoiseach only. The Dáil is summoned and dissolved by her on the advice of the Taoiseach under Article 13.2.1.

The President is required by the provision of Articles 13.3 and 25.2.1 to sign bills passed by both Houses of the Oireachtas, thereby giving them the force of law; and in addition she must, under Article 25.4.2 (except in cases where reference to the people or the Supreme Court is involved) promulgate each new legislative measure by publishing in the *Iris Oifigiúil* (the official gazette) a notice stating that the bill has become law.

The President may, after consultation with the Council of State, communicate with the Houses of the Oireachtas and she may address a message to the nation on any matter of national or public importance. Article 13.7.3 states that every such message or address must have received the approval of the government. The Constitution is silent on whether the President can make a statement, of a political nature, without the consent of the government. Successive governments have tended to believe that the President could not speak publicly on any issue without their approval. While it is not appropriate for the President to be involved in confrontation with the government on legislative or policy matters, Kelly (1984: 65–6) holds that the

President retains the ordinary rights of a citizen in regard to freedom in expressing her opinions or, in particular, replying to criticism.

Under Article 13.6, the President has the right to commute the sentences of criminal offenders, but by virtue of Article 13.9 she can exercise this power only on the advice of the government. Only three cases of the receipt of a pardon are reported and all of these occurred during the period in office of Ireland's first President, Dr Douglas Hyde.

The supreme command of the Defence Forces is vested in the President by Article 13.4, but this is followed by a provision requiring that the exercise of this command is to be regulated by law. Section 17 of the Defence Act 1954 provides that the military command of and all executive and administrative powers in relation to the Defence Forces shall 'under the direction of the President' be exercisable by the government through the Minister for Defence. Acting under the Defence Act 1954 and on the advice of the government, the President makes appointments to the following offices in the Permanent Defence Forces: Chief of Staff; Adjutant-General; Quartermaster-General; Inspector General; and Judge Advocate General. Under Article 13.5.2 of the Constitution, all commissioned officers of the Defence Forces hold their commissions from the President.

While Article 13.10 permits the conferring by law of additional powers and functions on the President, this is qualified by the provision of Article 13.11 referred to above. The Republic of Ireland Act 1948 provides that 'The President on the advice of the government may exercise the executive functions of the State in or in connection with its external relations.' For this reason, it is to the President that foreign ambassadors present their credentials, and it is the President who, on the advice of the government, accredits Irish diplomatic representatives abroad. The President represents Ireland abroad. Finally, in the declaration of war or emergency no function is allotted by the Constitution to the President under Article 28.3.

Among the additional powers which have been conferred on the President by law under Article 13.10 are formal powers of appointment. These include the appointment of Council members and senior professors of the Dublin Institute for Advanced Studies (under SS 8 and 9 of the Institute of Advanced Studies Act 1940); of the Governor of the Central Bank (under S. 19 of the Central Bank Act 1942); and of the Ombudsman (under S. 2 of the Ombudsman Act 1980). The Red Cross Act 1944 provides that the President of Ireland shall, by virtue of her office, be President of the Irish Red Cross Society. These additional powers are exercised by the President either on the advice of the government or pursuant to a resolution of the Oireachtas. The President also presents the centenarian's bounty, a once-off payment of £250 made to Irish citizens living in Ireland who have reached the age of one hundred years.

The provisions of the Constitution relating to the impeachment of the President effectively establish the supremacy of the legislature over a

President whom it deems to be unfit for office. Article 12.10 provides for the impeachment of the President for 'stated misbehaviour' after a charge made against her by either House of the Oireachtas is sustained by the prescribed two-thirds majority. When such a charge has been preferred, the other House will investigate it or cause it to be investigated. The relevant constitutional provisions are designed to ensure that this serious step will only be undertaken on a matter of widespread public concern.

The Constitution does not define or specify 'stated misbehaviour' or in any way limit the nature of the charge to be brought against the President. It provides, however, that in addition to proving the charge, the House responsible for the investigation must also pass a resolution that the misbehaviour that was the subject of the charge was such as to render her unfit to continue in office. This elasticity leaves it to the wisdom of that House to decide whether the particular charge, if proved, is or is not, in the special circumstances of the case, such as to render the President unfit to continue in office. (McDunphy 1945: 23)

The Constitution provides at Article 12.3.1 for the removal from office of a President whose permanent incapacity has been 'established to the satisfaction of the Supreme Court consisting of not less than five judges'.

There is no Vice-President of Ireland. The Constitution ensures that there is no gap in continuity as regards the powers, duties and functions of the office. A Presidential Commission discharges the powers and functions of the President in the event of her absence, or her temporary or permanent incapacity, or in the event of her death, resignation, removal from office or failure to exercise and perform the powers and functions of her office. This Commission consists of the Chief Justice, the Ceann Comhairle of the Dáil, and the Cathaoirleach of the Seanad. The Commission may act by any two of its number. In the event of the removal from office or death, resignation or permanent incapacity of the President, an election for her successor must take place within sixty days (Article 12.3.3).

DISCRETIONARY POWERS OF THE PRESIDENT

While the President acts on the advice of the government and has limited discretion in the making of certain appointments and decisions, she has, however, six independent powers which she may exercise on her own initiative independent of the government. These are outlined below.

(1) Article 26 of the Constitution enables the President, after consultation with the Council of State, to refer any bill (with certain exceptions) to the Supreme Court for a decision as to its constitutionality. Mr de Valera referred to this when he explained that the President 'in exercising these powers . . . is acting on behalf of the people who have put him there for that special purpose. He is there to guard the people's rights and mainly to guard the Constitution' and is invested

with certain functions and powers to do this. (*Dáil Debates*, 11 May 1937, col. 51). This power of a President is politically sensitive and has involved one incumbent in controversy which led to a constitutional crisis. The exercise of the power and the crisis of 1976 are examined in detail on pp 101–4.

(2) The second, and arguably most important, independent power of the President is the very wide power under Article 13 which enables her, in her absolute discretion, to refuse to dissolve the Dáil on the advice of a Taoiseach who has ceased to retain the support of a majority in the Dáil. Where she does so refuse, it is presumed the Taoiseach concerned would have to resign, and the Dáil would then have an opportunity of nominating a successor. Mr de Valera explained that the wise exercise of this power 'by the President may mean that he is maintaining the supremacy of the people at a time when it is vital that the people's supremacy should be maintained'. (*Dáil Debates*, 11 May 1937, col. 45) Three occasions have arisen when this crucially important power could have been used. Having considered all the options, however, the President on each occasion granted the dissolution (in 1944, in January 1982, and in November 1982). McDunphy (1945: 47, 52) comments:

> Here we find the President endowed with the authority entirely his own, independent of the Taoiseach, independent of the Government, independent of the Oireachtas, not answerable even to the Supreme Court, which is the final authority on matters of constitutional validity. The President's power in the matter is absolute; in its exercise he is governed only by his personal judgement of what is best for the people, and his decision, when made is final and unchallengeable . . . This power is unique in the Irish Constitution. It is the only case in which the President has an absolute and unquestionable right to act in direct opposition to a constitutional request from the Head of the Government, to reject an advice which in other matters is equivalent to a direction, which must be complied with as a matter of course.

There is no evidence that, as regards the dissolution of the Dáil, the President has declined to act on the advice of the Taoiseach on an occasion in which the support of a majority in the Dáil was lost. The President cannot dissolve the Dáil without the request of the Taoiseach. A President who refused such a request from the Taoiseach would invite controversy, yet in McDunphy's words (1945: 51); 'The Constitution gives no indication as to the evidence which would entitle the President to decide that a Taoiseach has in fact ceased to retain the support of a majority in Dáil Éireann.' Clarification of this point might have had a decisive effect in reducing the uncertainty generated by three general elections in rapid succession in 1981–2.

This discretionary power of the President was at the centre of a political controversy which erupted during the presidential campaign of 1990. Following the collapse of the Fine Gael/Labour coalition government in January 1982 after its defeat in the Dáil on a budgetary provision, Fianna Fáil issued a public statement that it was available for consultation with the President if he was going to exercise his absolute right of not dissolving the Dáil, and it was widely reported that efforts were made by senior members of the party to contact the President. Such an attempt to contact the President after the collapse of the government was not necessarily improper, and the President's discretion might be better exercised with full information and advice on the situation. It would, however, be wrong if *advice* became *pressure*; and it was subsequently alleged that telephone calls were made to Áras an Uachtaráin in January 1982 in an attempt to persuade the President to secure a transfer of power without an election. This claim appeared to receive substance from the admission made in the course of an interview in 1990 by Mr Brian Lenihan, a presidential candidate, that he had telephoned Áras an Uachtaráin on the night in question. Mr Lenihan later retracted this statement and requested a meeting with President Hillery to obtain his confirmation that the telephone call had not been made. On the following day, however, he withdrew his request in order to avoid drawing the President into the election campaign.

(3) Article 13 enables the President at any time, after consultation with the Council of State, to convene a meeting of either or both of the Houses of the Oireachtas. In this situation the President has the freedom to ignore the advice of the government. This power could become important if, for example, an unpopular government tried to avoid criticism by not calling a meeting of the Dáil. The power has never been exercised in the circumstances envisaged by the Constitution (although the President summoned a joint meeting of the Dáil and Seanad on 2 January 1969 to commemorate the fiftieth anniversary of the first meeting of Dáil Éireann). In an interview with the *Cork Examiner* on 8 October 1991 President Robinson envisaged the possibility of using this power, while acknowledging that it had to be a matter of timing and circumstance and that it could not be done at a time of political sensitivity.

(4) Under Article 27, a petition may be addressed to the President by a majority of senators and at least one-third of the members of the Dáil, requesting her not to sign a bill until it has been approved by the people either at a referendum or at a general election. The President then decides whether or not the bill 'contains a proposal of such national importance that the will of the people thereon ought to be ascertained'.

This provision is designed for a situation in which a matter of fundamental national importance is passed in the Dáil but is almost unanimously rejected in the Seanad. It applies to bills in respect of which the Seanad has been overruled by the Dáil in exercise of the powers given by Article 23. The President can act only after consultation with the Council of State. Where the President accepts a petition, the bill cannot become law until it has been approved by the people at a referendum or by resolution of the Dáil passed after a dissolution and reassembly. No bill has so far been referred to the people under these provisions.

(5) Article 22 enables the President, at the request of the Seanad, to refer the question whether a bill is or is not a money bill (a bill relating to the finances of the state) to a Committee of Privileges, a committee consisting of an equal number of members of the Dáil and of the Seanad with a judge of the Supreme Court as chairman. For the discussion of money bills, the Seanad has only twenty-one days, although it has three months for the discussion of an ordinary measure. Mr de Valera explained: 'To prevent any fraud upon the Seanad by compelling them to discuss within twenty-one days and practically not to interfere with the bill which they would have a perfect right to discuss if it came in the guise of an ordinary measure, and to prevent the possibility of mistakes by the Chairman of the Dáil, there is an appeal to the President against a certificate of the Ceann Comhairle. There can be an appeal made by the House affected, that is the Seanad.' (*Dáil Debates*, 11 May 1937, col. 49)

The Seanad may complain to the President that the bill was certified a money bill in error and may accordingly ask her to set up a Committee of Privileges to determine whether the bill was or was not a money bill. This function has not been exercised.

(6) The final independent power of the President relates to the need to get legislation passed quickly during a state of emergency. Under Article 24, when a bill is 'urgent and immediately necessary for the preservation of the public peace and security, or by reason of the existence of a public emergency whether domestic or international', the time for its consideration by the Seanad may be shortened. There may be occasions in which the very safety of the state may depend upon making a quick decision. The President has to agree with the government's view that a bill is in this category before this procedure can be adopted. The Dáil can then compel the Seanad to reach a decision within a very limited period; and if the Dáil does not accept this decision, the law can be enacted without the approval of the Seanad.

It is in order to diminish the chances of a misuse of this power, that the President's consent has to be obtained. She has to agree with the Dáil before the power of the Seanad can be curtailed. She is put in a very responsible position to act as umpire to see that the Dáil acts in accordance with the spirit of the Constitution. It would have to be a clear and an obvious abuse of power before the President would interfere. No attempts appear to have been made to avail of the powers given by this article.

THE COUNCIL OF STATE

The Council of State aids and counsels the President. It is composed of: (1) (as *ex officio* members) The Taoiseach, the Tánaiste, the Chief Justice, the President of the High Court, the Ceann Comhairle of the Dáil, the

Cathaoirleach of the Senate, and the Attorney General; (2) every able and willing person who has held office as President, Taoiseach and Chief Justice; (3) a maximum of seven other persons whom the President may appoint at her own discretion. Members in the third category serve only during the term(s) of the President who appoints them, and she has the power to remove them for any reason she deems sufficient. Their appointment enables the President to make the Council of State 'as representative as possible' (*Dáil Debates*, 13 May 1937, col. 430). The term of office of the Council of State is the same as that of the President who appointed it.

Members of the Council of State take an oath to 'conscientiously fulfil duties' as members and meet only when summoned by the President. The meetings are held *in camera*, and the President is not bound to follow the advice she receives; the final decision on the matter in question is hers alone—Article 32 of the Constitution states that 'The President shall not exercise or perform any of the powers or functions which are by this Constitution expressed to be exercisable or performable by him after consultation with the Council of State unless, and on every occasion before so doing, he shall have convened a meeting of the Council of State and the members present at such meeting shall have been heard by him.'

Article 14 provides for the establishment of a Commission, consisting of the Chief Justice, the Ceann Comhairle and the Cathaoirleach, to exercise the powers and functions of the President in the event of her absence, temporary incapacity or at any time when the office of the President may be vacant. In any contingency not provided for in the situation envisaged by Article 14 the Council of State may exercise its sole power to make such provisions as to them may seem necessary for the exercise and performance of the President's powers and functions.

REFERENCE OF BILLS TO THE SUPREME COURT

Under Article 26 (referred to earlier), the President is given the special function of highlighting the fact that a particular bill, or section of a bill, may be against the Constitution and of stopping it before it becomes law. If the President is of the opinion that the measure, if passed, might be invalid by being contrary to the Constitution, she has the power of referring that measure for decision to the Supreme Court. It is not the President who decides whether it is against the Constitution or not. Her function is simply one of referral to the Supreme Court, which makes the ultimate decision. It is an important power, because if the President did sign the bill into law, some of its consequences might well be irreversible.

Every reference of a bill to the Supreme Court by the President must be made not later than the seventh day after the date on which the bill is presented to her for signature by the Taoiseach. The President is not permitted to refer money bills, bills to amend the Constitution, or bills whose time for consideration by the Seanad had been abridged under Article 24. The Supreme Court must deliver a single decision, with no dissenting or separate judgments, not later than sixty days after the date of reference.

The advantages of the Article 26 procedure are that it allows the President to take action in good time to prevent legislation which is unconstitutional from getting on to the statute book. Furthermore, it saves the citizen from the trouble and expense of contesting the legislation later in the courts. It has the further advantage of deterring governments from introducing legislative proposals which might be repugnant to the Constitution.

The disadvantages are, firstly, that testing at this stage may be unsatisfactory, as there is no experience of operating the legislation. Furthermore, Article 34.3.3 provides that 'no court whatever shall have jurisdiction to question the validity of a law' which has been cleared through the Article 26 procedure. This means that although the act may have disclosed highly objectionable aspects in its operation, which were unforeseen at the time of the Article 26 reference, it cannot subsequently be challenged. In addition, commentators have noted that the leading constitutional court decisions have been taken in the course of ordinary proceedings brought in the courts. It is also argued that the Supreme Court is the ultimate arbiter and, as such, is the real guardian of the people's rights in the Constitution.

In the case of a reference of a bill under Article 26, the Attorney General (or counsel on his behalf) argues the case in favour of the constitutionality of the bill, and counsel assigned by the court argues the case that the bill is repugnant to the Constitution, largely by drawing attention to hypothetical results of its enactment. Such hypothetical argument is often difficult because it is not always possible to envisage the consequences of the bills if enacted.

Eight bills have been referred by the President to the Supreme Court under Article 26. These were:

(1) the Offences Against the State (Amendment) Bill 1940;

(2) the School Attendance Bill 1942;

(3) the Electoral (Amendment) Bill 1961;

(4) the Criminal Law (Jurisdiction) Bill 1976;

(5) the Emergency Powers Bill 1976;

(6) the Electoral (Amendment) Bill 1983;

(7) the Housing (Private Rented Dwellings) Bill 1987;

(8) the Adoption (No. 2) Bill 1987.

Three of these were declared to be repugnant to the Constitution. They were: the School Attendance Bill, which, in the opinion of the court, infringed the rights of parents to decide how their children should be educated; the Electoral (Amendment) Bill 1983, which, in extending voting rights, was · deemed to conflict with other basic provisions of the Constitution; and the Housing Bill, which was deemed to interfere with the property rights of owners of particular dwellings. The bills of 1940 and 1961 were amendments of legislation which had already been declared unconstitutional.

The 1967 Report of the Committee on the Constitution stated in relation to Article 26: 'We feel that, on the whole, this kind of provision is useful in the Constitution, and we are unable to agree, therefore, that it should be deleted. While we are unanimous in this opinion that Article 26 should be retained, we feel that some changes are necessary, but we have been unable to agree on the best approach to the problem.'

The Emergency Powers Bill 1976

In September 1976 President Cearbhall Ó Dálaigh referred the Emergency Powers Bill 1976 to the Supreme Court under Article 26 of the Constitution, as he was entitled to do, for a decision as to its constitutionality as the bill conferred great powers on the authorities. The government's view was that the exemption provided by Article 28.3.3 meant that the bill could not be declared unconstitutional as the Supreme Court did not have jurisdiction to review the bill, because it was for the purpose of securing the public safety of the state. The Supreme Court found that the bill was not repugnant to the Constitution, but stated:

> As to the right of the President to refer the bill to this Court, it is clear that he has power to do so notwithstanding that the bill is one passed by both Houses of the Oireachtas by reference to the provisions of subsection 3.3 of Article 28. The power of the President to do so has not been questioned in these proceedings.

The exercise of this independent power under Article 26 involved the President in political controversy. The Minister for Defence, Mr Patrick Donegan, publicly criticised the President 'in a clearly improper manner' (Chubb 1982: 200) in a speech delivered at Columb Military Barracks, Mullingar, on 18 October 1976 when he referred to the President as 'a thundering disgrace', adding: 'The fact is that the army must stand behind the state.' The President in a letter to Mr Donegan dated 19 October 1976 asked the question 'Can this sequence be construed by ordinary people otherwise than as an insinuation that the President does not stand behind the state?'

The Taoiseach, Mr Liam Cosgrave, referred to the Minister for Defence's outburst as no more than 'excessive verbal exuberance', and a Dáil motion calling on the minister to resign was defeated by 63 votes to 58 on 21 October. On the following day, moved by the government's failure to take action against the minister, President Ó Dálaigh resigned. He took this course of action to assert publicly his personal dignity and independence as President of Ireland and—a matter of much greater importance for every citizen—to endeavour to protect the dignity and independence of the Presidency as an institution. The Minister for Defence had apologised by letter for what he had said, telling the President that he deeply regretted the use of the words 'thundering disgrace'. Immediately after resigning Mr Ó Dálaigh published the correspondence exchanged between himself and the minister, in the course of which he had written:

> The President's role in relation to the Defence Forces is honorary in character; nevertheless, a special relationship exists between the President and the Minister for Defence. That relationship has been irreparably breached not only by what you said yesterday, but also because of the place where, and the persons before whom, you chose to make your outrageous criticism.

Thus the combination of the roles of guardian of the people's right under the Constitution and ceremonial head of state can involve the President in political controversy in the exercise of the independent powers bestowed on him by the Constitution, particularly in so far as they have been designed and fall to be exercised at times of crisis and where a conflict of opinion may emerge.

CONCLUSION

The President of Ireland is head of state with very few powers or functions which may be exercised independently of government control. This accords with constitutional practice in most other countries where the government is led by a prime minister; it differs radically from the United States, where the powers usually found in the hands of the nominal head of state are vested in the President together with the real executive power of government. In Ireland the Taoiseach is the head of the government and the President is ceremonial head of state.

The Constitution spells out the President's powers in detail so that conflict over spheres of authority between the cabinet and the President should not arise. The President's powers are directly circumscribed, and she normally acts on the advice and authority of the government. Any appointments which she makes under the Constitution (with the exception of the seven appointees to the Council of State, a purely consultative body) are made following the advice of a third party. Such independent powers as she possesses are intended for use only in emergencies, and to date only two of these independent powers have been exercised. The constitutional crisis of October 1976 which led to the resignation of President Ó Dálaigh resulted from the exercise by him of one of his independent powers under the Constitution.

From time to time there has been discussion as to how far it is possible or desirable to develop, within the existing constitutional controls, a new and more open style of Presidency in which each individual incumbent can make a distinctively personal contribution. In this connection, Erskine Childers, on the announcement of his candidature for the office of President in 1973 declared:

I have learned by experience that outside the party political field, some leaders should give guidance to the people, some leaders should reflect the most reasonable aspirations of the people on matters where discussion and debate will not create fundamental national division, but will encourage enlightened examination. Now that is the first thing I wanted to say to you, that the President in my view has an obligation to encourage discussion of this kind. The President should be able to look into the future and speak on the shaping of the nation; not the nation of 1973 but the nation of 1980, the nation of 1990.

Chubb notes (1983: 51) that President Childers did not follow this strategy with much vigour, partly because of the generally unfavourable reaction among politicians of all parties to this suggestion, and partly because of his untimely death. Clearly, it would be extremely difficult for a President to combine the diverse roles of titular head of state, guardian of the people's rights under the Constitution, and advocate of enlightened examination of social issues without falling foul of political controversy, criticism and misunderstanding.

President Childers also outlined his views on how the Presidency could have an inspirational role in giving leadership to the community:

The President above all other people in the state should inspire social patriotism. He should encourage mutual understanding between the differing social groups within the community . . . He should encourage the idea of how people can contribute themselves individually to the shaping of the national life.

Similarly, in her inauguration speech on 3 December 1990 President Robinson described her aim as a Presidency of 'justice, peace and love'. She said she would be representing a new Ireland which would be open, tolerant and inclusive as well as being proud of its heritage and culture, and in which the President could play a part in encouraging initiative in local communities:

As President, I will seek to the best of my abilities to promote this growing sense of local participatory democracy, this energising movement of self-development and self-expression which is surfacing more and more at grassroots level. This is the face of modern Ireland.

President Robinson also expressed the hope of adding an outward-looking dimension to her Presidency by acting as a symbolic representative on behalf of emigrants of Irish descent around the world, by fostering the spirit of reconciliation in Northern Ireland, and by contributing to the international protection and promotion of human rights. She undertook a ten-day visit to the USA in October 1991 and has repeated her desire to visit Northern Ireland in an effort to encourage reconciliation.

Questions have occasionally been raised about the necessity for the office of President. However, surveys conducted by *The Irish Times* and by the Market Research Bureau of Ireland in November 1989 and November 1990 (the latter just before the presidential election) found that 57 per cent and 65 per cent respectively of the respondents were in favour of continuation of the office. Support was strongest among young people. The 1967 Report of the Committee on the Constitution considered a proposal that the separate office of President should be abolished and set out the arguments advanced for and against. The arguments put forward in favour of abolition include: (1) that the President is largely a figurehead; (2) that the President's formal duties as head of state could without difficulty be discharged by the Taoiseach, who could act both as head of government and head of state; (3) that the abolition of the separate office of President would give rise to substantial financial savings. However, it can be reasonably argued that it would be neither desirable (in view of the President's function as guardian of the Constitution) nor practicable to combine the offices of Taoiseach and President; nor would it result in any significant financial saving.

The President is in constitutional theory elected by the people to safeguard their rights under the Constitution and is an important part of the system of checks and balances on the power of the legislature. While the President has very few independent powers under the Constitution, it is clear that these independent powers are potentially very important because they are designed to act as a check in circumstances of conflict or crisis. The fact that these powers have not often or never been exercised does not diminish their potential importance.

REFERENCES

Chubb, Basil, *The Government and Politics of Ireland*, 2nd ed. (London: Longman, 1982)

Chubb, Basil, ed., *A Source Book of Irish Government* (Dublin: Insitute of Public Administration, 1983)

Farrell, Brian, 'The Constitution and the Institutions of Government: Constitutional Theory and Political Practice', ed. F. Litton, *The Constitution of Ireland 1937–87* (Special Issue of *Administration* Vol. 35. No. 4. 1987)

Irish Times/Market Research Bureau of Ireland, *Satisfaction Ratings: Government and Party Leaders, Party Support and Other Issues* (Dublin MRBI, Nov. 1989)

Kelly, John M., *The Irish Constitution* (Dublin: Jurist Publishing, 1984)

McDunphy, Michael, *The President of Ireland: His Powers, Functions and Duties* (Dublin: Browne & Nolan, 1945)

6

The Civil Service

The civil service comprises that body of persons who have been selected by the Civil Service Commission to serve the organs of state defined by the Constitution, namely the President, the Houses of the Oireachtas, the judiciary, the Taoiseach and his ministers, the Attorney General, and the Comptroller and Auditor General. The term can be used roughly to describe those who work in government departments. The legal basis for the civil service is provided in the Ministers and Secretaries Act 1924. That act authorises each minister to appoint the civil servants in his department (except the secretary) in such numbers and grades as the Minister for Finance approves. The secretary of each department is appointed by the government on the recommendation of the minister concerned. The procedure by which appointments are made is described below.

Technically there are two categories of civil servants. Those employed in parts of the civil service not under the direct control of ministers are *civil servants of the state*, for example the staff in the Houses of the Oireachtas. All other civil servants—the vast majority—who are employed in the government departments are *civil servants of the government*.

The tables in Appendix G show the total number of civil servants in various years between 1975 and 1990 and the present number in each department. On 1 January 1991 there were 27,311 persons in the civil service (excluding industrial civil servants such as craftsmen and general operatives, of whom there are about 1,700). Although this is a lot less than the number of persons employed in the local authorities, the health services or the state-sponsored bodies, the civil service occupies a key position in the public service in that it is the part of that service which is closest to ministers and government and, therefore, more immediately involved in the making of policy. Moreover, its supervisory influence extends to the various other parts of the public service, on whose activities it impinges in one way or another, whether in matters of policy, finance, organisation, pay or personnel management. It is at the hub of the wheel of government, so to speak.

The prime purpose of the civil service as a whole is, of course, to serve the public, and the first duty of a civil servant is to help his minister meet his responsibilities to the Oireachtas. He works continuously for, with and under politicians in a system which responds to a complex series of demands which emerge in various ways: from political parties, organisations, groups and the media; from administrators themselves through their perception of needs, their appreciation of the problems hindering development and their concern to get these resolved; from decisions of the courts and other appellate bodies; from Ireland's membership of international organisations, such as the EC; and from developments abroad generally, such as economic recession or war.

An interesting aspect of the Irish civil servant is that although politicians and ministers change, the civil service is permanent. There is something of a paradox in this, in that the civil service is at one and the same time the permanent servant of the state and also the servant of the administration which is for the time being in power.

RECRUITMENT

Civil servants (with some exceptions noted beneath) are recruited as a result of competitions held by the Civil Service Commission under the Civil Service Commissioners Act 1956. The commissioners are the Ceann Comhairle of the Dáil, the secretary to the government and an assistant secretary in the Department of Finance. The commission operates under the aegis of the Department of Finance, but is independent of the minister in its selection procedures, though it is the minister who answers parliamentary questions relating to the policy of the commission.

The competitions can be of different kinds and may consist of one or more of the following: a written, oral or practical examination, an interview, or any other test considered appropriate. Candidates fall into two broad categories. The first category is that of persons seeking admission on the basis of the school certificate examinations or tests specially set by the commission. In addition to an examination, such candidates are usually obliged to undergo an interview before being appointed, as for example, potential executive officers. The second category is that comprised of persons who have technical qualifications usually acquired after some form of third-level education or who have certain prescribed experience. Generally, persons in this category (for example, engineers) are selected after interview. These competitions are described as open competitions, i.e. they are open to persons outside the civil service who fulfil the conditions laid down.

For each competition by interview, a special interview board is set up, normally consisting of three members. The commission uses the services of interviewers drawn from all sections of the community. A detailed scheme of marking is provided by the commission for each board so as to give it a framework within which it may make its assessments.

Canvassing on behalf of competition candidates is prohibited, and this is a rule which is rigidly enforced. No matter what criticism may be levelled against the commission for its seemingly bureaucratic procedures, there has never been any suggestion that these are anything other than completely fair. Even politicians, who spend a great deal of their time making representations to other civil service offices, have discovered the waste of time in approaching the Civil Service Commission.

As the minister in charge of each department is legally the employer of all the staff in that department, the names of those selected by the commission are submitted to departments to get ministers' approval to their appointment. No alternative names are provided, and invariably those recommended are appointed.

The exceptional appointments referred to above relate to persons appointed in the public interest, to those in the broad category of skilled worker, porter and cleaner, and to short-term or contract appointments such as temporary seasonal staff for the Passport Office. Those appointed in the public interest are usually persons who have particular skills or talents which the civil service lacks, for example a geologist with special experience or an expert in nuclear energy. Where such appointments are made, the Civil Service Commissioners have no function to perform. The procedure is that the minister to whose department the person is to be appointed obtains first the consent of the government, after which a notice must be published in *Iris Oifigiúil*, the official gazette. If any questions are raised in the Dáil or elsewhere, the minister and the government must be prepared to defend the appointment. For other types of non-competitive appointment specified above, the manner of recruitment is left to individual departments. The usual procedure is for the jobs to be advertised and then filled by interview.

CAREER STRUCTURES
The civil service may be divided into three main career structures: general, departmental and technical. Within these categories are the grades (described below).

General Service
The general service grades are described by the Devlin Report (1969) as consisting of 'a central core of general service officers who are recruited to perform the general duties of departments from the routine clerical operations to the higher policy, advisory and managerial work. These officers are recruited at varying educational levels from primary school to university

degree standard. The emphasis is on a general education, and every recruit can, if he obtains the necessary educational qualifications and experience, aspire to the highest positions in the civil service.'

Departmental

Departmental grades are confined to a few departments or offices, such as the Department of Foreign Affairs, the Office of the Revenue Commissioners, the Houses of the Oireachtas, and the Office of the Comptroller and Auditor General. The various posts are held by officers who have been assigned to specialised work within a particular department. They are recruited with a general educational qualification, but are also given extensive on-the-job training which will enable them to become specialists in their own fields. Examples include customs and excise officers, tax officers, and ambassadors.

Technical

There are technical officers employed in nearly all departments. They are recruited to the civil service for the performance of specialised work and already possess a qualification related to the work to be performed. The qualification is usually a formally recognised degree, diploma or certificate. In so far as it is possible to generalise, their role is to bring expert knowledge, skill and experience in specialist fields to bear on the determination and execution of government policy, for example in advising on the interpretation of the law, on health schemes, on environmental issues, or on the development of natural resources. These are the solicitors in the office of the Chief State Solicitor, the doctors in the Department of Health, the engineers in the Department of the Environment, and the geologists in the Department of Energy.

GRADES

The civil service is divided into about 700 grades, that is to say, that within the three categories outlined above there are about 700 job titles. There are not, however, that many pay scales, since many grades have the same scales, and there are many grades with only one person in them, such as the Director of the Meteorological Service or the Registrar of the Supreme Court.

There is no legal definition of a grade; persons are appointed to what are called 'positions' in the civil service. What happens is that positions requiring broadly the same level of qualifications and with comparable levels of work, responsibility, pay and conditions of service are grouped by the Department of Finance into grades. Examples of grades are the executive, engineering, librarian and draftsman grades. The general service is made up of grades which are common to two or more departments; these are described below.

The work of the general service grades has not, even at this remove from the beginning of the state, yet been closely defined, with the result that the lines of demarcation between contiguous grades are far from clear. The confusion which this causes for outsiders is compounded by the fact that job descriptions are not common in the civil service. Persons moving from one job to another within a grade, or moving to a higher grade, on promotion, seldom get a statement showing what their new duties are. For the absence of job descriptions there are two main reasons. The first is the tedium of preparing them, when there is no rule saying they should be prepared. The second is that to have them would reduce the freedom of managers at all levels in allocating tasks and would lead to claims for increases in pay where the work done was not exactly in accord with that set down in the job description. Those in the various general service grades are expected to be able to perform efficiently any work assigned to them. This arrangement has, however, enabled the civil service to take in its stride, more or less, the embargo on recruitment which has obtained for several years and which has led to many officials at all levels having to carry out tasks not appropriate to their grade because there was no one else available to do so.

Clerical Staff

Clerical staff perform work which includes filing, the operation of machines, the recording of information, checking accounts and making payments, less difficult analysis and presentation of findings, and the drafting of letters and memoranda which follow established practice and seek or give factual information. In general, they deal with work which requires substantial dependence on acquired knowledge and experience. The receptionists in public offices are generally from the clerical grades.

Executive and Higher Executive Officers

The executive grades, which are generally referred to as the middle management grades, could be regarded as the most central to the smooth working of every government department. At entry level they include the brightest of the school leavers, while each year a certain number of places are reserved for university graduates.

The work of executive officers includes presenting all the important aspects of complicated cases in a logical and readable sequence, summarising accurately the particular issues, recommending a course of action where there are a number of options, preparing briefs for, and reports of, meetings, analysing statistical material and accounting for unusual developments.

The work of higher executive officers is an extension, at a higher level, of the work of the basic grade. Higher executive officers have to make more difficult decisions and give directions where there are exceptions to standard procedures.

They and their staff perform a wide range of tasks. Some are charged with large areas of responsibility, such as the payment of salaries in the Department of Education (teachers), Justice (Gardaí) or Defence (army); travelling expenses of the advisers and inspectors employed by the Department of Agriculture and Food; social welfare allowances; and housing grants. Many are engaged in what is known as case work, for example: examining proposals and making suggestions about the provision of a new school or health clinic; for the introduction of a youth help scheme; for a new measure to deal with an environmental problem. Some are engaged in monitoring the progress of ongoing measures such as fisheries protection, energy conservation or projects to attract tourists. Many, such as those in the Ferries and Aviation Divisions of the Department of Transport, Tourism and Communications, oversee the operations of state-sponsored bodies. Very many are involved in EC work. Some are engaged in the work of the other international organisations of which Ireland is a member, such as the World Health Organisation, the General Agreement on Tariffs and Trade or the Organisation for Economic Co-operation and Development, and regularly attend meetings of these bodies abroad. Very many also are engaged in the operation, maintenance and enhancement of computerised systems, as, for example, those who are responsible for the processing and payment of claims in the Department of Social Welfare. They implement the provisions of legislation (such as the collection of taxes) and assemble information for new legislation, consulting the legal officers as required on this and on the taking of prosecutions under existing legislation. Officers in the Department of Justice ensure the smooth operation of the judicial system and the daily running of the courts. Nearly all officers in all departments at one time or another have to prepare replies to parliamentary questions. The above examples are only a small and random selection of the varied work undertaken by higher executive officers.

The Higher Civil Service
Those in the general service grades from assistant principal upwards, sometimes referred to, following British practice, as the administrative grades, constitute the higher civil service. Their work is broadly concerned with the formulation of policy, pursuing and examining proposals for change, offering alternative lines to ministers, preparation of legislation, organisation of projects or schemes and the general management of large blocks of executive work. They are responsible for the administration of the state and for the execution of policy and are expected, on a continuous basis, to devise ways of improving efficiency. These grades also supply the advisers who accompany ministers when meeting deputations or attending meetings abroad.

In general, the higher an officer moves up the administrative grades, the greater and wider will be his policy role, while his executive role will be correspondingly diminished.

Civil Service Grade Structure

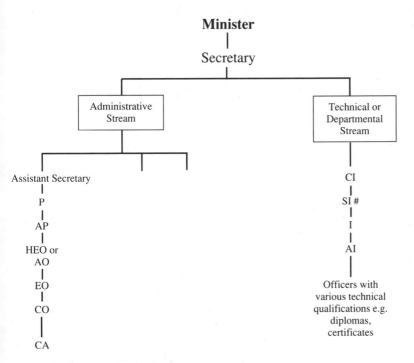

P – Principal (4 or 5 to each Assistant Secretary)
AP – Assistant Principal
HEO – Higher Executive Officer
AO – Administrative Officer (Graduate Entry Grade)
CO/CA – Clerical Officer/Assistant
CI – Chief Inspector (Engineer, Doctor, Architect, Veterinary Surgeon)
SI – Senior Inspector (as above)
– Numbers vary up to about 6 Senior Inspectors to each chief
I – Inspector
AI – Assistant Inspector (Graduate Entry Grade)

Principal and Assistant Principal

The grade of principal is a central one in the sense that principals are in charge of large divisions of their departments' work. Each department has a finance and personnel division. Other examples of divisions are those dealing with old-age benefits, national school buildings and petroleum products in the Departments of Social Welfare, Education and Energy respectively.

Where a principal is engaged on policy work relating to broad national issues, the work is divided into sub-areas with an assistant principal in each, putting forward proposals for dealing with the issues in his sub-area. Where the work involves national schemes, it could be divided on a geographical basis. Each principal has, in the normal course, the help of at least two assistant principals. The area of work controlled by an assistant principal is normally called a *branch*.

The officials who accompany ministers on their appearances in the Dáil in connection with routine parliamentary business are usually in the grades of assistant principal or principal.

Assistant Secretary

The duties of assistant secretaries are rather similar to those of principals, but on a higher level of responsibility and usually in a broader field. A main feature of the assistant secretary's role is his access to the minister; the terms and frequency of this access depending on the attitudes of individual ministers and secretaries.

On major parliamentary occasions, such as the presentation of the budget or of departmental estimates, or when the issues being debated are otherwise politically important or sensitive, the official accompanying the minister in the Dáil is usually an assistant secretary.

Secretary

The secretary is the chief adviser to the minister and is the apex of the pyramid. He is, in effect, the managing director of the department. All of the policy proposals which have been formulated within the department, all of the matters on which the minister's views or directions are sought or which are considered desirable to be brought to his notice are submitted to the secretary for presentation to the minister. The secretary is personally responsible to the minister for the overall management of the department, including the regularity and propriety of all transactions and the efficiency and economy of administration in the department.

The secretary is also the accounting officer for his department's vote. What this means is that he has primary responsibility for the administration of the money voted each year by the Dáil for the department. This is an important exception to the principle of ministerial responsibility. At the end of each year he must prepare an account, called the appropriation account, showing how the money voted by the Dáil for the department has been spent—in effect to show that it has been properly spent in the manner approved by the Dáil. (The appropriation account of the Department of Finance for 1989 is reproduced in Appendix H.) The secretary must be satisfied that adequate arrangements exist to ensure the correctness of all payments from the vote under his control and the bringing to account of all receipts connected with the vote. This account is presented to the Comptroller and Auditor General and subsequently to the Public Accounts Committee (PAC). When the committee is examining the report, the secretary is the principal witness. He answers the questions of the committee and otherwise explains matters as requested.

WORK OF THE CIVIL SERVICE

The Principle of Accountability

The Ministers and Secretaries Act 1924 contains a far-reaching provision which largely determines the way in which the civil service performs its work. This is the provision that each minister, as head of his department, is a corporation sole with perpetual succession. The effect of this is that the acts of a department are the acts of its minister, for which he alone is responsible; and that, legally speaking, unless there is an exception provided by law (which there is, for example, in the case of civil servants determining tax liabilities in the office of the Revenue Commissioners), no civil servant can in law give a decision. In effect, the minister *is* the department, and his servants have no separate existence. Every decision made by a government department comes, strictly speaking, from the minister. As it is obvious that ministers cannot personally make all the decisions, owing to the demands on their time and the lack of the necessary detailed knowledge, the vast majority of the decisions are in fact made by the civil servants. How the system works in practice is that the civil servants' decisions are regarded as being those which the minister would have made had the issues being brought to his personal notice. The work is carried on through a system of implicit delegation from the minister to the secretary of the department and on down through the various grades. Hence the conventional opening phrase in letters from government departments: 'I am directed by the Minister for X to state . . .'

This system has a major impact on the way in which the civil service does its work. It is the minister who is answerable to the Dáil and ultimately to the electorate for all the activities of his department; and as he may be questioned in the Dáil about them, the discretion and freedom of action of civil servants is limited. As a result, they are often regarded as being over-cautious. This caution arises from their anxiety to ensure that none of their actions/decisions are such as to cause the minister any embarrassment which could in turn reflect on the individual official. There is, in particular, a need for consistency in dealing with individual cases; and this in turn leads to a reliance on precedents, which may not be quite apt in every instance. The overriding emphasis on equity and impartiality is marked in all aspects of civil service work.

Accountability through the minister to parliament and to the public is an integral part of the daily life of many civil servants. This entails keeping detailed records, taking decisions at a higher level than may appear necessary, documenting discussions and negotiations leading to decisions, carefully drawing up and meticulously observing the rules relating to the making and receipt of payments, and having more centralised arrangements for financial control then are found in the private sector. Commenting on this aspect of the work, FitzGerald notes (1991: 54) 'I came to appreciate also the commitment to thoroughness which, while sometimes frustrating in the slow tempo it imposes on change, protects the system against egregious error.'

The Non-Commercial Principle

A large part of the work of the civil service has no commercial counterpart. Drafting and applying legislation, taking measures to protect the environment, making social welfare payments and arranging for the certificate examinations in second level schools are typical of the tasks which are unique to government. Government is judged not on its profitability but on its social, political, cultural and economic achievements, subject to some overall limitation upon its total demands for taxation. The level of taxation is judged in general terms; it is seldom linked to specific outputs. Thus, up to the present time, the efficiency and effectiveness with which departments conduct their business have not been the dominant factor in determining the flow of funds towards them. Hence departments have not generally found much benefit in deploying the kinds of management systems common in the private sector. This situation is, however, changing, albeit slowly. (see Chapter 12)

Basic Functions

The civil service has two main tasks: to assist ministers in the making of policy, and to carry out policy decisions. Policy formulation means analysing the problems that exist, defining the issues they present, and finding out how they should be dealt with. Among the major questions to which civil servants have addressed themselves in recent years are: What should be done to keep beaches free from pollution? Do the criminal justice laws need to be amended? Are the provisions for the welfare of children adequate? Does policy on neutrality require examination? How can tourism be advanced? Are changes in secondary education necessary?

Having thoroughly examined all aspects of the problems laid before them, civil servants then inform their ministers of the various alternatives open to them, making a recommendation as to which should be selected. Thus the decisions of a minister are considerably influenced by what has gone on before. The calibre of mind that civil servants bring to their appraisal of the facts of a specific problem influences, and often determines, the character of the minister's decision. The nature and importance of the policy-making process illustrates the necessity for civil servants to have ability, professional knowledge, integrity and independence of thought. Generally ministers have a relationship with their advisers in which no one feels restrained from freely expressing their views. FitzGerald, however, adverts to an occasion on which he considered that the Department of Finance attempted to challenge a government decision. He went on to say that this action was, nevertheless untypical, noting that 'civil servants rightly consider it to be their duty to advise ministers fully of the possible adverse consequences of proposed political decisions; they would be failing in their duty were they to do otherwise. It is also humanly understandable that they should often tend to feel that the status quo, the product largely of their own and their predecessors' efforts, has a certain merit and deserves to be preserved unless very cogent arguments are put forward for altering it. Some resistance to change is thus to be expected from the civil service, each department of which tends to have its own attachment to policies developed in the past.' (1991: 301). When decisions are taken, civil servants at all levels seek faithfully to implement them, irrespective of whether or not they accord with the advice given. The situation is neatly expressed in the well-worn phrase 'minister on top, civil servant on tap'. The relationship between a civil servant and his minister is one in which the former is publicly silent and the latter generally has little to say. In the course of their work in advising ministers and in seeing that decisions are implemented, the types of task are many and varied. Some typical examples follow.

Legislation

When legislation is needed to implement some new policy or to change an existing policy, one of the senior officials in the field of work where the new measures are to be taken usually has the task of preparing a background memorandum setting out why the legislation is necessary; why the present position in regard to the matter at issue is regarded as unsatisfactory; what benefits will accrue from passing the legislation (and what disadvantages, if any); what parties or activities are likely to be affected and in what respects; what changes will be required in existing cognate activities as a result of the new legislation; what the cost will be, and so on.

When the proposals have been approved by his minister and by the government, the civil servant then attends on the Attorney General during their drafting into the form of a bill for presentation to the government and subsequently to the Dáil or Seanad. He prepares the speeches which the minister delivers on the various stages of the bill, provides the minister with a detailed brief on every provision of the bill, and waits on the minister during all stages of the debates. He takes notes on the points made by members, arranges for the inclusion in the bill of any amendments accepted, and prepares the minister's concluding speech which deals with the various points raised.

When legislation has been passed by the Oireachtas (or otherwise when decisions have been taken by the government) requiring the introduction of new schemes or changes in existing schemes, a number of consequential matters have to be considered. These might include staffing, publicity, forms and procedures, discussions with bodies and groups who will be affected, and systems to provide management information.

Meetings Abroad

Over the last twenty years or so civil servants have increasingly taken part in the work of numerous international organisations, most notably the European Community. Attendance at meetings abroad is now a feature of the work of many civil servants, mainly those at middle and senior level. As far as possible, attendance is shared evenly among those engaged on a particular aspect of their department's work, and staff transfers take account of the desirability of providing this type of experience for as many persons as possible.

The EC process involves the representatives of national governments in the preparatory and decision-making functions of the Council of Ministers. Officials from the Department of Foreign Affairs, Finance, Agriculture and Food, Industry and Commerce, and Environment attend frequently and regularly at meetings in Brussels (and officials of the other departments less regularly). There they advance the views and interests of their departments and respond to initiatives from others. In a typical instance the Commission initially invites member countries, in effect officials from the departments concerned, to bilateral discussions on some proposal it hopes to put forward for the ultimate approval of the Council of Ministers. Typical examples of proposals are a project to reduce unemployment, the tightening of regulations about the use of heavy lorries, the revision of the subsidy arrangements for milk, and provision for Community-wide recognition of architects. After the bilateral discussions a draft regulation or directive is examined, first by a working group consisting of officials of the member states, and then by higher-level committees—the Special Committee on Agriculture if it is of an agricultural nature, and the Committee of Permanent Representatives (Coreper) when it relates to any other issue—which seek to resolve any conflicts.

This involvement in a wide range of issues for debate at Community level as well as the scope for 'package deals' calls for co-ordination and agreement at national level. Overall co-ordination is achieved through a committee of senior officials from the departments concerned meeting frequently in Dublin (see p. 208). During the period of the Irish presidency of the EC in 1990 the Irish officials served as chairmen of over 1,200 working groups. The work calls for a thorough knowledge of the subject-matter and for the negotiating and diplomatic experience necessary to know when to stand firm, when to concede, and when to support an alternative viewpoint.

General

Other activities which help to give an insight into the work of the civil service (in addition to those already mentioned and others more obvious) include the operation of the national scheme for the eradication of bovine tuberculosis; the inspection of primary and secondary schools; the management of commercial harbours; the erection and upkeep of public buildings; the division of commonages; the meteorological service; the valuation of land and buildings; the protection of wildlife; the issue of passports and visas; the national archives, library, gallery and museum; consumer affairs; the geological survey; grant of patents; the state laboratory; driver testing—all these in addition to constantly meeting deputations, replying to letters from politicians on behalf of their constituents, and liaising with other public service bodies. The list is endless!

A useful general description of the work of an Irish civil servant is provided by the account of his own work given by a senior officer in Britain:

> You will spend a fair amount of time in your office writing and answering letters to members of the public, other civil servants, outside bodies with which your department deals; preparing memoranda, writing minutes, suggesting how to initiate, implement or alter policy; telephoning or being telephoned; interviewing visitors; discussing informally with colleagues how or what to do; consulting with specialists with whom the administrative civil servant has more and more contact: architects, engineers, cost accountants, doctors, inspectors of several kinds. In many departments of government, principals and some assistant secretaries have territorial responsibilities which necessitate periodic visits away from the office. These visits can refresh as well as inform. In this age of government by committee you will have to attend at committees or at an outside body's committees as your department's representative. An ability to speak intelligibly, briefly and cogently is needed as much in the Home Civil Service as in the Foreign Office. The opportunities for travel tend to grow, even in the social service departments; for we are all internationally minded now. (William Reid, quoted in Chapman 1970: 60).

CODE OF CONDUCT

Integrity

Civil Servants are bound by the Corruption Acts 1889–1916. These provide penalties for corrupt acceptance of gifts or other considerations as rewards or inducements for doing or not doing some act or for showing favour or disfavour in relation to the business of their departments. The use of official information for private gain is also regarded as a corrupt practice. In addition to their statutory obligations, civil servants are expected to preserve a proper sense of integrity in all their work, whether in relation to their advisory or their executive role.

It must be noted, however, that the fundamental concept of public service has for some years been in a state of change, reflecting the general atmosphere of change prevalent throughout Irish society as a whole. The old conventional practices such as the unquestioning acceptance of rules and regulations and the instinctive obedience to authority are now being challenged in a way unthinkable to previous generations of civil servants. Former certainties, now seem less well established and increasingly irrelevant, and changing values and priorities are giving rise to new and less restrictive attitudes regarding what is right, important and acceptable in the conduct of public affairs.

Confidentiality

The obligations here derive from the Official Secrets Act 1963, which prohibits civil servants from communicating official information unless authorised to do so. Such information includes not only documentary material such as papers, minutes, briefs, letters and so on, but also views, comments and advice acquired or transmitted verbally. The prohibition also applies to those who have retired, in relation to information to which they had access before retirement.

Further, a civil servant may not publish without the agreement of the head of his department any material touching on the business of his own or of any other department. To a certain extent, no doubt, this accounts for the paucity of written information generally available on the workings of government departments. It also largely accounts for the fact that civil servants are very rarely heard on radio or television programmes discussing matters for which their departments are responsible.

Party Politics

The rules on this subject are of very long standing. Their purpose is, generally speaking, to prohibit civil servants from participating in party politics. Originally they applied to every civil servant but were modified in the 1970s along the lines indicated below, following representations from some staff associations. Essentially the argument of the associations was that all civil servants, because of their experience of the administrative machine, are particularly well qualified for service in parliament; and that it is inconsistent with the natural rights of a civil servant as a citizen, and harmful to the public interest, if he is not allowed to offer himself for this other form of public service and to serve the community in another capacity, without being expected to sacrifice his career, security of employment and pension rights. They pointed to the practice in a number of other member states of the European Community where even senior civil servants are allowed to pursue political activities, including standing for parliament. Civil servants there may resume their posts if unsuccessful in an election or when they wish to retire from parliament.

Successive governments and the Department of Finance, on the other hand, have long been apprehensive of the results of civil servants playing an active role in party politics. They point out that it is in the public interest that civil servants should be politically impartial and that confidence in their impartiality is an essential part of the structure of government in Ireland.

The modification referred to above permits clerical staff, analogous grades in the technical area and industrial workers to engage in politics (though not to stand for election to the Oireachtas), subject to the proviso that the permission could be revoked in the case of officers engaged on a particular category of work. Civil servants engaged in the framing of policy proposals remain completely barred from political activity. In practice this means the executive, middle and senior grades. Civil servants in these grades are, in general, happy with the present position, and there are no moves to change it. They rarely discuss party politics, and the vast majority of civil servants do not know how their colleagues vote at elections. They tend to be very critical of the occasional colleague who may be seen to be overtly political. Civil servants in Ireland display a total loyalty to the minister of the day, no matter what party he belongs to.

Outside Occupations

Those in technical grades such as engineer, doctor or solicitor are prohibited from engaging in private practice or from having connections with outside business. In other cases civil servants are not actually prohibited from taking on other work for remuneration outside office hours, for example teaching or taking part in a business. They are, however, obliged to ensure that any outside business activities do not conflict with their official duties and are not of such a nature as to hinder the proper performance of such duties. (Thus a civil servant would probably be debarred from doing any work for a firm with which his department did business.) Where there is any doubt, an officer is obliged to reveal his position to the secretary of his department and to abide by the latter's decision on the matter.

EMPLOYMENT ARRANGEMENTS

Pay

Civil servants generally have pay scales which provide for a number of annual increments or for pay points on reaching a certain age. There are long scales for the basic recruitment grades (up to fourteen points in some cases); medium-length scales for those in the middle grades (about seven points); short for lower grades and also for grades at the highest levels (three in the case of paper-keepers and assistant secretaries). Secretaries have flat salaries. The secretaries of the Departments of the Taoiseach, Finance and Agriculture and Food have higher salaries than the others, as has the Chairman of the Revenue Commissioners. The system of increments is designed to provide incentives, and before an increment is granted the head of the department or someone on his behalf (usually the head of the personnel section) must certify that the officer has done his work satisfactorily during the preceding year.

The civil service is divided into broad groups for the purpose of determining pay. The first and largest group is that comprehended within the conciliation scheme for the civil service. This scheme embraces those having salary scales up to the maximum of principal. The arbitrator is normally a lawyer and is appointed by the Minister for Finance after consultation with the staff associations. The second largest group is that of the industrial workers, whose rates are dealt with by a joint industrial council under the aegis of the Labour Court. The smallest group contains those with salaries higher than principal. Recommendations on the pay of this group are made to the government by the Review Body on Higher Remuneration in the Public Sector. The ultimate decision on matters of pay rests with the government, but in practice the rates are fixed by the Minister for Finance under the powers conferred on him by the Civil Service Regulation Act 1956.

The pay structure in the civil service is much less flexible than the pay arrangements in ordinary commercial employment. With a view to providing more incentives and encouragement towards greater effectiveness, the white paper *Serving the Country Better* (1985) announced the introduction of merit pay. It indicated that measured, outstanding performance would be rewarded by a cash bonus. To preserve the incentive element, merit payments would be made to not more than ten per cent of staff in any grade or department. The size of payment would vary with the degree of outstanding performance within a range equivalent to five to ten per cent of annual salary. In 1986 the Review Body on Higher Remuneration in the Public Service was asked to consider the application of performance-related pay to the senior grades of the civil service. Having set out all the arguments for and against, the review body concluded that the potential advantages of properly designed and appropriately introduced performance-related pay schemes outweighed the possible disadvantages, for all the civil service grades within its remit except that of secretary. (This exception was made in order to avoid involving ministers as appraisers, which would be undesirable for reasons of practice and principle.) Accordingly, in reply to a parliamentary question in May 1991, the Minister for Finance indicated that a merit pay system for assistant secretaries and some other grades at that level had been introduced. The system is based on variable progression through a pay range by reference to annual assessment of performance against predetermined work objectives. The minister further indicated that he had no proposals to extend this system to other grades. In general, the proposal for merit pay has not received a welcome from either civil servants themselves or from their unions. They point to the difficulties of performance assessment and the dangers of favouritism.

Promotion

Promotions are technically regarded as appointments and are, therefore, governed by the Ministers and Secretaries Act 1924 and, as already indicated are made by the minister in charge of the department concerned. Promotions to the more senior posts (from principal upwards) require also the concurrence of the Minister for Finance. Where promotions are not done in the customary way, that is in the normal grade-to-grade progression, the approval of the Civil Service Commissioners must be obtained. Promotions not in the customary way are very rare. Examples would be promotion from executive officer to assistant principal (skipping a grade) or from engineer to assistant principal (crossing a work category barrier).

The principle is accepted that those seeking promotion should be selected on merit. Before an officer is promoted, the head of his department must certify not only that he is fully qualified for the vacant position but also that he is the best qualified of all those eligible. Up to recent years it had been left to the head of each department to select the most meritorious persons for promotion to vacancies occurring in his own department. Increasingly, however, particularly in the general service grades, the net is now being cast wider than the officers serving in the department where the vacancy exists. Thus, for promotion to the clerical officer grade about a quarter of the vacancies arising are filled from interdepartmental competition, and for the executive, higher executive, assistant principal and principal grades about one-half of the vacancies are so filled.

For the highest posts in the civil service a new system was introduced in 1984. Since then appointments to posts at the level of secretary, and assistant secretary (including technical posts at the same level) are made by the government (in the case of secretaries) or by the appropriate minister, with the approval of the Minister for Finance (in the case of other grades). These appointments are made on the basis of reports from the Top Level Appointments Committee (TLAC), established in 1984, which interviews all applicants. Secretaries appointed under the new system may serve for a period of not more than seven years; if aged fifty-five years or more at the time of appointment, they must retire after five years' service.

Conditions

The Civil Service (Regulation) Act 1956 makes provision for the regulation, control and management of the civil service and empowers the Minister for Finance to make such arrangements to this end as he sees fit. The act provides that every established civil servant holds office at the will and pleasure of the government. What this means is that only the government can dismiss such a civil servant. In practice, however, this power is used very rarely and then only for grave reason involving serious misconduct. Civil servants are rarely dismissed because of poor work performance, partly because of the difficulties of assessment, partly because job descriptions do not exist, partly because of a tendency to make generous allowances for incapacity, and partly because of a feeling that the state can afford it and that 'there but for the grace of God go I'. It is sometimes said that an Irish civil servant's tenure is, legally, the most insecure in the world, but that, in practice, it is the most secure.

Among the other provisions of the act are that civil servants must retire at the age of sixty-five years, but that they may be required to retire at the age of sixty; that they may be suspended without pay for grave misconduct; and that they may be reduced in pay or in grade.

Job-sharing and Career Breaks
A scheme to facilitate the sharing of jobs was introduced in 1984. In general, job-sharers have the same arrangements pro rata as their full-time colleagues in regard to pay and other conditions of employment.

Career breaks (in addition to those granted for domestic or educational reasons) of between one and five years are available where the demands of the work permit, excluding grades with specialist skills. Those returning to the civil service after a career break have a guarantee of re-employment in a relevant grade (but not necessarily in their original department) within a period of twelve months of the date on which they planned to return to work. Up to the end of 1990 about 3,500 had availed themselves of this facility. These arrangements bring a measure of flexibility and opportunity in a time of scarcity of promotional outlets.

Redeployment
This important concept and practice which had hitherto proved virtually impossible has been a feature of civil service manpower policy since 1982 for all grades and in all work categories of the civil service. Persons in grades such as those of executive officer, customs and excise officer and building inspector who were found to be surplus in certain work areas of their own departments were, for example, transferred to priority work relating to the collection of revenue and to the making of social welfare payment. In addition, persons in certain of the state-sponsored bodies which had a surplus staff were redeployed into the civil service following competitions arranged by the Civil Service Commission.

Disabled Persons
The employment target set by the government is 3 per cent. Information available suggests that this target has not been achieved. The majority of disabled are employed in the clerical or subordinate grades.

Local Offices

In accordance with government policy, the work of the civil service is increasingly being carried out from local offices, and numbers of civil servants have been transferred from Dublin to these offices. This development is frequently referred to as decentralisation, though some commentators prefer to call it dispersal or relocation, since nearly all the decisions continue to be made at departmental headquarters. Appendix I shows the locations of these staff.

MANAGEMENT IN THE CIVIL SERVICE: REFORM PROPOSALS

Improving management practices in the civil service is an issue which has been raised at various times over the past twenty years or so. The Public Services Organisation Review Group identified the need for a more effective system of management and communication as being among the major issues which faced the civil service. It therefore concentrated on devising and articulating such a system and devoted a considerable part of its report to the arguments for its adoption. It accepted the constraint of the Ministers and Secretaries Act 1924 which determines the minister as corporation sole, but it sought to exploit the loophole which allowed for the establishment of state-sponsored bodies which could operate under the aegis of government departments without the minister being responsible for their every act. Accordingly the report of the review group (The Devlin Report, 1969) recommended the legal creation within each department of an 'Aireacht' responsible for policy matters and a number of executive agencies to implement policy decisions.

The recommended extension of the state-sponsored body concept has not been accepted, largely because of the lack of political interest and the absence of intellectual support, including support within the civil service itself. Ministers and departmental staff alike proved to be far more concerned with the Devlin Report's proposals regarding departmental structure and the distribution of functions than with its scheme for effective and accountable management. Similarly, in 1973 the debate on the bill to set up the Department of the Public Service (essentially to facilitate the management of departments) was very poorly attended. Only five deputies contributed to the debate which was marked throughout by a preoccupation with parliamentary control, an apprehension that parliament might lose some of its power, and a feeling that democracy would suffer as a consequence.

The proposed agencies have not been set up, except in a few cases such as the Air Navigation Office and the Social Welfare Services Office. Even these offices, however, have no statutory basis, so that while in practice they operate as if they had autonomy, the legal position is nevertheless that the ministers concerned remain responsible for all of the work of the offices and answer parliamentary questions about the way it is carried out. This is the arrangement clearly preferred by politicians, who are unwilling that full responsibility for the detailed operation of grant schemes, licences, favours for constituents, etc. should be removed from the ministers, to whom they have ready access both personally and through parliamentary questions, and given instead to officials, who cannot be so readily approached.

Another of the recommendations of the Devlin Report was that management advisory committees be established in all departments. While most departments have set up such committees (at least nominally), in many departments they meet infrequently, and when they do they focus on *ad hoc* issues rather than on how well a department is performing. Again, while many departments have attempted to outline detailed objectives, little progress has been made on identifying and costing results, the assignment of budgets to individual managers, or on the daily monitoring of service delivery. Performance monitoring is new to the civil service, and experience thereof is very limited.

The next major effort at reform was the publication in 1985 of the white paper *Serving the Country Better*. It was devoted almost entirely to the civil service and emphasised the need for change therein. It stated that 'At the centre of the government's plans for tomorrow's public service is a management programme which will involve the introduction in all departments of management systems based on corporate planning and emphasising personal responsibility for results, costs and service.' Each department was expected to report at the end of each year on the progress of the reform achieved.

Following the change of government in 1987, there was a change of emphasis on civil service issues, and the plans outlined in the white paper were discontinued. The new government abolished the Department of the Public Service as a separate department and merged its activities with those of the Department of Finance. The published programme for the government formed in 1989 contains no reference to reform in public service management.

In spite of the apparent lack of government concern, there has in recent years been a questioning of the need to continue traditional work practices and career patterns. This has arisen as a result of political demands for the curtailment of the cost of the public service, which is being sought through a combination of restricted recruitment and promotion, pay restraint, and the deployment of staff across traditional functional boundaries in order to conform with changing working priorities. These developments, together with the volume and speed of information which the new technology is making available throughout the civil service, seem likely to force a critical evaluation of the existing structure and the decision-making processes. Though the signs are slow in emerging, this may eventually result in a reduction in the number of grades and the delegation of responsibility to lower levels. These issues are elaborated in Chapter 12.

REFERENCES

Report of Public Services Organisation Review Group, 1966–69 [Devlin Report] (Dublin: Stationery Office, 1969)

Serving the Country Better: A White Paper on the Public Service (Dublin: Stationery Office, 1985)

Chapman, Richard A., *The Higher Civil Service in Britain* (London: Constable, 1970)

FitzGerald, Garret, *All in a Life* (Dublin: Gill & Macmillan 1991)

Appendix G

Total Numbers of Civil Servants

(i) Total Number of Civil Servants at Five-Year Intervals, 1975–90

Year	Number of civil servants	
	Industrial	Non-industrial
1975	3,121	24,206
1980	3,159	30,844
1985	2,600	29,903
1990	1,723	26,666

(ii) Total Number of Civil Servants serving by Department/Office

	1 January 1991	
	Industrial	Non-industrial
President's Establishment		10
Oireachtas		196
Taoiseach		292
Central Statistics Office		473
Comptroller and Auditor General		79
Finance		590
Revenue	35	6,032
Office of Public Works	1,556	836
State Laboratory		61
Valuation Office		149
Ordnance Survey		298
Civil Service Commission		104
Ombudsman		34
Attorney General		32
Chief State Solicitor's Office		114
Director of Public Prosecutions	..	16
Justice		4,648
Environment		790
Education		823
National Gallery		42
Gaeltacht		67
Marine	159	270
Energy		227
Industry and Commerce		522
Tourism, Transport and Communications		1,058
Defence	6	438
Social Welfare		3,779
Health		334
Foreign Affairs		781
Labour		562
Agriculture and Food	74	3,654
Totals	1,830	27,311

Appendix H

Appropriation Account of the Department of Finance for 1989

Office of the Minister for Finance   Vote 7

Account of the sum expended, in the year 31st December, 1989, compared with the sum granted, for the s .laries and expenses of the Office of the Minister for Finance including the Paymaster-General's Office, and for the payment of certain grants and grants-in-aids.

Service	Grant	Expenditure	Expenditure compared with Grant	
			Less than Granted	More than Granted
	£	£	£	£
A.1.—Salaries, Wages and Allowances ...	10,454,000	10,028,869	425,131	—
A.2.—Consultancy Services	920,000	577,642	342,358	—
B.1.—Travelling and Incidental Expenses	811,000	866,741	—	55,741
B.2.—Office Machinery and other Office Supplies	1,205,000	1,208,012	—	3,012
B.3.—Office Premises Expenses	490,000	411,673	78,327	—
C.—Postal and Telecommunications Services	599,000	488,655	110,345	—
D.—Management of Prize Bonds	1,600,000	1,482,600	117,400	—
E.—Central Computing Service	1,240,000	1,017,128	222,872	—
F.—Information Technology Initiatives	700,000	674,012	25,988	—
G.—Economic and Social Research Institute —Administration and General Expenses (Grant-in-Aid)	1,008,000	1,008,000	—	—
H.—Institute of Public Administration (Grant-in-Aid)	1,024,000	1,024,000	—	—
I.—Grants for County Development Work	381,000	365,066	15,934	—
J.—Payment to Western Development Fund (Grant-in-Aid)	750,000	750,000	—	—
K.—Repayment of Advances	450,000	180,513	269,487	—
L.—Losses in respect of Certain Loans for Industrial Development Purposes Advanced by Industrial Credit Corporation PLC	3,500,000	3,571,837	—	71,837
M.—Fund for distribution of surplus of National Lottery (Grant-in-Aid)	55,000,000	47,685,092	7,314,908	—
N.—Civil Service Arbitration Board	20,000	7,056	12,944	—
O.—Review Body on Higher Remuneration in the Public Sector	18,000	11,674	6,326	—
P.—Contribution to the Common Fund for Commodities	200,000	—	200,000	—
Gross Total	80,370,000	71,358,570	9,142,020	130,590

Surplus of Gross Estimate over Expenditure £9,011,430

	Estimated	Realised	
Deduct—			Deficiency in Appropriations in Aid realised
Q.—Appropriations in Aid	870,000	761,444	£108,556

Net Surplus to be surrendered £8,902,874

Net Total	79,500,00	70,597,126	

A.2. — This saving arose because certain studies provided for were not undertaken.

B.1.— The excess was mainly due to expenditure on (i) home travel, (ii) non-EC foreign travel and (iii) incidental expenses being greater than anticipated.

B.3. — The saving was due to (i) maintenance and (ii) heat, light and fuel costs being less than expected.

C.— The saving arose because expenditure on both postal and telephone services was less the anticipated.

D. — The saving arose because the transfer of the Scheme to a new operator took less time than had been anticipated.

E. — The saving was due to the deferment of the purchase of a number of software packages and expenditure of hardware maintenance and computer stationery being less than anticipated.

K. — The saving arose because losses which were expected to arise in the year of account did not materialise to the extent expected.

M. — The savings arose because Lottery-funded projects proceeded less rapidly than had been predicted.

N. — The saving arose because there were fewer sittings of the Board than had been anticipated in the first half of the year.

O. — The saving arose mainly because the level of specialist assistance was less than anticipated.

P.— The saving arose because Ireland's voluntary contribution to the Fund was not requested in 1989.

Appropriations in Aid

	Estimated	Realised
1. Receipts from An Post and Bord Telecom Éireann	16,000	16,700
2. Receipts from computer services rendered by Central Computing Service	635,000	529,569
3. Recoupment of salaries, etc., of officers on secondment	107,000	108,486
4. Recoupment of certain travelling and subsistence expenses from the EC, etc.	100,000	97,867
5. Miscellaneous	12,000	8,822
	£870,000	£761,444

1. The surplus arose because the use by An Post and Telecom Éireann of the services of the Acting Chief Medical Officer was higher than expected.
2. The deficit arose because repayments from Health Boards and other Health Agencies due in 1989 were not made until 1990.
3. The surplus arose because the amounts to be recouped were higher than anticipated.
4. The deficit was due to the frequency of travel on EC business being less than anticipated.
5. The deficit was due to receipts being less than anticipated.

Extra Remuneration

Twenty officers received sums ranging from £627 to £2,231 for roster duties. Five officers received sums varying from £732 to £5,721 for performance of higher duties. One officer received £2,919 in respect of special duties.

Sixteen officers received allowances ranging from £477 to £1,972 in respect of duties as delegates at meetings abroad. Three officers received gratuities of £500, £850 and £1,000 in respect of extra attendance.

Two hundred and eight officers in all received sums in respect of overtime. One hundred and nineteen of these received amounts ranging from £407 to £7,412. The total amount paid in respect of overtime was £204,371.

The total number of officers who received extra remuneration was three hundred and four.

Notes.

Ex-gratia lump sums totalling £31,407 were paid to one hundred and sixty- three officers of Assistant Principal and Principal grades in respect of certain outstanding adjudication awards. Amounts varied between £40 and £1,702 (E.107/6/88).

This account includes the sum of £34,162 in respect of an Irish Staff Member with the European Institute of Public Administration.

One Principal Officer received the sum of £1,400 in respect of membership of the Legal Aid Board. This Account includes expenditure of £34,023 in respect of staff on loan without repayment to other Departments.

Ex - gratia payments amounting to £162 were made to six officers in respect of loss and damage to personal property in the course of official duties. (E.109/41/41).

A sum of £20 unaccounted for in a petty cash account of March 1989 was written off (Per/Gen.127).

In addition to the grants - in - aid from the Vote, extra amounts of £15,190 and £11,000 respectively were issued to the Economic and Social Research Institute and to the Institute of Public Administration from the Vote for Increases in Remuneration and Pensions (No 46).

Total Expenditure in respect of Commissions etc. on account of which payments were made in the year ended 31st December, 1989.

Commission or Committee	Year of Appointment	Total expenditure to 31st December, 1989
		£
Civil Service Arbitration Board	1950/51	345,670
Review Body on Higher Remuneration in the Public Sector	1969/70	650,089

Department of Finance,
30th April, 1990

S.P. CROMIEN,
Accounting Officer.

I have examined the above Account and the appended Accounts in accordance with the provisions of the Exchequer and Audit Departments Act, 1921. I have obtained all the information and explanations that I have required, and I certify, as a result of my audit, that in my opinion the Accounts are correct.

P.L. McDonnell.
Ard-Reachtaire Cuntas agus Ciste.

FUND FOR DISTRIBUTION OF SURPLUS OF NATIONAL LOTTERY (GRANT-IN-AID)

Account of Receipts and Payments in the year ended 31st December, 1989

	£
Grant-in-Aid, 1989 (Subhead M)	47,685,092
Payments (see Schedule)	47,685,092
Balance at 31st December, 1989	NIL

SCHEDULE

	£
Department of Defence	620,000
Department of Education	22,262,539
Department of the Environment	5,880,000
Department of Health	6,969,000
Department of the Taoiseach	4,990,000
Department of Social Welfare	900,000

Department of Foreign Affairs	530,664
Office of Public Works	2,243,000
Roinn na Gaeltachta	3,269,389
Department of Finance	20,500
	£47,685,092

Department of Finance,   S.P. CROMIEN,
30th April, 1990   Accounting Officer.

NATIONAL LOTTERY SUSPENSE ACCOUNT
Account of Receipts and Payments in the year ended 31st December 1989

	£
Balance at 1st January, 1989	NIL
Receipts from Fund for distribution of surplus of	
National Lottery (Grant-in-Aid Account)	20,500
	20,500
Payments - Gaeleagras na Seirbhise Poibli	28,946
Balance at 31st December, 1989	£8,446 (Dr.)

Department of Finance,   S.P. CROMIEN,
30th April, 1990   Accounting Officer.

PUBLIC SERVICE EARLY RETIREMENT SCHEME
Account of Receipts and Payments in the year ended 31st December, 1989.

		£
Balance at 1st January 1989		93,193 (Dr.)
Receipts		
Vote 45	90,318	
The Department of Labour in	1,544	
respect of Statutory redundancy		
Entitlement		91,862
Balance at 31st December		£1,331 (Dr.)

Department of Finance,   S.P. CROMIEN,
30th April, 1990   Accounting Officer.

WESTERN DEVELOPMENT FUND

Account of Receipts and Payments in the year ended 31st December, 1989

	Receipts		Payments
Balance at 1st January, 1989	457,775	Grants (see Schedule)	1,024,170
Grant-in-Aid (Subhead J)	750,000		
Repayments	3,000	Balance at 31st December, 1989	186,605
	£1,210,775		£1,210,775

Note

A Company in respect of which a repayable advance of £24,413 (including interest) was outstanding at 31st December, 1989 is in liquidation.

Department of Finance,
27th April, 1990

S.P. CROMIEN,
Accounting Officer.

Grants.

	£
Galway County Council (Workspace), Galway	28,212
Shellfish Research Laboratory, Carna, Co. Galway	40,000
Jamie Young, Renvyle, Co. Galway	26,726
IRD Waterville, Co. Kerry	12,500
Longford County Council (Workspace), Longford	67,628
Killala Community Council, Co. Mayo	5,253
Cuilmore Leisure Ltd, Boyle, Co. Roscommon	18,400
Western Mushrooms Ltd, Strokestown, Co. Roscommon	31,862
Ballyleague Community Co-operative Society Ltd, Co. Roscommon	43,600
Sligo Market Yard Craft Centre, Sligo	78,273
Messrs Cawley & Scanlon, Ballymote, Co. Sligo	62,000
Charles P. Henry, Ardtarmon House, Sligo	5,904
North West Fur Farms, Sligo	7,450
Miscellaneous Small Grants (under £5,000)	596,362
Total Payments from Fund	£1,024,170

Repayable Advance Outstanding at 31st December, 1989

	£
Ballybay Tanners Limited, Ballybay, Co. Monaghan, (in liquidation)	24,413

Value of Computer time rendered to other Public Departments during the year ended 31st December 1989 without repayment

Number of Vote	Department, etc.	Amount
4	Central Statistics Office	893,012
8	Comptroller and Auditor General	772
10	Public Works and Buildings	2,832
15	Valuation and Ordnance Survey	2,387
16	Civil Service Commission	5,633
19	Office of the Minister for Justice	69,558
25	Environment	188,344
26	Office of the Minister for Education	125,360
30	Marine	16,638
32	Agriculture and Food	153,667
33	Labour	32,464
34	Industry and Commerce	14,568
35	Tourism and Transport	4,332

37	Defence	57,747
39	Foreign Affairs	207,190
41	Social Welfare	11,142
42	Health	57,153
43	Energy	2,130
		£1,844,929

Appendix I

Numbers of Civil Servants Working in Offices outside Dublin, by Departments

Place	Agric.	Defence	Educ.	Energy	Env.	F. Aff.	Gaelt.	Just.	Marine	OPW	OS	Rev.	SW	T & T
Carlow	47							11			1	1	22	
Cavan	210							90	1			20	18	
Clare—Ennis	75							9					30	
Clare—Remainder	10				59			11				48	1	316
Cork—Cork City	196	2	21			3		258	8	14	5	386	147	43
Cork—Bandon	11							4					2	
Cork—Bantry	4							1	1			4	8	
Cork—Cobh		5						89					8	
Cork—Mallow	13							6		1		1	3	
Cork—Skibbereen	5												1	
Cork—Remainder	93							11	2		11	14	5	15
Donegal—Lifford	11							10				28		
Donegal—Letterkenny	20		1					8		5		60	40	
Donegal—Remainder	97						8	6	8	1		60	55	16
Galway—Ballinasloe	1							4						
Galway—Galway City	97	186	19	1				31	4	9	3	131	66	4
Galway—Tuam	16							4					2	
Galway—Remainder	48						28	5	1	8	8		11	
Kerry—Killarney	13							3			11		5	
Kerry—Tralee	69						3	26	1	1	4	72	48	
Kerry—Remainder	48						2	3	1			1	31	44
Kildare—Naas	33							16					3	
Kildare—Remainder	56	2									9		25	
Kilkenny	73							20		3	8	92	28	5
Laois—Portlaoise	35							394		3			4	
Laoise—Remainder	8							1			2			
Leitrim—Carrick-on-Shannon	11							9					15	
Leitrim—Remainder	8							1				2	9	
Limerick—Kilmallock	1												1	
Limerick—Limerick City	85		13					249		10	2	220	89	
Limerick—Remainder	31							2		7		4	22	
Longford	43							10					27	
Louth—Drogheda	18							10			2	9	38	
Louth—Dundalk	20							15		2	1	193	43	
Louth—Remainder	5									1		40	2	
Mayo—Ballina	21				256			5		2		3	35	
Mayo—Castlebar	126			3				20	9	2		54	19	
Mayo—Claremorris	16							2					1	
Mayo—Westport	2							2				1	13	
Mayo—Remainder	38						2	3	1		2	21		
Meath—Kells													2	
Meath—Navan	46							1						
Meath—Remainder	18							14		8			2	
Monaghan	74							14		8	5	74	5	5
Offaly—Birr	4												1	5
Offaly—Tullamore	35							10		1		8	3	
Offaly—Remainder	9										6		1	
Roscommon—Castlerea	8							2					1	
Roscommon—Remainder	92							12		5			2	
Sligo	100		10					19		7		64	354	
Tipperary—Clonmel	19							20				4	22	
Tipperary—Nenagh	52							2		1			3	
Tipperary—Thurles	12							5		5	3	56	17	
Tipperary—Remainder	70							11		5			3	
Waterford	89							28	1	8	1	160	57	

Place	Agric.	Defence	Educ.	Energy	Env.	F. Aff.	Gaelt.	Just.	Marine	OPW	OS	Rev.	SW	T & T
Westmeath—Athlone	17	2	107					12		4	1	79	33	
Westmeath—Mullingar	51							13		5		1	18	5
Westmeath—Remainder	8									1				
Wexford—Enniscorthy	46							1				3		
Wexford—Gorey	2							7						
Wexford—Remainder	35							21		1	13	118	37	6
Wicklow—Bray								6		9			29	
Wicklow—Remainder	7							54		1	4	5	17	
No Fixed Station								12					30	
Serving Abroad	10		1			219						16		

OPW Office of Public Works. OS Ordnance Survey. SW Social Welfare. T & T Tourism and Transport.

7

Local Government

Ireland has had local government since the Middle Ages. The original authorities charged with its administration were the county sheriffs, assisted by the grand juries. In later years these were supplemented by a number of *ad hoc* bodies established to meet the needs created by various social and economic changes (town commissioners, poor law guardians, sanitary authorities, boards of governors of hospitals and asylums, harbour authorities, etc.). The old system was essentially judicial in its mode of operation and thoroughly unrepresentative in character. It survived until 1898, when the Local Government (Ireland) Act inaugurated a comprehensive reform based on the principles of efficiency and democracy. It set up a number of multi-purpose authorities and extended the franchise to householders; these provisions, with subsequent modifications, form the basis of the local government system of today.

The system as it now operates is made up of elected and non-elected statutory bodies. The elected local authorities consist of town commissioners (30), boroughs (6), urban district councils (49), county boroughs (5) and county councils (27). The non-elected bodies include vocational education committees, joint library committees and harbour authorities.

Councillors do not receive any salary, nor is there any payment for loss of earnings or expenses (other than travelling). A mayor of a borough may, however, receive such remuneration as the council decides. (The Lord Mayor of Dublin receives £19,000 per annum and allowances for entertainment up to £30,000.)

The county councils and the county boroughs exercise the full range of local government functions. The boroughs and urban district councils have responsibility for most of these functions within their areas. The town commissioners have limited responsibilities. Each local authority has two arms, the elected council, which makes policy, within limits prescribed by legislation, and the executive, which carries out the policy.

POWERS

Local authorities receive their powers through legislation. That legislation specifies what they can, or must, do and in some cases how they must do it. It also specifies whether, and to what extent, they are responsible to central government or, more specifically, to particular ministers. Local authorities are permitted to carry out only those functions entrusted to them by law. The range is relatively narrow, and it is common to find local authorities elsewhere involved in public transport, police, primary and second-level education and municipal undertakings of various kinds, such as, for example, the provision and operation of theatres. If an Irish local authority carries out a function not specifically entrusted to it by an act, it is acting ultra vires and can be challenged in court. They have however, the power to make by-laws governing local affairs, such as traffic movements or the regulation of behaviour in public parks.

ELECTIONS

All counties, county boroughs and the larger boroughs and urban districts (Bray, Drogheda, Dundalk and Sligo) are divided into local electoral areas under orders made by the Minister for the Environment. The smaller urban districts and towns with commissioners constitute single electoral areas. The number of councillors in each local authority is determined by order (except in the case of boroughs and county boroughs, where the number is fixed by statute), as also is the number of councillors to be elected for each electoral area. County councils have between 20 and 78 members; county boroughs between 15 and 52; boroughs usually 12 (Dún Laoghaire has 14); urban district councils usually 9, and town commissioners the same number. There are 1,618 elected members in all. There is no prescribed councillor/population ratio; in practice, the ratio varies considerably, even within one class of local authority.

The law provides that elections are to be held every five years. However, it also provides that they may be postponed, and they have been on several occasions, the most recent being 1990. Postponement is effected by ministerial order which must be confirmed by both Houses of the Oireachtas. The system of voting, as for national elections, is by proportional representation. Those over eighteen years of age on the date the electoral register comes into force (15 April each year) are entitled to vote, irrespective of nationality. Polling day must, by law, be in June; the actual date is fixed by the minister. Each candidate must lodge a deposit—£10 for county council and county borough elections, and £5 for other local authorities—which is forfeit if the candidate fails to reach one-third of the quota at some stage. As for Dáil elections, political party affiliations may be shown on the ballot paper.

Certain persons are disqualified from being elected, including those who have served, or are serving, prison sentences, those guilty of misconduct while members of local authorities, and persons who are active members of the defence forces. In addition, certain officials of local authorities—generally those above the grade of clerical officer—may not retain their employment if they are elected to and wish to serve on their own or a neighbouring local authority. Restrictions also apply to civil servants: those in the executive grades and upwards may not put themselves forward.

MEETINGS

The number of meetings to be held each year is prescribed by law. So is the procedure for calling meetings and the size of the quorum. Provision is made for the calling of special meetings by the chairman or a specified number of numbers. (In October 1990 a special meeting of Dublin Corporation was called at the request of five members to consider the nomination of another member for election to the Presidency of Ireland.) Subject to this, a local authority may make its own standing orders to regulate its meetings. Decisions are made through majority vote.

The public has no legal right to attend council meetings; it is a matter for each local authority to decide whether or not to admit them. The press is not entitled as a matter of right to attend meetings of the borough councils. In the case of other elected local authorities, the press may not be excluded from council meetings unless the Minister for the Environment so authorises. Very rarely are either the public or the press excluded from meetings.

Council meetings are presided over by a chairman or, in the case of a borough, by the mayor. These officers must be elected annually by the council; a vice-chairman may also be elected. They have no executive role and are not responsible for administration. This is the responsibility of the manager. The chairman has, however, special power to obtain information from the manager—a right which no other individual councillor has—and the manager normally meets him regularly to keep him informed.

THE MANAGEMENT SYSTEM

The city and county management system owes its origin to the United States of America. There in the early part of the century the idea of running municipal affairs in the same manner as business affairs took hold. This was the idea that, instead of elected members being in charge of all activities, they and a manager should operate in the same way for a city as a board of directors and a general manager for a business. This idea spread rapidly in the United States and reached Ireland in the early 1920s. Thus, when the Dublin and Cork Corporations, which had been dissolved in 1924 and replaced by commissioners, came to be reconstituted in 1929, legislation provided for a city manager in each case to run the cities with the elected members. Roche (1982: 101) notes that the original dissolution in Dublin, at any rate, was received with equanimity by the citizens, who seemed to share the accepted view of the corporation as a combination of corruption and inefficiency. Subsequently, Limerick and Waterford got city managers, and the counties got county managers.

The functions of local authorities are, under the management system, divided into *reserved functions* discharged by the elected members, and *executive functions* performed by the city or county manager. While the law provides for an exact division of functions so that responsibility may be defined, in practice they are complementary; managers and councillors do not act independently of each other. The relationship is outlined below. The manager is the experienced whole-time administrator responsible for the efficient discharge of day-to-day business without making an undue demand on the time of the elected members, who are part-time.

The Manager: Appointment and Area
City and county managers are appointed by the local authority on the recommendation of the Local Appointments Commission, the three-man body set up in 1926 to select and recommend to local authorities persons for appointment to the principal offices. Internal promotions to the post of manager are not permitted. Nearly all managers have had previous service with local authorities, and it is exceptional when a person outside the local authority service succeeds in being recommended by the commission.

The same person acts as manager for the county council and all boroughs, urban districts and towns in the county. County borough corporations have their own managers, except in Dublin. Dublin city and county are unique because of size. Following recent re-organisation, Dublin has a city manager and the county has three county managers. At the time of writing three new authorities are to be set up to replace Dublin County Council and Dún Laoghaire Corporation.

Reserved Functions
The main functions which are reserved to elected members include the adoption of the annual estimate of expenses, the fixing of the annual rate to be levied to meet these and the amount to be borrowed, the making of development plans and by-laws, house-building programmes, and assisting other local bodies in providing service and amenities. The various functions can be exercised only on the passing of a resolution. The manager may not, save with the consent of the members, exceed the amount provided for any particular purpose.

Executive Functions
Executive functions are in practice all of those not reserved. They include arrangements made by the manager in relation to staff, acceptance of tenders,

making contracts, fixing rents, making lettings, and deciding on applications for planning permissions.

Manager/Council Relations

The sharp legal distinction made between the reserved and the executive functions does not, however, quite reflect the way in which business is actually carried out. Managers and councillors work in close co-operation, and the manager attends and participates in council meetings as if he were a member (though he has not the right to vote). The councillors appreciate that the manager is the expert in administration, having normally spent his whole life in local government. Indeed the manager has often been described as the power-house of local government. Even in policy areas, therefore, which are their prerogative, they rely on him for guidance as to what can and cannot be done. He has a greater knowledge than they have because of his wider experience of the forming and execution of policy. Collins (1987: 59) writes of the advantage enjoyed by the manager 'because he is the centre of a wide communications network involving the central government, other managers, his staff, the public and other politicians. A manager is liable to be in contact with the local business community, state agencies for economic development and a range of social institutions. Such a network keeps the manager abreast of possible sources of advantage or difficulty for his own plans. He is also able to use his administrative and technical staff to store and assess the information available to him.'

For his part, the manager goes beyond the mere legal obligation to keep his councillors informed about the business of the council, about new works, or about the way in which he proposes to carry out any particular executive function. Because they now hold the power formerly vested in the council, managers generally are careful to retain the goodwill of members, and they like to keep them informed about matters affecting their constituents. Managers recognise the brokerage role expected of the individual councillor, and recognise also that their own overall policy responsibilities are not compromised by the occasional marginal adjustment to facilitate individual citizens.

Council policy is articulated by the manager. In doing so he is normally careful to be circumspect about appearing influential and freely refers to the assistance of individual councillors in helping the council to arrive at decisions. Such a line of action reflects the manager's recognition of the wealth of local knowledge and collective wisdom of his council. Real conflict is rare, though there may frequently be a semblance of conflict when councillors at meetings may wish to be seen as championing the interests of those who elected them as against the tyranny of the bureaucracy. Certainly the conflict anticipated at the introduction of the management system is not in evidence today: both sides have learned to live in harmony with the system.

The manager has absolute authority in regard to control and supervision of staff, and this is an authority which the councillors are happy to leave with him.

However, if the number of staff or their remuneration is to be changed, the council must agree.

Staff

In many ways the local authority service is a single service with a standard pattern of grades and uniformity in methods of recruitment, pay and conditions of service. Local authorities employ about 26,000 people. About 9,000 of these are in managerial, clerical and technical grades. The officials in these grades have uniform conditions of appointment and, in general, have the same permanent tenure of office as established civil servants.

The standard county administrative organisation is: county manager; county secretary; finance officer; administrative officer; senior staff officer; staff officer; assistant staff officer; clerical officer; clerk-typist and clerical assistant. The first three grades are appointed following competitions conducted by the Local Appointments Commission. (The commissioners are the Ceann Comhairle of the Dáil and the Secretaries of the Departments of the Environment and of Health. The commission is staffed by civil servants and is housed in the same building as the Civil Service Commission; the staffs are interchangeable.) The promotions to the four intermediate grades are made by competitons held locally and usually open to the whole local government service.

On the technical side, the grades include engineers, architects, librarians, solicitors, coroners and fire officers.

Dublin Corporation and Dublin County Council are exceptions to the general rule about appointments. Vacancies in many senior, but not the top, posts are filled by promotion from among eligible officers serving with these bodies. It is considered that the numbers employed in the two bodies are sufficiently high to warrant this departure from the normal practice.

About 17,000 persons are employed in the skilled, semi-skilled and manual grades. These have the same conditions as persons in equivalent jobs outside the public service.

FUNCTIONS OF LOCAL GOVERNMENT

Almost all of the functions of local authorities derive from legislation emanating from the Department of the Environment, whether acts of the Oireachtas or statutory instruments made by the minister. There are, however, some tasks carried out on behalf of other departments, such as the dipping of sheep against scab, vocational education and grants for higher education, and certain traffic control measures.

In the day-to-day work there is constant contact between the officials in the Department of the Environment and the managers and other staff of the local

Local Authority Estimates, 1990
EXPENDITURE BY PROGRAMME GROUP

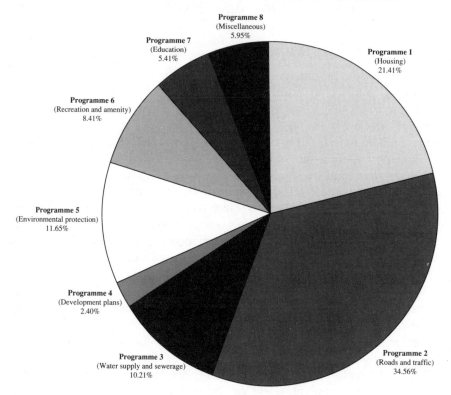

Programme 8
(Miscellaneous)
5.95%

Programme 7
(Education)
5.41%

Programme 1
(Housing)
21.41%

Programme 6
(Recreation and amenity)
8.41%

Programme 5
(Environmental protection)
11.65%

Programme 4
(Development plans)
2.40%

Programme 3
(Water supply and sewerage)
10.21%

Programme 2
(Roads and traffic)
34.56%

Stationery Office, Dublin

authorities. Managers and departmental staff meet frequently. Information is exchanged, plans are discussed, and new proposals are sounded out. Managers themselves hold monthly meetings to compare experiences and discuss common business. Where the minister attaches particular importance to an issue or project, the managers are invited specially to the department, as, for example when they were called to the Custom House in September 1990 to hear the minister's concern that they were not doing enough to protect the environment.

The services provided may be classified under eight broad headings: (1) housing; (2) roads and traffic; (3) water supply and sewerage; (4) development plans; (5) environmental protection; (6) recreation and amenity; (7) education; (8) miscellaneous. The total estimated expenditure for 1990 under these headings was £1,062.15 million. The percentage allocated to each heading is shown in the above diagram.

(1) Housing

National housing policy is that, as far as resources permit, every family should have a house of good standard in an acceptable environment at a price or rent the family can afford.

There are, of course, many bodies as well as local authorities involved in housing. These include building societes, the associated banks, assurance companies and the Housing Finance Agency (a specialised agency through which local authorities fund house purchase loans). The role of the local authorities can be regarded as a residual one—to provide access to housing for those who cannot afford to get their own houses or who have difficulty in qualifying for loans from the recognised lending agencies. Local authorities may assist in providing houses by administering loans financed by the Housing Finance Agency; by building houses for letting and possible subsequent sale to the tenants; by providing serviced sites for individuals or co-operatives who wish to build their own houses; and by providing in addition to what might be termed normal housing, special-category accommodation such as sheltered housing for the elderly and serviced halting sites for travellers. The provision of sites for travellers has a high political profile, with the result that the management acts have been amended to give the manager rather than the council the greater control in this area.

(2) Roads and Traffic

County councils, county boroughs, boroughs and urban district councils are road authorities under the various Road Acts and are responsible in law for maintaining the public roads system. In practice, however, the state has accepted responsibility for the national primary roads (the main routes from Dublin to the principal cities and towns) and the national secondary roads (the routes between the major national centres) and makes 100 per cent grants to the roads authorities to cover the cost of maintaining and improving these. The upkeep of the other roads in the country which are classified as county and urban is financed from local authorities' own resources and from government grants. Through the grant mechanism, the minister largely controls the location and timing of road works.

Two recent developments have been the introduction of tolls to finance road construction and the establishment of the National Roads Authority. The legál basis for the former type of venture is contained in the Local Government (Toll Roads) Act 1979, which allows road authorities to enter agreements with private interests for the construction, maintenance and management of toll roads and bridges. A formal toll scheme must be made (this is a reserved function of the elected members), and if there are objections, a public local inquiry must be conducted by a person appointed by the minister, after which the minister may confirm, or refuse to confirm the scheme.

The National Roads Authority was set up in July 1988. The intention is that this will be a statutory body. Its tasks are (1) to plan the roads of the future, to recommend how they should be paid for, and then to make the payments, and (2) to arrange for the design of road improvement projects, the placing of construction contracts, and the promotion of private investment in roads.

The promised Roads Bill was introduced in the Dáil in April 1991 and at the time of writing awaits debate. Its purpose is 'to provide for the construction and maintenance of public roads, to establish a National Roads Authority, to provide for motorways, busways and protected roads, to provide for the tolling of public roads, and to provide for other matters connected with the matters aforesaid'.

The local authorities will, however, continue to have a major role in the development of national roads; they will continue to own, maintain and manage them. They will also continue to have responsibility for non-national roads, which account for 94 per cent of total road mileage.

Responsibility for road traffic matters generally, such as the specification of standards for vehicles and the preparation of 'rules of the road', rests largely with the Department of the Environment, in consultation with the Department of Tourism, Transport and Communications, and the Gardaí. Local authority responsibilities include the provision of traffic signs and road markings, the preparation of traffic studies and the application of traffic management techniques, the employment of road safety officers and co-operation in road safety campaigns, the operation of meter-parking schemes, and the employment of traffic and school wardens. The Gardaí are responsible for the making of by-laws relating to traffic matters generally, including stopping places for buses and stands for taxis, but local authorities must be consulted in the exercise of this function.

Motor taxation and the licensing of drivers are carried out by the local authorities as agents of central government. The moneys collected are paid into the Exchequer, and the administrative costs are recouped to the local authorities.

Public lighting is provided by the county councils and the urban authorities, through arrangements made with the Electricity Supply Board. Only Dublin Corporation has its own public lighting department. Grants are available from the Department of the Environment towards the provision of new and improved lighting on main roads in built-up areas but not towards maintenance or operating costs.

(3) Water Supply and Sewerage
County councils, county borough and borough corporations and urban district councils are designated sanitary authorities with an obligation to provide adequate supplies of water for domestic, agricultural and industrial uses and systems for the safe and environmentally acceptable disposal of sewage and

other water-born wastes. Technical advice and other assistance (for example, access to a public mains supply) is provided to groups who organise their own supply of water through group schemes, The Public Capital Programme provides each year for investment in water and sewerage facilities. This money is divided by the department among the various authorities in accordance with proposals on hand and the needs of each area.

Local authorities have charged for water supplies for many years, mainly to commercial users and to those domestic users connected to a public water supply. However, up to 1983 the charges did not apply to domestic users in urban areas. (Since the vast majority of houses in urban areas had a water supply, they were regarded as paying for this through their ordinary rates.) With the abolition of rates on private dwellings in 1978, the position changed, and subsequently in 1983 the powers of local authorities were extended to enable them to charge for services generally. A decision to levy charges is a function reserved to the elected members.

(4) Development Plans

The Local Government (Planning and Development) Act 1963 constituted county councils, county boroughs, boroughs and urban district councils as planning authorities and obliged them to prepare a development plan within three years of the passing of the act and to review the plan at five-yearly intervals. A development plan is a statement of development objectives, supported by maps. The objectives must include the zoning of land for different uses, the development of roads and public utilities such as water and sewerage, the preservation and extension of amenities and urban renewal. It may include a wide range of additional objectives to assist local interest groups, for example provisions for community and recreational development and measures to encourage the local economy.

The plan is the framework within which development, both public and private, is to take place. Its adoption is a reserved function of the elected council. Before adoption it must be prepared in draft form and displayed publicly for three months in order to give the public the opportunity to make representations. These representations must be considered (but not necessarily accepted) by the local authority before it formally adopts the plan.

While the development plans are not subject to the approval of a central authority, the Minister for the Environment nevertheless has power to take whatever measures are necessary to co-ordinate the development plan objectives of the eighty-seven separate planning authorities and to resolve any conflicts that may arise between them. For example, he may require a number of authorities to work together, or he may direct that the provisions of a plan be varied.

Control of development is ensured through the operation of a system of planning permissions and refusals. Most developments may not proceed without permission from the authority or, on appeal, from An Bord Pleanála (the body set up by statute in 1976 to deal with appeals). Certain classes of development are exempt from the requirement of planning permission, for example small extensions to domestic dwellings, agricultural and forestry development, and developments by government departments. Decisions on planning applications are a matter for the city or county manager, but the council may intervene to alter managers' decisions. Planning permissions lapse after a period of five years if the development is not undertaken.

(5) Environmental Protection

As a result of the establishment of the Office of the Environment in 1989, with its own minister of state, considerable emphasis is now being given to the protection of the environment. In this connection, local authorities engage in a diverse set of activities. These include the prevention of air and water pollution by industrial plants and other industrial concerns, the provision of notices and the erection of fencing at dangerous places such as quarries, rivers and cliffs. They must collect, or arrange to collect, refuse and to clean streets. Litter wardens may be appointed and offenders prosecuted.

Other responsibilities undertaken by the local authorities include the inspection of buildings to prevent fire hazards, civil defence arrangements (under the guidance of the Department of Defence) and the control of dogs, including their licensing.

(6) Recreation and Amenity

Under this heading the services include the provision of libraries and museums and the giving of assistance to local festivals and exhibitions. Facilities for sport and for community development include the provision of parks and open spaces and of land free or at reduced prices for sports grounds or community halls. Some local authorities provide direct amenities such as golf courses, tennis courts and swimming pools, and some also provide caravan and camping sites directly, such as Dublin, Wexford and Wicklow.

(7) Education

County councils, county borough corporations, the borough corporations of Drogheda, Dun Laoghaire, Galway, Sligo and Wexford, and the urban councils of Bray and Tralee are each required by law to establish a Vocational Education Committee to provide and manage vocational schools. The committees, which have their own corporate status, do not come within the city and county management system. The main funding for these schools comes from the Department of Education, but the local authorities also provide some.

Under the national scheme of higher education grants, the local authorities make the payments. The cost of the grants is met, in the first instance, by the local authority, but all expenditure over and above the amount provided in the year 1967–68 by local authorities themselves for certain former scholarship schemes (post-primary and university) is refunded by the Exchequer.

Local authorities in urban areas and in towns may provide school meals. County councils can provide meals in Gaeltacht areas only.

In the county boroughs of Cork, Dublin and Waterford and in Dun Laoghaire school attendance committees comprised of representatives of the local authority, the Minister for Education, parents and managers enforce the School Attendance Act 1926. Elsewhere the act is enforced by the Gardaí.

(8) Miscellaneous

The activities under this heading include administration, purchase of plant, the preparation of the list of electors for all elections, and the appointment (in Dublin area only) of inspectors to check weighing scales used in shops and such places.

FINANCE

Local authority expenditure is divided into capital and current. Capital expenditure, generally speaking, represents expenditure on fixed assets such as housing, including loans to house purchasers, water and sewerage schemes, libraries and swimming pools. Among the items in the Public Capital Programme of the government each year are sums to meet the needs of local authorities. The Minister for the Environment allocates these sums between the individual authorities, on the basis of proposals from them, the level of need in each area, and the state of ongoing works. Where borrowing is necessary, e. g. for the provision of offices, recourse is had to the Local Loans Fund or, more frequently, to the banks. The vast bulk of capital expenditure by local authorities—on roads, housing, sanitary services, fire stations and libraries—is now financed by 100 per cent grants from the Exchequer.

Sources

There are three main sources of current account revenue: government grants of a general and specific nature (about 44 per cent); income from goods and services (about 24 per cent); and rates on industrial and commercial property (about 22 per cent).

Local Authority Finance, 1990

Expenditure and Receipts

A summary of the estimated expenditure and receipts for 1990 is as follows
with comparative out-turn figures for 1989.

	Estimated Current Receipts and Expenditure of Local Authorities, 1990					
	County Councils £'m	County Boroughs £'m	Urbans £'m	Miscellaneous Bodies[1] £'m	Total 1990 £'m	Provisional Outturn '89 £'m
Expenditure	695.63	279.96	83.98	2.58	1062.15	1,030.84
Financed by Government Grants/ Subsidies	365.57	77.17	22.25	1.09	466.08	440.80
Goods/ Services	216.34	93.14	39.37	0.97	349.82	368.28
Commercial Rates[2]	100.66	105.44	33.59	0.34	240.03	229.76
County Demand	12.27	—	(11.87)	—	0.40	—
Total Receipts	694.84	275.75	83.34	2.40	1,056.33	1038.84

Notes
1. Includes Town Commissioners, Joint Drainage Boards, Burial Boards and other
miscellaneous bodies.
2. Includes rates on ESB property.

The general grants, known as rate support grants, are compensation for the
fact that rates are no longer levied on land or domestic dwellings and have
never been levied on government property. These grants may be spent by the
local authorities as they see fit. The specific grants, which are mainly for
roads, social employment schemes and higher education grants, give local
authorities less discretion as to how they are to be spent.

Income derived from goods and services includes house loans repayments,
rents, charges for water, refuse collection and planning applications, and
employees' pension contributions.

Rates are levied on the basis of valuations placed annually on all
immovable property by the Commissioner for Valuation. Certain places are
exempt from valuation, such as places of religious worship, or from rating,

such as secondary schools, domestic dwellings or land. The remaining buildings which attract rates are primarily those used for industrial or commercial purposes. The aggregate property valuation in each local authority area forms the basis for the levy of rates. The procedure is that each local authority is required to prepare and adopt an estimate of expenses for the year ahead. The estimate shows projected gross expenditure and the anticipated receipts available to meet that expenditure. The gap is bridged (on each of the eight programmes outlined) by dividing the residual amount by the aggregate valuation, thus producing a rate in the pound. Town commissioners are not rating authorities. They prepare an estimate, and the cost of their services is sought from the county council. The county council then levies 'town charges' on the council rates and applies that higher rate in the town only.

Audit
Accounts of receipts and expenditure are audited by auditors appointed by the Minister for the Environment. The auditors have power to disallow payments made without authority and to surcharge those responsible for making them. On occasion councillors, generally for political reasons of their own, vote against the advice of the manager for some project which is not lawful or not approved.

Surcharges may, and usually are, appealed to the minister, who has the power to remit them and often does so. Managers are obliged to warn council members about the loss of money through decisions arising from the use of their reserved powers which lack legal authority.

LOCAL GOVERNMENT REFORM

Fundamental Considerations
Any consideration of the local government system must be influenced by two basic determinants. On the one hand, local authorities are providers of services involving very substantial public expenditure (in excess of £1,062.15 million on current items in 1990, as already shown). It is necessary, therefore, that local authority structures should be such as to ensure the efficient and effective operation of the local government system. This implies fairly large authorities having the necessary resources to meet this requirement.

On the other hand, the local government system is not merely a provider of services, but is also one of the essential elements which go to make up the democratic nature of the state. In Irish terms, local democracy connotes small units, which may, however, be so small as to be unable to perform effectively and efficiently in the major services areas, but which must nevertheless be financed from public funds.

The arguments for reform, therefore, tend to turn on these two principles of efficiency and of local democracy and on the relative importance attached to each.

Reform Proposals
Reform of local government has been under consideration by successive
governments since about 1971. In that year a government white paper
proposed that town commissioners and many of the urban district councils
should be abolished and their functions transferred to the county council; that
a single authority should be established for the entire Dublin area; and that the
law relating to local government should be modernised. None of these
proposals had been implemented before the government left office in 1973.

The new government produced in 1973 a discussion document which largely
rejected the proposals in the white paper and proposed some limited changes of
its own. The document proposed transfer of functions from smaller to larger
authorities and the achievement of greater co-ordination throughout the local
government system by such means as agency arrangements. No changes had
been made by the time the government left office in 1977.

In 1978 and in 1983 domestic rates and rates on land were, respectively,
terminated. As a result, the burden of financing local government has been
fundamentally altered. This has led to increased central influence because
much of that finance is now provided by the Exchequer.

Before the 1987 general election the Fianna Fáil party (which after the
election formed the government) published a *Programme for National
Recovery* which included a number of proposed reforms in the local
government system. These were the retention of the existing counties and
county boroughs as the main units of local government; the creation of new
district (rather than town) councils to which functions would be assigned by
the relevant county or borough council; the devolution of functions from
central government to local authorities; the giving to local authorities of a
wider role in promoting local enterprise and of a role in the fight against
crime. At the close of that government's term of office no action had been
taken to implement these proposals.

The government programme for the years 1989–93 stated that a select
committee of the Oireachtas would be established to examine the whole
question of local authority funding, structures and functions; it was to issue its
report within a year.

The government announced in April 1990 that a sub-committee of six of
its members working in tandem with a seven-member committee of experts,
would examine the structures and functions of local government, but not the
funding. As regards the funding, the committee was invited to make
recommendations 'on the criteria on which the contribution from central
funds to local authorities should be made on a statutory basis'. The
committee's report was considered by the government early in 1991. Among
the proposals contained in it were the establishment of a three-tier system of
local government (at regional, county and sub-county or district levels),

means of devolving more power from central to local government, and the further examination of the criteria to relate to funding.

The government announced that the reform programme would be put in place on a phased basis. Thus the Local Government Act passed in May 1991 did not provide for comprehensive reform measures. Its main provision was to enable the elections for all county and county borough councils (which had been deferred from 1990) to proceed, while at the same time it authorised the postponement of elections to sub-county authorities. Other provisions related to extending the competence of local authorities and to making certain changes in functions and in administration, for example in regard to planning applications and to expenses.

Legislation to provide further reform and to consolidate and modernise local government law is promised.

REFERENCES

Local Government Reorganisation and Reform (Dublin: Stationery Office, 1991)

Collins, Neil, *Local Government Managers at Work* (Dublin: Institute of Public Administration, 1987)

Roche, Desmond, *Local Government in Ireland* (Dublin: Institute of Public Administration, 1982)

8

The State-Sponsored Bodies

DEFINITION

The description of state-sponsored bodies provided by FitzGerald (1963: 5) remains perhaps the most succinct. He defined them as autonomous public bodies, neither temporary in character nor purely advisory in their functions, whose staff is not drawn from the civil service but to whose board or council the government or ministers in the government appoints directors etc. They exclude bodies which (1) have some autonomy vis-à-vis government departments and which are staffed by civil servants, such as the Adoption Board or the Civil Service Commission; (2) are mainly advisory in function and permanent in character, such as the Animal Remedies Consultative Committee; (3) are advisory and temporary in character, such as the Commission on Taxation; and (4) are local authorities. Each body operates under the general control of a minister, who is responsible for ensuring that the body carries out the tasks for which it is set up but who does not intervene in the day-to-day carrying out of these tasks.

State-sponsored bodies are therefore part of the system of government, and the government is ultimately responsible for their performance. This situation underlines the fundamental difference between private sector companies, who are responsible to shareholders, and state-sponsored bodies, whose shareholder is ultimately the Minister for Finance, and it leads to endless debate on the degrees of freedom and of control appropriate in the case of these bodies.

The state-sponsored bodies form a large part of the public sector. They may be divided into two broad categories according to their basic purpose: the commercial (trading) bodies, and the non-commercial. Both categories, and the reasons for their establishment are discussed below, and a full list of them is given in Appendix J.

There is no standard framework for the setting up of state-sponsored bodies; their legal status, terms of reference and mode of operation tend to be determined empirically as the need arises. Each is established by means of a constituent document (act, statutory instrument or some other form of written directive) which deals with such matters as functions, board membership, staff, funding, and the relationship between the minister and the board. It is possible to distinguish six different methods of incorporation; these too are briefly outlined below.

REASONS FOR ESTABLISHMENT

The 'corporation sole' concept introduced in the Ministers and Secretaries Act 1924 meant that civil servants would be the employees of ministers and would carry out all the functions of government in the name of ministers. After only three years, however, it became clear that if certain tasks desirable in the national interest were to be undertaken, and if the only body in a position to undertake these was the state, it would become necessary to loosen the control of ministers. The rigidity of the civil service system was considered unsuitable for the running of the commercial operations which were becoming necessary. Thus, in order to cut through the red tape that often constrains speedy direct action by government the first of the commercial bodies (the Electricity Supply Board and the Agricultural Credit Corporation) were established in 1927: many others followed, one of the most recent being Coillte (the Forestry Board) in 1989. Ministers were placed at one remove, so to speak, from these bodies; they were responsible for what the bodies were set up to do (i.e. for their policy) but not for the details of the way in which they did their work.

From the beginning these bodies have been established for practical reasons. Something needed to be done, and the best, or sometimes the only, way of having it done was through direct public intervention. Thus the system of state-sponsored bodies emerged in a haphazard fashion in order to perform certain specific tasks which could not readily or appropriately be undertaken within the structure of government departments or local authorities, such as the manufacture and sale of products, marketing, or the provision of transport services. There has been little of the ideological motivation common else-where, as, for example, in Britain.

The management of the semi-state bodies is also determined by practical considerations. In contrast to the civil service (whose structure is designed essentially for the purpose of assisting ministers), they have freedom to adopt the structures most suitable for the efficient performance of the duties assigned to them. They also have greater freedom in matters such as recruitment. A further advantage is that the system enables the state to assemble boards of directors who have experience in the private sector.

Up to recent years the tendency was to set up a new body to meet each new need or opportunity as it arose. In many cases these new bodies engaged in tasks which were formerly carried out by government departments. For example, the work of Telecom Éireann and An Post was formerly carried out by the Department of Posts and Telegraphs, that of Córas Beostoic agus Feola (the Meat and Livestock Export Board) by the Department of Agriculture and Food, and the work of Coillte by the Department of Energy. In recent years, however, following close financial scrutiny, some state-sponsored bodies have been abolished and their work assigned to government departments (as in the case of Bord na gCapall and An Foras Forbartha). In other cases tasks have been amalgamated, as in the case of Eolas (merger of the National Board for Science and Technology and of the Institute for Industrial Research and Standards) and Teagasc (merger of the Agricultural Research Institute and the National Agricultural Advisory and Training Service).

Commercial Bodies
These bodies are sometimes called public enterprises because they operate in the market place, providing goods and services from whose sale they derive the greater part of their revenue. There are about twenty-five of these enterprises, employing about 72,000 people. They include bodies which provide an infrastructural base for the whole economy, the undertaking of which the private sector found either unattractive or beyond its resources at the time the need for the activities arose, (e. g. Aer Lingus and the ESB). They also include bodies to develop natural resources (e. g. Bord na Móna and An Bord Gáis); bodies set up as a rescue operation by the state when a private undertaking was threatened with financial difficulties (e. g. the British and Irish Steam Packet Company—the B & I); and bodies to provide finance for certain sectors (e. g. the Agricultural Credit Corporation) or to promote a particular industry (e. g. the Racing Board or Bord na gCon).

The basic assumption behind the establishment of the commercial bodies is the belief that the business and entrepreneurial skills employed in the private sector may be utilised to equal effect in the service of the state. In accordance with this view, it is maintained that a business task is best performed by a body with a definition of objectives and a clear mandate which, because of the changing political scene, government departments do not generally have; that a board of directors which includes people who have what is termed 'outside experience' bring such experience, freshness and skills to augment the civil service in the conduct of public service tasks; and that the practice results in the harnessing of the talents of persons who might wish to give public service and who might not otherwise have the opportunity of doing so. In this way, the argument runs, the best of both worlds is achieved.

Non-Commercial Bodies
These bodies carry out a wide variety of tasks such as the promotion of Irish goods (An Bord Tráchtála), agricultural and industrial research and advice (Teagasc and Eolas), the provision of health services (the Blood

Transfusion Service and Dublin Dental Hospital) and the regulation of certain professions (the Opticians Board and the Nursing Board). Other areas of activity include industry (the Industrial Development Authority), training and employment (FÁS), education (the Higher Education Authority and the National Council for Educational Awards), tourism (Bord Fáilte), culture (the Arts Council) and research (the Health Research Board).

These are all activities which in some other countries are carried out by government departments. The Public Services Organisation Review Group (in the Devlin Report, 1969) noted that most of the activities of the non-commercial state-sponsored bodies are such as are, were or could be carried out within the civil service. The group referred to a tacit acceptance by ministers, officials and the public generally that functions such as the bodies carry out are best performed outside the civil service with its existing organisation and constraints. They pointed out, however, that every decision to allocate a new function to a state-sponsored body while similar functions are left in the civil service structure represented a failure to face the problems of the efficiency of the machinery of government or at least to think through the roles of the parts of that machinery. This critical reappraisal of the role of the non-commercial bodies may have been partly responsible for some of the terminations and amalgamations referred to earlier.

METHODS OF ESTABLISHMENT
State-sponsored bodies are set up in various ways, as follows:

(1) the statutory corporation which derives its powers and authority directly from the act which sets it up. Its relationship with the sponsoring minister, its functions and powers are laid down in the act. Examples of bodies set up in this manner are Teagasc and FÁS.

(2) the public company set up pursuant to a statute and incorporated by registration under the Companies Act. In these cases the act provides for the setting up of a company which is subsequently established by memorandum and articles of association issued under ministerial authority. Examples are the B&I and the National Stud.

(3) the private company incorporated by registration under the Companies Act in accordance with company law. The objects of the company and the special conditions governing its operations are contained either in the memorandum and articles of association or in administrative directions from the parent department. Examples of companies set up in this way are Aer Rianta and the Irish National Petroleum Corporation.

(4) the corporate body set up under a statutory instrument made by a minister. For example, the Health (Corporate Bodies) Act 1961 and the Local Government (Corporate Bodies) Act 1971 provide for the establishment, by orders issued by the Ministers for Health and the Environment respectively,

of bodies to provide health and environmental services—the National Rehabilitation Board and the National Safety Council.

(5) bodies set up as private companies limited by guarantee and thus legally independent of ministers, but which, because of their large dependence on the state for finance, are sometimes regarded as being state-sponsored bodies. Organisations in this category include the Institute of Public Administration and the Economic and Social Research Institute.

(6) bodies which have no governing legislation or articles of association, whose constitution amounts to a statement from the government or the minister concerned as to what their tasks are, such as the Combat Poverty Agency.

Clear criteria as to when some of the above methods should be used are not discernible. The company mould, at least in the earlier days when the commercial bodies were being set up, seems to have been preferred for the reason that the public might be encouraged to take up some of the shares. (There has, however, been no large take-up though some of the bodies, for example Arramara Teo. and the Industrial Credit Corporation, have private shareholders). There was also the consideration that changes in direction could be more flexibly be provided for without going through the elaborate procedure of an amending statute.

PRESCRIBED FUNCTIONS

The functions are normally prescribed in such a way as to enable board and management to exercise a certain amount of discretion. Sometimes the prescription can be so broad as to lead to problems of interpretation as to what the functions really are; such problems do not, however, normally emerge into public view, being dealt with between the department and the body concerned. A broad prescription can lead to such wide diversification of activities that it raises questions about state-bodies entering into competition with private firms, for example in the case of the hotel and catering services of Aer Lingus or the sale of appliances by the ESB. On other occasions the functions can be prescribed in such detail as to leave little discretion with the body and to raise the question why the sponsoring department did not itself carry them out. For example, the functions of FÁS, the body set up under the Labour Services Act 1987 to provide training and employment schemes and job services, are set out in considerable detail, amounting to about 1,000 words.

BOARDS

Board members are all part-time, save for those very few bodies (e. g. CIE) which have a full-time chairman, and those many bodies where the chief executive is also a member of the board. The number of directors is normally prescribed in the governing legislation and varies from board to board. In general, six is about the lowest membership and ten or twelve the norm.

Selection

In the selection of directors ministers have almost unlimited discretion and choice. In practice, ministers notify their colleagues informally at the meetings of the government of appointments they propose to make. In some cases, however, the legislation provides that certain organisations must be represented on the board: for example, in the case of FÁS, employers and unions must be represented; and in the case of Teagasc, farming organisations. But even in such instances ministers may choose from names submitted to them. In some cases there must be representatives of the workers on the board. Members of the Oireachtas and of the European Parliament are debarred from board membership.

In order to meet persistent criticism that many directors owed their appointments to their services to a political party rather than to professional competence, a scheme to regulate the selection of board members was announced in December 1986. It involved, on the one hand, the introduction of a register of suitable appointees, to be prepared in consultation with bodies such as the Irish Congress of Trade Unions and the Irish Management Institute; and, on the other hand, the drawing up by ministers of a range of required competences for boards under their aegis, so that these could be matched with the abilities of prospective appointees. Although such a register is now in use, the criticism persists. The Programme for Economic and Social Progress (1991) states:

> The primary considerations which should apply in the appointment of directors to state companies are the experience and expertise of the individuals concerned. The chairman should be consulted prior to the appointment of directors in order to provide the minister concerned with the necessary information on the experience, talents and qualifications required for the board of the company in question.

This principle is accepted by the government.

Worker Representation

Worker representation on the boards of a number of state bodies (Aer Lingus, Aer Rianta, Bord na Móna, B&I, CIE, ESB, NET, An Post, Telecom Éireann and the National Rehabilitation Board) is provided for under the Worker Participation (State Enterprise) Acts 1977–88. The reasons for worker participation were given by the Minister for Labour when introducing the arrangement in 1977. These were: the entitlement of workers to participate in company decision-making, the need to harness the total resources of a company, and the beneficial effect on industrial relations. In introducing the

1988 bill, which added Aer Rianta and the National Rehabilitation Board (the only non-commercial body in the list) to those provided for in 1977, the minister referred to the need to extend what the EC Commission referred to as the 'democratic imperative' to representative arrangements in the workplace.

Under these arrangements, one-third of the seats on the boards of the designated bodies are reserved for worker representatives. Elections among the workers employed by the bodies are held every four years under the auspices of the body concerned. The successful candidates are then appointed by the minister.

The contribution of workers' representatives to the business of boards has not yet been substantively evaluated. Clearly ministers and trade unions are happy with the arrangements. Not so happy—though it is difficult to get firm evidence on this—may be the chairmen and chief executives of the bodies concerned. They have referred to conflicts of interest, and also to problems of confidentiality which can arise, for example, when worker representatives return from a board meeting to their fellow-workers (i.e. their own electorate), who may not fully appreciate the need for discretion regarding the proceedings at the meeting. On the other hand, a summary report of the National Productivity Centre in 1982 in relation to seven bodies pointed to certain benefits such as the provision of two-way communication between shop floor and boardroom, the bringing of practical experience to discussions, and improved industrial relations.

Civil Service Representation

In some cases ministers have appointed senior officials in their departments to boards under their aegis. The practice is however, neither common nor uniform. The arguments for it have not been advanced by ministers, but they are accepted as being the desirability of providing a direct and useful flow of information between the body concerned and the department, to the advantage of both.

The appointment of civil servants to boards is not always acceptable to some chief executives or to some of the other members. They regard such appointments as inhibiting and interfering, and point out that they can cause conflicts of role in that civil service appointees are often called upon, as part of their departmental responsibilities, to evaluate and adjudicate on proposals from boards of which they are members. They also point to the risk of such appointments cutting across the lines of communication that should normally obtain between the chairman of a board and the minister.

Fees

Membership of some boards carries a fee, but, again, the practice is not uniform, nor is the amount of the fee. In general, the members of the boards of the commercial bodies receive a fee which varies from board to board.

Fees, where payable, are of the order of £1,000 to £1,500 a year for the chairman (but there are a few exceptions where the fee is higher) and £500 to £800 for ordinary members. In no cases are fees payable to civil servants for board membership, on the grounds that their work on the board is merely an extension of their work in their departments. Travelling and subsistence expenses at the highest rates applicable to the civil service are in all cases paid for attendance at meetings on the business of the board.

It is sometimes asked why board members are prepared to act for such relatively low fees, and some for no fee. There is, however, no shortage of people who are willing, not to say anxious, to be members of state boards. Such appointments are widely regarded as conferring a certain status on those who receive them. The fact that, at the time of writing, fees have remained unchanged since 1974 points to this.

FINANCE

Commercial Bodies

The commercial bodies are financed in three main ways: from the Exchequer, from internal sources, and through borrowing from the banks and other financial institutions at home and abroad.

The Exchequer provides loans, share capital and subsidies. In the case of statutory corporations, the financial structure is subject to statutory control. Limits on the aggregate of loans for individual corporations are prescribed in the establishing legislation and increases over these limits require further legislation.

The Minister for Finance is the sole or main shareholder in all of the commercial state-sponsored bodies which are public liability companies. The share capital structure is prescribed in the establishing statutes and increases in that capital also require further legislation.

It is government policy that the commercial state-sponsored bodies should operate, as far as possible, without Exchequer assistance, i.e., that they should make ends meet from their own resources, e.g. from the fares charged by the transport bodies and from the sales of products and services in other cases. Some of them, such as the Electricity Supply Board and the Voluntary Health Insurance Board, are required by law to break even, taking one year with another. Despite these aspirations and legal imperatives, however, it is not unusual that for other reasons, of a social or political nature, one finds that the policies of the government make attainment of these more difficult. This happens, for example, when it delays price increases, as it does sometimes in the case of CIE or when it seeks to delay the termination of a loss-making activity, as in the case of the closure of post offices by An Post.

Some of the bodies raise a proportion of the capital they need through borrowing abroad, since in many recent years the interest rates available there have been lower than those available in Ireland. (The bodies have to weigh the advantages of the lower rates available against the possible disadvantages of exchange rate fluctuations and devaluation.) In some instances the borrowing is guaranteed by the state. The incidence of guarantees is being greatly reduced in line with current government policy. Where guarantees are given, the Department of Finance must be satisfied that the money to be borrowed is to be used for properly authorised projects and that the terms of the loans are reasonable. What this means, in effect, is that no state body has the authority to incur obligations that ultimately fall upon the Exchequer unless the Minister for Finance agrees. (The collapse of the previously successful Irish Shipping in 1984 was due to its having entered a number of highly speculative, long-term, fixed-rate agreements fundamental to the future of the company, without the knowledge of the Minister of Finance. The government refused to underwrite the massive costs arising from these unauthorised agreements.)

Non-Commercial Bodies
The non-commercial bodies employ about 7,500 people and depend mainly on the Exchequer for their funds. As indicated earlier, these bodies were not set up to trade and in very many cases are performing tasks which could be carried out by government departments. The normal procedure is that they get a specific sum of money called a grant-in-aid from their parent department. The sum is arrived at by consultation between officials of the body concerned, the parent department and the Department of Finance. The final determination is made by the government. One body, FÁS, receives a considerable amount of its finance from the European Community.

Accounts
All state-sponsored bodies prepare annual statements of accounts. In some cases these are certified by the Comptroller and Auditor General and in others, mainly the commercial bodies, by auditors in the private sector. In the latter cases the accountants responsible for certification must be approved by the Minister for Finance, who can also prescribe the format of the accounts. In all cases the accounts must be submitted to the parent department; and, where the establishing legislation so provides, they must be submitted to the government prior to subsequent presentation to the Dáil (in effect making them available in the Oireachtas library).

THE MECHANISM OF CONTROL

Ministerial Control
Ministerial control derives mainly from the act or other document setting up the body, but also from the fact that the minister is a member of the government, which has ultimate control. The constituent document, in

addition to prescribing the functions of the board, normally lays down that certain powers may not be exercised except with the approval of the minister, and that such reports and information as he requests must be made available to him.

Individual sections within the departments concerned are responsible for carrying out the duties directly arising from the operations of the state bodies under their aegis. These duties can range from the preparation of the warrants of appointment of directors to examining new proposals and answering parliamentary questions. The normal lines of communication are between the chairman of the board and the minister, between the chief executive and the assistant secretary in charge of that work, and otherwise between officials in the body and in the department at various levels, exchanging information and making suggestions.

The degree of ministerial control depends to some extent on the attitude of individual ministers. Some are very interested in the performance of the bodies under their aegis and meet their boards frequently; some meet them only occasionally; some never meet them.

On the rare occasions when boards are reluctant to accept government policy they can earn themselves a ministerial reprimand, as when in April 1978 the Agricultural Credit Corporation did not accept that government pay policy applied to their chief executive; or removal of the chairman and the board, as when in November 1972 RTE did not accept a government ban on a broadcast interview with an IRA leader. The latter is a power that a minister will feel able to apply only in the last resort.

Oireachtas Control
The state-sponsored bodies are answerable to the Oireachtas in a number of ways:

(1) They are obliged to present annual reports and accounts. Even though, as with the annual reports and accounts of most companies, these may not reveal a great deal about the thinking behind the bodies' policies, the presentation nevertheless affords members of the Oireachtas an opportunity to have discussion initiated by way of a motion in either House.

(2) Parliamentary questions may be asked. In answering, however, ministers seek to ensure that the bodies are not subjected to such degree of scrutiny as would disclose commercial information or undermine their proper managerial prerogative. Usually, therefore, ministers do not answer questions which relate solely to day-to-day matters; the conventional reply is that the minister has no function in these.

(3) When amending legislation in relation to a particular body is being debated, deputies and senators have wide scope for raising issues relating to the body concerned.

(4) The annual presentation by ministers of the estimates for their departments affords members of the Dáil an opportunity of commenting on the affairs of those bodies for which funds are being provided in the estimate.

(5) Individual members of the Dáil or Seanad may at any time table motions relating to the affairs of individual bodies or of the bodies as a whole.

By and large, however, the above means of inquiring into the affairs of state bodies are not greatly availed of, that task being left mainly to the joint committee on these bodies.

Joint Committee on Commercial State-Sponsored Bodies

This committee was originally appointed by the Dáil and the Seanad in 1976. The life of each committee is coterminous with the life of the Dáil which appointed it. It normally consists of eleven members—seven deputies and four senators—with a chairman who is a member of the party in government. Its task is to examine the reports and accounts and overall operational results of specified bodies, as well as matters relating to responsibility, structure and organisation, accountability and financing, together with relationship to central government and to the Oireachtas, and to report on these to the Oireachtas, with recommendations as appropriate. The committee may also undertake more general studies of the common problems of the bodies and make such reports as it sees fit.

The committee itself selects the bodies for its examination, normally taking them in rotation. The body selected is asked to submit a memorandum on its activities, current and envisaged. A similar memorandum setting out the government's views and concerns is requested from the relevant department, and the public is also invited to make submissions. In addition, the committee takes account of previous reports on the body concerned made by organisations such as the Economic and Social Research Institute or the National Economic and Social Council or by consultants, and of debates in the Dáil or Seanad or in the media. Having established the key issues and questions, the committee conducts a formal examination of representatives of the state-sponsored body (usually the chairman and two or three members of the board, together with the chief executive). The committee has the power to demand, and be provided with, reports and documents. The questioning can be intensive and, when considered of interest to the public at large, is widely reported in the media. In addition, a full report of the proceedings is published. It is difficult to measure the impact of this publicity, but there is little doubt that in so far as it bears directly on consumer affairs, both the body and the relevant minister take note.

Members of the committee complain from time to time about the inadequacy of their powers. They are not empowered to call ministers, nor to demand by subpoena the appearance of others whom they wish to hear. Besides, the question of privilege for statements made before the committee is unclear. Further, its reports are not debated by either the Dáil or the Seanad, though laid before the Houses. At the same time, it has been said that membership of the committee helps to provide members with information on a wide sector of state activity, leading to more informed discussion in both houses.

The Public Accounts Committee
This committee, composed of members of the Dáil only, with a chairman drawn from the main opposition party, is the last link in the chain of the state's finances. A description of the work of the committee is given in Chapter 3.

The Ombudsman
Only the two largest of the commercial bodies comes within the remit of the Ombudsman, namely An Post and Telecom Éireann. Where the Ombudsman receives a complaint about either of these bodies he can investigate it at no cost to the complainant. However, the latter must have pursued the matter fully with An Post or Telecom Éireann before approaching the Ombudsman. The greatest volume of all complaints received by the Ombudsman are those in relation to Telecom—1,032 out of a total of 2,727 in 1990. By contrast, 53 were received about An Post.

THE DEBATE ON ACCOUNTABILITY AND CONTROL
As the state-sponsored bodies have been established in the national interest, it is accepted that the government and the Oireachtas should be in a position to measure adequately whether they are carrying out efficiently the tasks assigned to them. At the same time, it is accepted also that the very fact of the setting up of such bodies to carry out specific functions outside the civil service structure and without direct ministerial responsibility is an indication of an intention to give them a reasonable amount of freedom and scope for initiative. There is something of a dilemma here, and it is reflected in a general lack of definition concerning the relationship between the bodies and their departments. The accountability and control of the state-sponsored body is as yet an unsolved problem, and the failure to devise a precise and comprehensive system has meant that the level of control tends to depend on such factors as the political visibility of an organisation (e.g. RTE), its geographical spread (e.g. CIE), its financial performance (c.g. B&I), and the attitudes of individual ministers and boards.

Government policy over the years has, in broad terms, been to allow the state-sponsored bodies as much freedom as possible consistent with the achievement of the objectives for which they were established. More recently it has been explicitly indicated that the commercial bodies must achieve commercial results within a competitive framework, without benefit of financial help from the state. In so far as the non-commercial bodies are concerned, performance is to be measured not so much financially as by innovativeness in generating revenue, increasing industry involvement in their task, and achieving set targets and improved productivity. They can no longer rely on incremental increases in their annual grants.

The question of the appropriate nature and degree of control over the state-sponsored bodies has long been debated. The debate has become more intensive in recent years because of the severe strain on the Exchequer imposed by some of the bodies in the general context of a relentless national drive for efficiency and economy. The respective cases for freedom of action and constant government intervention were set out in the NESC report *Enterprise in the Public Sector* (1979). Accountability and control and the problems of performance associated with them also received considerable attention in the government programmes *The Way Forward* (1982) and *Building on Reality* (1984), in the report *Proposals for a Plan*, 1984–87, and in a white paper on industrial policy published in 1984. This latter document cited a number of reasons for the worsening financial performance of many of the commercial bodies. Among them were the lack of clarity of objectives and confusion between social and strategic roles, most obvious in bodies such as CIE, Irish Steel and Gaeltarra Éireann. 'This was borne out by the different priorities adopted by public firms in response to the recession. Taken as a whole, the public sector bodies tended to maintain investment and employment levels, while information on private sector companies suggested that they gave priority to the maintenance of financial liquidity.' (O'Neill 1985: 32)

This concern led to the government deciding in 1986 that a system of information to enable ministers to anticipate problems rather than have problems thrust upon them was necessary and, accordingly, that each commercial body should prepare a corporate plan for its activities for a period of five years ahead which would be rolled over on an annual basis. It was indicated that such a plan would encourage a systematic approach to planning and would provide standards for the evaluation of performance, especially in such areas as finance, investment and employment. The plans are submitted to the parent departments, where they are evaluated in consultation with the Department of Finance. Other ameliorative measures, mainly providing for a more strictly regulated system of submission of reports and accounts, were also recommended by the Minister for Finance. It is not clear to what extent these changes have been implemented. In 1991, for example, Telecom Éireann and An Post found themselves, as a result of the intervention of the Minister for Communications following public outcry, unable to implement certain proposals concerning, respectively, revised telephone charges and the closure of local post offices.

The chief executives of the commercial bodies do not like some of these arrangements. They maintain that what they describe as the dead hand of bureaucracy is creeping more and more relentlessly into the management of the bodies. They are unhappy also about government control over remuneration, which, they say, should be left free for their boards to determine. This is a long-standing grievance. The chief executives point to what they call the illogicality of giving boards responsibility for spending millions of pounds and yet not giving them responsibility for the pay of their staff. The government answer to this is that all parts of the public service must conform to its guidelines on pay which, because of the relative size of public sector employment to total employment in the country, are vital to the economy because of the spin-off effects. It is in addition sometimes pointed out that when control over pay was not exercised centrally, many boards were excessively generous in rewarding their staff.

As regards the corporate plans specifically, the chief executives say that they have got little response from departments, and that, where responses were received, they were shallow and lacking in depth. In their view, this is not surprising, since departments do not generally engage in corporate planning and have little experience in this area.

THE DEBATE ON PRIVATISATION

The final issue which has dominated the debate on state-sponsored bodies in recent years is the question of privatisation. Privatisation may include: charging for services previously supplied at prices unrelated to use by government agencies; injecting private non-voting capital into the financial structures of nationalised undertakings; opening up their markets to competition from private sector firms; full-scale denationalisation, involving the sale of a majority shareholding to the private sector.

It is this latter concept of privatisation which has been the main focus of debate in Ireland to date. Normally behind a debate such as this there is a clash of ideologies, a clash of views as to the role of the state in society. One view is that government is a burden on society, that all creative forces are in the market place, and that the state is largely an obstacle to economic progress. The other view is that the state is a moral system superimposed on the disorder of nature and that the mission of government is to bring order and justice to an unjust world. The state, according to this view, has to provide social justice. It has to make up for market failure.

Apart from Irish Sugar and the Irish Life Assurance Company, which were privatised in 1991, the bodies mentioned in the debate about privatisation have included Telecom, Aer Lingus, Aer Rianta, the Agricultural Credit Corporation, the Industrial Credit Corporation and the B&I Company.

The arguments in favour of privatising the state bodies include:

(1) Efficiency. Public sector enterprises have difficulty in measuring their efficiency, since they have to satisfy conflicting social and commercial objectives. Such enterprises are inevitably constrained in their actions by

political considerations. Greater speed and flexibility in decision-making could be possible if there were not the need for frequent reference to government departments or to the government.

(2) Funding. Public ownership would provide companies with opportunities for further development by means of funding secured in the private sector if national budgetary considerations precluded the financing of such developments by the Exchequer.

(3) Wider public interest. Providing shares to the general public would increase their interest in the companies, would be to the benefit of democracy, and would provide better for the interests of the consumer.

(4) Improved performance. The sale of shares to employees, sometimes by means of preferential offers, is said to increase the sense of employee involvement in the concern and to act as a stimulus to improved performance on the part of employees and, consequently, of the firm.

(5) The public sector borrowing requirement. The reduction of this requirement could help in dealing with the problem of high taxation and the national debt.

The arguments against privatisation:

(1) There is no certainty that the free market will automatically lead to the optimum economic outturn. Nor will it lead to social equality. The only way in which these goals can be achieved is through state intervention; otherwise the profit motive will prevail.

(2) Benefits for private investors. Potential purchasers in the private sector will be interested only in those state concerns which are profitable and will leave the state with the bodies which continue to be a drain. Such private investors will reap the benefit of large amounts of taxpayers' money which over the years have been injected into the state sector. Thus privatisation would bring profit to the few at the expense of the community.

(3) Employment. Employment is a vital part of community interest. Its provision would not, however, be given its due importance should a state enterprise be privatised.

(4) Efficiency. There is no evidence that state bodies are any less efficient than private business, as witness the collapse of the Private Motorists' Protection Association and the Insurance Corporation of Ireland.

(5) Removal of constraints. The question is asked why the state bodies were set up in the first place and whether the situation has changed. Any weakness caused by the constraints of state ownership could be remedied by dealing with such constraints, while retaining the bodies in state ownership.

The view of the government on the question of privatisation, as communicated to a symposium on the development of state-sponsored bodies held by the Institute of Public Administration in September 1990, is that the debate thereon is largely academic and that the matter of ownership is not at issue.

The government has adopted a pragmatic view. What is important is that state-sponsored bodies work, that they contribute to economic activity and growth, and that they compete fairly in the open market place. The government will retain or dispose of the bodies on a practical case-by-case basis.

THE EC AND STATE BODIES

The Treaty of Rome sees market forces as the prime motor of a trans-national economy. It regards these forces as being capable, subject to adequate supervision, of bringing about 'harmonious development of economic activities, a continuous and balanced expansion, an increase in stability, an accelerated raising of the standard of living and closer relations between the states belonging to it' (Article 2). There is no 'community role' for public enterprise.

Essentially the EC requires both private and state commercial organisations to be bound by the same rules of competition, i.e. that there be no discrimination in favour of state bodies. It points to the fact that the state in relation to its bodies is generally looking for results, among which profit may not always be the major consideration, and that a state body can be in direct competition in its activities with those of other undertakings, whether public or private, in its own or other countries. The risk (as far as the EC is concerned) of distortions of competition between undertakings becomes real at this point and is highlighted by the difficulty of defining normal market behaviour.

It was against this background that the Community adopted in 1980 a directive on the transparency, or openness, of the financial relations between member states and their public enterprises. The directive imposes on member states the obligation to supply on request certain information on these relations; it also defines certain types of financial relationship to which the EC considered it particularly important that transparency should be applied. Examples of these relationships are the foregoing of a normal return on public funds and the compensation for financial burdens imposed by the state. The directive was not acceptable to some member states (Ireland did not object), who challenged it in the European Court of Justice; this challenge was unsuccessful.

It was in the light of this general situation that, even before the directive, Bord Bainne (the Dairy Board) had to change its status from being a state-sponsored body to that of a co-operative. An Bord Gráin (the Grain Board) and the Pigs and Bacon Commission were forced to terminate their activities. At the time of writing the activities of the Dublin and Cork District Milk Boards are in course of being wound up and the boards abolished.

CONCLUSION

It is difficult to disagree with the assessment given by Barrington (1980: 65): 'Overall [the Irish state-sponsored body] has shown itself to be a very considerable instrument for development. It has played a big part in raising the level of management in this country. In an unstructured, unplanned sort of way, the state-sponsored bodies have contributed very effectively to the development of the country, and represent a most interesting adaptation of a form of organisation from the private business world to the needs of public administration. This has not been without its problems, and there are other problems still to be faced; but, overall, one cannot but be impressed by the record. This record, if accepted, poses major challenges, and opportunities, for the future of Irish public administration.'

REFERENCES
Barrington, T. J., *The Irish Administrative System* (Dublin: Institute of Public Administration, 1980)
FitzGerald, Garret, *State-Sponsored Bodies* 2nd ed. (Dublin: Institute of Public Administration, 1963)
O'Neill, Stephen, 'Corporate Planning and State Bodies', *Seirbhís Phoiblí*, Vol. 6, no. 3 (1985)

Appendix J
List of State-Sponsored Bodies
This comprehensive list of Irish state-sponsored bodies (both commercial and non-commercial) is based on information supplied by ministers in response to parliamentary questions in May 1991. The bodies are listed under the relevant government department, together with their dates of establishment.

Agriculture and Food	
Commercial	
National Stud	1945
Racing Board	1945
Bord na gCon	1958
Non-commercial	
Córas Beostoic	
agus Feola	1979
Teagasc	1988
An Bord Glas	1990
Education	
Non-commercial	
Dublin Institute for Advanced Studies	1940
Higher Education Authority	1972
National Council for Educational Awards	1979
National Council for	
Curriculum and Assessment	1987
Energy	
Commercial	
Electricity Supply Board	1927
Bord na Móna	1946
Bord Gáis Éireann	1976
Irish National Petroleum Corporation	1979
Coillte	1989
Non-commercial	
Nuclear Energy Board	1973
Environment	
Commercial	
National Building Agency	1960
Housing Finance Agency	1982
Custom House Docks	
Development Authority	1986
Non-commercial	
An Comhairle Leabharlanna	1948
An Foras Forbartha	1964
Medical Bureau of Road Safety	1968
Local Government Staff Negotiations Board	1971
Local Government Computer	
Services Board	1975
An Bord Pleanála	1977
Fire Services Council	1983
National Safety Council	1987
Environmental Research Unit	1988
National Roads Authority	1988
Finance	
Commercial	
Agricultural Credit Corporation	1927

Industrial Credit Corporation	1933
Non-commercial	
Central Bank of Ireland	1943
National Treasury Management Agency	1990
Gaeltacht	
Non-commercial	
Bord na Leabhar Gaeilge	1952
Bord na Gaeilge	1978
Údarás na Gaeltachta	1980
Health	
Commercial	
Voluntary Health Insurance Board	1957
Non-commercial	
Pharmaceutical Society of Ireland	1875
Therapeutic Substances Advisory Committee	1933
Hospitals Trust Board	1938
St Laurence's Hospital Board	1943
National Health Council	1947
An Bord Uchtála (Adoption Board)	1952
Bord na Radharcmhastóirí (Opticians Board)	1956
Board for the Employment of the Blind	1957
Comhairle na Nimheanna	1961
Dublin Dental Hospital Board	1963
Blood Transfusion Service Board	1965
Cork Hospital Board	1966
National Rehabilitation Board	1967
Comhairle na nOspidéal	1970
Eastern Health Board	1971
Midland Health Board	1971
Mid-Western Health Board	1971
North-Eastern Health Board	1971
North-Western Health Board	1971
South-Eastern Health Board	1971
Southern Health Board	1971
Western Health Board	1971
St James's Hospital Board	1971
General Medical Services Payments Board	1972
Hospital Bodies Administrative Bureau	1973
Beaumont Hospital Board	1977
Medical Council	1978
Postgraduate Medical and Dental Board	1978
Leopardstown Park Hospital Board	1979
Tallaght Hospital Board	1980
National Social Services Board	1984
An Bord Altranais (Nursing Board)	1985
Dental Council	1985
Health Research Board	1986
National Drugs Advisory Board	1986
Drug Treatment Centre Board	1988

St Luke's and St Anne's Hospital Board	1988
Food Safety Advisory Committee	1989
National Council for the Elderly	1990
National Cancer Registry Board	1991

Industry and Commerce
Commercial

Irish Steel Ltd	1947
Nitrigin Éireann Teo.	1987

Non-commercial

Shannon Free Airport Development Company	1959
Kilkenny Design Workshop Ltd	1965
Industrial Development Authority	1969
National Development Corporation	1986
Eolas	1988
An Bord Tráchtála	1959

Justice
Non-commercial

Legal Aid Board	1979

Labour
Non-commercial

Council for Education, Recruitment and Training for the Hotel, Catering and Tourism Industries (CERT)	1963
Employment Equality Agency	1977
An Foras Áiseanna Saothair	1988
National Authority for Occupational Safety and Health	1989
Labour Relations Commission	1991

Marine
Commercial

Arramara Teo.	1952
Bord Iascaigh Mhara	1952

Non-commercial

Foyle Fisheries Commission	1952
Central Fisheries Board	1980
Eastern Fisheries Board	1980
Northern Fisheries Board	1980
North-Western Fisheries Board	1980
Shannon Fisheries Board	1980
Southern Fisheries Board	1980

South-Western Fisheries Board	1980
Western Fisheries Board	1980
Salmon Research Agency	1990

Social Welfare
Non-commercial

Combat Poverty Agency	1986
Pensions Board	1990

Taoiseach
Non-commercial

National Gallery of Ireland	1854
National Library of Ireland	1877
National Museum of Ireland	1877
National Theatre Society	1904
Irish Manuscripts Commission	1928
Arts Council	1951
National Economic and Social Council	1973
Law Reform Commission	1975
Irish Film Board	1981
National Concert Hall	1981
Irish Museum of Modern Art	1985
National Archives	1988
National Heritage Council	1988
Temple Bar Properties Ltd	1991
Temple Bar Renewal Ltd	1991

Tourism, Transport and Communications
Commercial

Aer Lingus	1936
Aer Rianta	1937
Aerlinte Éireann	1947
Córas Iompair Éireann	1950
Radio Telefís Éireann	1960
B&I Line	1965
An Post	1984
Telecom Éireann	1984
Bus Átha Cliath	1987
Bus Éireann	1987
Iarnród Éireann	1987

Non-commercial

Bord Fáilte Éireann	1955
Independent Radio and Television Commission	1988

9

The Health Service

The role of the state in health care has been evolving since the late eighteenth century from the locally funded provision of essential basic services, mainly for the very poor, to the wide and sophisticated range of services provided on a national basis for the whole community in the latter part of the twentieth century. The rationale for the dominant role now adopted is that health is perceived in the modern state as a basic human right, the protection of which is accepted as a valid function of the state.

The current role of the state in relation to health services might be described as involving three aspects: that of regulating and setting standards for inputs to the health system; that of providing services, (health services staff are, in the main, state employees, and many hospitals, health centres and so on are in the ownership of the state); and that of funder of services. The dominant source of funding is currently the Exchequer.

The major responsibility for health policy in Ireland lies with the Minister for Health and the Department of Health, established in 1947. Legislation and regulations setting the broad structure within which better health services for the nation can be developed are introduced by the minister and department and approved by the Dáil and Seanad. The functions of the department may be summarised as supporting the Minister for Health in the discharge of ministerial and parliamentary functions, the formation of policy, the determination of programmes for the implementation of agreed policy, the co-ordination, appraisal and review of the effectiveness of policies and the overall organisational arrangements of the delivery of health services, and the co-ordination of the international activities of the service. It is responsible for the prevention and cure of disease, the treatment and care of persons suffering from physical defects or mental illness, the regulation and control of the training and registration of persons for health services and control over the appointment and conditions of service of appropriate local officers. Other responsibilities are for health research, ensuring that adequate nutritional standards apply in certain foods, preventing the sale of impure and contaminated food, controlling proprietary medical and voluntary preparations, registering births, deaths and marriages and compiling health statistics.

The Department of Health is divided into three line areas (hospital services, community health services and community welfare services) and four staff units (finance, personnel, planning and organisation). The overall control of the department lies with its secretary, who has the main responsibility for seeing that the minister's policies are carried out.

Figure 1: The General Structure of Ireland's Health Care System

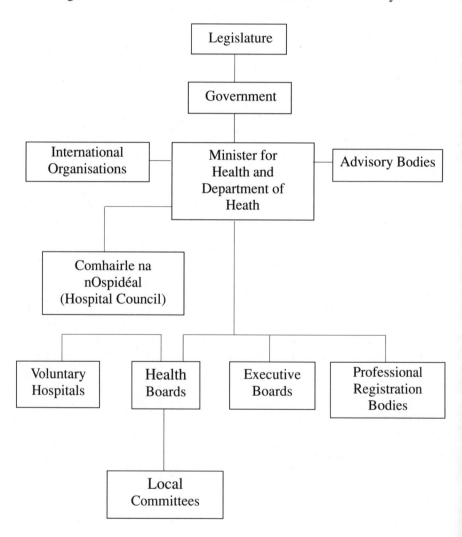

The Irish health service is a large and complex service employing a vast range of expertise and skills in over 300 grades in approximately 150 hospitals, which provide acute in-patient care. In addition, mental handicap homes, psychiatric hospitals, community health centres and general practitioners provide essential health services. The system encompasses a mix of public and private care, involving the same institutions and personnel, and with a degree of interaction in funding arrangements. The administrative structure of the system is shown in Figure 1.

There are over 64,000 people employed in the public health services in Ireland, and expenditure on staff represents about 67 per cent of current public expenditure on the health services. Public health expenditure accounts for almost one-fifth of total government spending and represents about 7 per cent of GNP. An estimated further 2 per cent is accounted for by private health expenditure. Expenditure quadrupled in real terms between 1960 and 1980 (a rate of growth twice that of the real growth in GNP). Expenditure in real terms has remained broadly constant since 1980. Health services represent the fastest growing claims on the resources of the community within the social services (since social security and assistance payments are essentially transfer payments).

THE HEALTH BOARDS
The statutory responsibility for administering the services provided for in health legislation and by ministerial initiative is vested in eight regional health boards established under the provisions of the Health Act 1970, which replaced the former system under which health services were administered on a county basis by twenty-seven main local authorities. The boards decide and administer the practical details and working of the health services at local level and are the largest employers of staff in the health service. In order to ensure that central policy decisions are implemented in a way acceptable to local interests, a majority of their members are appointed by the relevant local authorities for the areas served by each board.

The 1970 legislation arose from the necessity to make the organisation and administration of the health services as efficient and economic as possible. As the state had the major financial interest in the health services and this interest was increasing, it was desirable that a new administrative framework combining national and local interests should be developed for services. It was also necessary to broaden both the geographical and the representational basis of the local bodies in charge of the health services so as to get a more balanced approach towards desirable changes such as the reorganisation of the general hospital services. Developments in professional techniques and equipment and management methods indicated that the county was too small an administrative unit to be the basis for health services and that better services could be provided on an inter-county basis. This was particularly true in relation to the hospital service.

Responsibilities of Health Boards

In addition to their responsibilities for health services, the health boards are responsible for a long and diverse list of functions under the health acts and various other acts ranging from the Rats and Mice (Destruction) Act 1919 to the State Lands (Workhouse) Act 1930. Certain welfare services are also provided by the boards: for example, they have responsibility for the payment of disablement allowances for the home help service, and for welfare homes for the aged. Health boards administer the supplementary welfare allowance scheme on an agency basis for the local authorities, thus facilitating co-ordination of health and welfare services. The boards also co-ordinate the work of voluntary organisations working in their areas.

The division between public, voluntary and private health agencies, however, means that a health board has limited power in determining overall health policy for its area, particularly if the major hospitals serving its catchment area are under private or voluntary control and funded directly by the Department of Health.

Structure of Health Boards

The total number of persons on a health board ranges from 27 on the North-Western Health Board to 35 on the Eastern Health Board. The membership is a combination of three main interests as follows: (1) elected representatives from county councils and borough councils, who account for more than half the membership; (2) professional representatives of the medical, nursing, dental and pharmaceutical interests, who are mostly officers of the boards; (3) nominees of the Minister for Health, of which there are three on each board; these were formerly used to represent excluded professional groups, but now tend to represent the consumers of medical services.

Interviews reported by Zimmerman in 1981 revealed general satisfaction with the mixture of elected public representatives and professionals on the health boards. The boards appointed in 1970 had a total of 235 members, including 61 medical doctors, 44 farmers, 32 shopkeepers, 17 nurses, 10 pharmacists, 8 dentists, 7 teachers, 6 solicitors, 6 trade union officials, 6 clerks and company directors. The overall mix has not changed significantly since then, although there is a movement towards giving greater representation to people from social service backgrounds.

Each health board has a Chief Executive Officer (CEO) who has responsibility for day-to-day administration. The Health Act 1970 provides for the appointment of this statutory officer who has specific responsibilities in the areas of staff appointments and pay, determining eligibility for health services and ensuring that budget allocations are not exceeded.

The board generally holds its meetings on a monthly basis. Business is conducted by means of various sub-committees, such as visiting, financial and other appropriate committees.

Management of Health Boards

The management structure of the health boards was devised in accordance with the recommendations of the McKinsey Report (1970). It is based on the concept of a management team with a Chief Executive Officer supported by programme managers and functional officers. These are full-time officers. The management team usually meets weekly under the leadership of the CEO.

Under the 1970 act, only a limited range of decisions, mainly relating to eligibility of individuals for services and personnel matters, are reserved to the Chief Executive Officer of a health board. Otherwise he and other officers of the board are required to act in accordance with the decisions of the board. In practice, however, the health boards have recognised the need for substantial delegation to their Chief Executive Officers of the day-to-day management of the services, while retaining ultimate control in their own hands.

For administrative purposes, the work of the board is divided into three broad programmes covering community care services, general hospital services and special hospital services (mainly the hospital services for the mentally ill). Each of these programmes is in the charge of a 'programme manager'. In the larger boards there is a separate programme manager for each of the three programmes, while in the three smaller boards there are two programme managers, one of whom deals with the two hospital programmes. In addition, there are functional officers in charge of finance, personnel, planning and management services. This group of officers, under the Chief Executive Officer, form the management team for the health board. Each member of the team has his/her own specific responsibilities, but they all act together as a group in evolving policy and advising the board on future lines of development. An outline of the three programmes is as follows:

Community care contains a diverse range of services, including the general practitioner services; the dental, opthalmic and aural services; services for mothers and children; the care of deprived children; and community services for the elderly and the handicapped.

General hospitals cover the treatment of patients in medical, surgical and maternity hospitals, including the treatment at out-patient consultant clinics associated with these hospitals. The services are provided either directly by the board in hospitals under its own control or by voluntary and private hospitals.

Special hospitals cover services provided for the mentally ill and the mentally handicapped. Services for the mentally ill are provided mainly by consultant clinics or by liaising with professionals in the relevant voluntary bodies. Services for the mentally handicapped are frequently provided by voluntary and religious organisations, and patients are maintained in their institutions by the board on a contract basis.

The health board and the Minister for Health can each delegate functions to the Chief Executive Officer. The 1970 Health Act distinguished between functions reserved to the health board and functions delegated to the Chief Executive Officer. This reflects a similar type of distinction in the local government area. Among the functions reserved to the board are: the drawing up of objectives for improved health services; deciding the allocation of the budget; selecting and starting capital projects; the decision on numbers and categories of staff appointed to the board; dealing in property and land. In law the powers of health board members appear to be wider than the powers in law of county council members.

Among the functions delegated to the Chief Executive Officer are: advising the board; executing its decisions; deciding on eligibility for services; responsibility for personnel matters and other functions as may be prescribed. Among the responsibilities of programme managers are the determination of the needs and targets for the services in their programme; the proposal of plans and estimates of the resources required for the services provided; the implementation and review of plans; ensuring a high level of efficiency in service provision.

To complete the overall structure of the health care system, in each of the eight health areas there are a number of local advisory committees. Each county and each county borough has a local committee composed of three councillors from each electoral area, together with the county manager, members of the medical profession and persons attached to voluntary organisations in the sphere of social services. The functions of these committees are purely advisory, and they do not have any decision-making powers.

It is difficult to assess the precise degree of autonomy enjoyed by the health boards. A 1973 Report issued jointly by the Department of the Public Service and the Department of Health described interventions by the Department of Health as extending 'to questions of range, scope and standards of service, control of and accountability for finance and personnel matters including numbers, types, remuneration and conditions of service. The essence of these interventions is that they achieve co-ordinated norms for the health boards as a group.'

OTHER EXECUTIVE BOARDS

Outside of the Department of Health, there are a number of bodies established on a permanent basis, such as the National Drugs Advisory Board, the National Council for the Elderly, and the National Rehabilitation Board, which provide a wide range of services and advice on their relevant areas of activity. For those aspects of the work on the health services not suited to localised operation, the practice has evolved of setting up special central executive agencies such as the Blood Transfusion Service Board.

In 1961 the Health (Corporate Bodies) Act introduced a new, more easily used procedure for the Minister for Health to set up specialist bodies. This enabled the minister by order to 'establish a body to perform functions in, or in relation to, the provision of a health service or two or more health services'. Such an order, which is liable to annulment by either House of the Oireachtas, specifies the constitution and functions of the body established and includes provision for the appointment of staff. The National Drugs Advisory Board is an example of a body established under this procedure.

In addition, as required, special broadly based working parties and committees are established from time to time to advise on specific aspects of the services. Notable among these are reports on the psychiatric services, the general medical services, and the care of the mentally handicapped, the elderly and the disabled.

The National Health Council is an advisory body which was established under the Health Act 1947, as amended by the Health Act 1953. Its functions are to advise the Minister for Health on regulations made under the Health and Mental Treatment Acts and 'on such general matters affecting or incidental to the health of people as may be referred to them by the minister and to advise the minister on such other general matters relating to the operation of the health services as they think fit'. Matters relating to the conditions of employment of health service staff and the amount or payment of grants or allowances do not come within the council's remit. These wide statutory functions give the council considerable flexibility in its consultative role.

The Council is a broadly based, representative body appointed by the Minister for Health. At least half of its members must be 'nominated by bodies representative of the medical and ancillary professions and of persons concerned with the management of voluntary hospitals'. It was established at a time when there were few bodies available to advise the minister. In the intervening period the situation has changed dramatically with the setting up of several specialist, advisory and executive bodies to carry out specific functions. The establishment of these bodies reflects the major expansion in the range of services being provided from public funds.

The statutory responsibility for the regulation of the number and type of appointments of consultant medical staff and senior registrars in hospitals is vested in Comhairle na nOspidéal. It also specifies qualifications for such appointments and regulates the appointment of certain hospital staff, such as senior biochemists, and advises the Minister for Health on matters relating to the organisation and operation of hospital services. It is not involved in the day-to-day administration of hospitals but rather in co-ordinating and control of service development and long-term medical manpower planning.

Comhairle na nOspidéal was an innovative mechanism, involving devolution of authority to medical experts for the provision of technical inputs into the hospital policy-making process. Fourteen of its twenty-seven members (each of whom is appointed for a three-year term of office) must be members of the medical profession.

ELIGIBILITY FOR HEALTH SERVICES

The primary aim of the eligibility criteria is to ensure that no person in need is denied access to a health service which he is unable to afford from his own resources. Health promotion is encouraged by making certain community protection services available to all persons without charge.

The 1953 Health Act provided for each group in the population the services which they could not afford. The 1966 White Paper on the health services and their further development outlined the then thinking on health service eligibility. It stated that the government did not accept the proposition that the state had a duty to provide unconditionally all medical, dental and other health services free of cost to everyone without regard to individual needs or circumstances. On the other hand, it stated that no service was designed so that a person must show dire want before they could avail of it. The preventative services designed to protect the community as well as to help the individual were available to all without regard to means.

There are two categories of eligibility for health services, and the category to which a person belongs determines what services he should pay for and what services he is entitled to free of charge. Category I includes all medical card holders, who are entitled to the full range of health services without charge. Eligibility is decided on the basis of a means test. About 35 per cent of the population are in this category.

Category II consists of the remainder of the population whose annual income is above the medical card limit. Persons in this category are entitled to a number of free services, including maternity and infant welfare service, all in-patient hospital services (including consultant services) in public wards, and outpatient specialist services.

The eligibility arrangements for public hospital services have recently been changed to allow everyone, regardless of income, the choice of being a public patient or a private patient. As agreed in the Programme for Economic and Social Progress (1991), everyone, from 1 June 1991, is entitled to avail of public hospital services (including consultant services).

Private and public patients are both liable for hospital charges; in addition, maintenance charges are payable for private and semi-private accommodation. For *out-patient* services arising from a particular medical condition, a single charge of £10 applies in respect of the first visit only. The *in-patient* hospital charge is at a rate of £12.50 per day, subject to a maximum of £125 in any period of twelve consecutive months.

Medical card holders are exempt from both out-patient and in-patient hospital services charges. The following categories of patients are also exempt:

(1) women receiving services in respect of motherhood;

(2) children up to six weeks of age, children suffering from prescribed diseases and disabilities, and children referred for treatment from child health clinics and school health examinations;

(3) persons receiving services in respect of prescribed infectious diseases;

(4) persons receiving services provided in accordance with EC regulations.

The 1966 white paper also set out the principles and objectives of providing a free general medical service to persons who are unable without undue hardship to arrange general practitioner medical and surgical services for themselves and their dependents. These principles were embodied in the Health Act 1970, which abolished the old dispensary system and provided in its place a choice of family doctor to the greatest extent practicable, thereby ending the discrimination implicit in the former system. During the 1970s there was a rapid expansion in health services and improvement in the standards of care available to the population in general. The Report of the Working Party on the General Medical Service (1984) found that there has been virtually universal satisfaction at the extent to which the scheme has met these objectives. Prior to March 1989, payment to the doctors was by way of fee per service; after that date a capitation-based system was introduced.

VOLUNTARY HOSPITALS

The health service has a unique mix of public and voluntary involvement. There are considerable numbers of voluntary organisations which on a national or local basis provide health services with the financial support of the minister. Voluntary hospitals which are owned and controlled by religious orders or by boards of governors, have traditionally played a major role in the Irish health services. Most of these hospitals enjoy teaching hospital status and retain significant autonomy in management. While the state, through the Department of Health and the health boards, provides most of the finance for hospitals in Ireland, only a proportion of these are managed and controlled by public authorities. Problems of co-ordination between and within the statutory and voluntary sectors and gaps in service provision have been identified. It is obviously desirable that all publicly-funded agencies, whether statutory or voluntary, work together effectively without jeopardising the independence of the voluntary sector.

About half the acute hospital beds in the country are provided in non-statutory voluntary and joint board hospitals with a range of private forms of management and control. In the Eastern Health Board area (Counties Dublin, Kildare and Wicklow) over 80 per cent of acute beds are outside the direct management of the health board 'as voluntary organisations have played a major role in the development of services in the Dublin region and will continue to do so in the future'. (Minister for Health, 18 September 1991)

Numerous voluntary organisations serving the elderly, the physically and mentally handicapped, the mentally ill and many other groups provide very valuable services both locally and often on a national basis. They include the voluntary hospitals and councils and associations for specific diseases or conditions and bodies concerned in the organisation of social services. Their role involves not just the delivery of services but also participation in the process of policy development. Statutorily, the hospitals and institutions involved, many of which are owned and run by religious bodies, provide services on behalf of health boards. Even the use of the term 'voluntary' is a misnomer for the most part, as these voluntary bodies are dependent for virtually all their funding on Exchequer sources.

Owing to the range and nature of the services they provide, these hospitals are significant spenders of money and employers of labour. Personnel employed by them enjoy broadly similar conditions of employment, including pension arrangements, pay rates and grading structures, to their health board counterparts. Mental handicap homes, which are owned and run by voluntary organisations, have similar arrangements to those which operate in the voluntary hospitals.

Voluntary organisations 'have been the foundation upon which statutory policy for community care has been developed in Ireland in the past' (National Planning Board 1984: 314). The relationship of the Department of Health with these bodies varies by reference to the service which they provide. Those providing institutional care are paid the costs of services provided on a budget basis, while those community-based groups providing health and welfare services are grant-aided by the health boards towards the costs of the services.

VOLUNTARY HEALTH INSURANCE BOARD

There has been considerable debate, in Ireland as in other countries, on the appropriate public/private mix in health care. In Ireland private insurance and private providers of services are integral parts of the health care system, with a close, complementary relationship with the public sector. Many people choose to supplement their statutory entitlements to health services by taking out voluntary insurance cover. The state pays a significant part of the cost through tax relief, while much of the income of the voluntary insurance scheme is, in turn, spent on the services of public hospitals. The state also pays private providers, such as general practitioners and pharmacists, for their services to certain categories of patient.

The Voluntary Health Insurance Board was established in 1957 following the report of an advisory body. It is a state-sponsored body whose members are appointed by the Minister for Health. It provides for persons who wish to supplement their entitlement to health services. The board is non-profit making and is mainly concerned with hospital costs, for which it provides a range of plans. Some £100 million is paid by way of subscriptions to the Voluntary Health Insurance Scheme each year for additional health care. It is an interesting aspect of the mix of private and public health care in Ireland that insurance for private medical costs is underwritten by a public enterprise which has a virtual monopoly.

Under the terms of the Voluntary Health Insurance Act 1957, it is illegal to offer health insurance without a licence from the Minister for Health. Other than the VHI there are fourteen licensed health insurance schemes which cater mainly for a workplace or union membership (such as, for example, the largest scheme, the ESB Staff Medical Provident Fund). The VHI plays a pivotal role in the delicate mix between public and private care in Ireland. At the end of February 1989 there were 1.3 million persons (almost 37 per cent of the population) covered by schemes operated by the board. The concept and practice of community rating is crucial in this regard. The VHI calculates insurance premia, which do not take account of the risk factors such as age and condition of health. Members invest for life, with the young subsidising the old.

HEALTH EXPENDITURE

In common with other Western countries, Ireland has experienced substantial increases in health expenditure over the last thirty years. The main reasons for this may be summarised as: technological advances which have been expensive and complement (rather than replace) existing facilities, thereby increasing total costs; demographic factors, particularly the proportion of elderly people in the population, since they account for a significant part of total health spending; manpower increases due to higher demands for services and growing specialisation; expanded scope of services, with an increased emphasis on welfare services for disadvantaged groups such as the disabled, the elderly and children at risk; the growth in coverage of services with extensions in eligibility; and the appearance of new diseases, most notably AIDS. The total spending on health services is the product of the unit cost per item of service and the number of services provided to individual patients and clients. While it is possible to influence costs to some extent through efficiency improvements, it is more difficult to control the number of people availing of the services. There is, of course, always a political awareness of the role of the health services as employers in a time of high unemployment.

The financial constraints on the public provision of health services have been very great in recent years and have obliged the health agencies to adopt various measures to reduce expenditure levels to within approved allocations. These measures included reductions in supplements to basic pay, reduced locum cover, delayed filling and non-filling of vacancies, deferred purchasing and reduced stock levels. Despite this, there were 7,000 more staff in the health services at the end of 1989 than there were in 1977. Attempts were also made to reduce activity especially at week-ends. The fact that there has been a declining resource base since 1981 has been a considerable inducement to concentrate on the provision of appropriate care. There has been strong emphasis on value for money, increased efficiency and cost-effectiveness. The health care system has moved from one led by demand to one very much constrained by supply considerations.

Throughout the 1980s the health services were a major electoral issue. The emphasis on the need for increased efficiency in public expenditure resulted in their coming under close scrutiny, both because they represent such a large proportion of spending and because they are so vital to the quality of life.

The Irish health system has historically reflected a bias towards institutional services which absorb 70 per cent of resources allocated to it. Political factors have reinforced this tendency, as shown in a statement by the Minister for Health in the Dáil in 1983:

> The incessant pressure is for £50 million hospitals all over the place. As a consequence, in recent years I estimate that we have spent £300 million to £400 million on acute hospital capital works when at least £30 million of that would have transformed the situation I have referred to. Psychiatric patients, disabled people, mentally handicapped people, do not have much voting power, not as much as consultants, doctors and nurses in hospitals. Politicians, regrettably, have responded in the wrong direction. (*Dáil Debates*, 30 Nov. 1983. Cols 697–8)

Considerable resources have been made available to the health boards in services and voluntary hospitals in order to stimulate improvements. Thus there have been developments in the use of new cost-containment methods, of cost comparisons between hospitals, and in the application of information technology. The current emphasis in the health services is on achieving accountability, cost effectiveness and efficiency. Planning guidelines, information systems, financial and personnel management systems are all geared towards achieving this objective. The Irish health services and health expenditure are kept constantly under review. For example, in addition to the Commission on Health Funding (see below), a Dublin Hospitals Initiative Group was established in 1990 and has produced several reports on problems in the management and delivery of acute hospital services in the Dublin region, and a Group was also set up in 1990 to examine the efficiency of aspects of the health care system. The decisions based on these reviews are outlined below.

Report of the Commission on Health Funding (1989)

The Commission on Health Funding was established in 1987 to examine the funding required to provide an equitable, comprehensive and cost-effective public health service and any changes in administration which seem desirable for that purpose. The Commission's report, published in September 1989, is a comprehensive analysis and reappraisal of the health services, recommending radical changes throughout the system, in accordance with its general finding: 'The kernel of the Commission's conclusions is that the solution to the problem facing the Irish health services does not lie primarily in the system of funding but rather in the way that services are planned, organised and delivered.' The Commission recommended a restructuring of the administration of the health services with clear roles and relationships between the department, the health boards and proposed area general managers. In this context, the commissions' declared aim was to separate hospital and executive functions in the health services. This aim is reflected in the way roles are assigned within the proposed new structure. The report was very critical of the present structure of health administration in Ireland and highlighted a number of weaknesses:

(1) It confuses political and executive functions, and therefore undermines both.

(2) It fails to achieve a proper balance between national and local decision-making.

(3) The decision-making process does not provide a sufficient role for information and evaluation.

(4) Accountability within the structure is inadequate.

(5) There is insufficient integration of related services.

(6) There is inadequate effective representation of the interests of individual patients and clients within the structure.

In the two years after the publication of the report, the majority of the Commission's key recommendations have been implemented or are in process of being implemented. This is covered in detail below. The Commission's evaluation of the deficiencies in the administration of services was of crucial importance in the development of plans for the reorganisation of the services. It recommended that overall responsibility for the management of health services should be transferred to a Health Services Executive Authority, the role of voluntary health agencies should be clarified, planning and service evaluation should be enhanced, and an independent appeals system should be established for patients. A Performance Audit Unit should be set up to assist the Minister for Health. The proposed administrative structure recommended by the commission is shown in Figure 2.

Figure 2: Administrative Structure proposed by the Commission on Health Funding, 1989

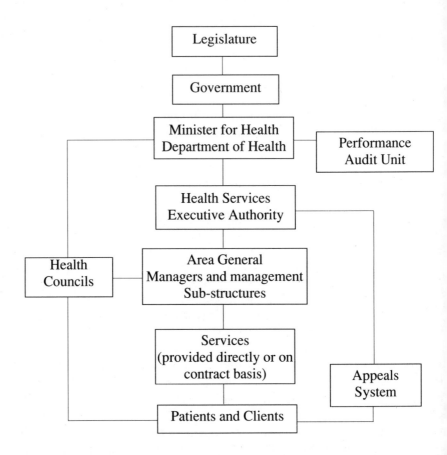

The Minister for Health, recognising the problems caused by the lack of coordination between autonomous bodies, particularly in the Dublin region, because of the multiplicity of these bodies, announced in September 1991 a major reorganisation of health services in the Eastern Health Board area (Dublin, Wicklow and Kildare). A single new authority will be responsible for all health and personal social services, replacing the Eastern Health Board, as well as taking some of the functions of the Department of Health. It will ensure that health services in the region are delivered in an integrated and coordinated way. The roles, relationships and accountability of various levels in the health service will be clarified and, where necessary, strengthened by amending legislation.

THE FUTURE

The Government have indicated their commitment to developing health services so as to ensure equality of access to services irrespective of means. The essentials of Ireland's approach to health policy do not depart significantly from the principles set down by the World Health Organisation in its 'Health for All by the year 2000' strategy and emphasise health promotion through the development of healthier lifestyles, and the prevention of disease and handicap on a multi-sectoral basis. This is in the context of a recognition of the fundamental role of primary care (non-hospital services such as those provided by general practitioners, dentists and public health nurses, and personal social services such as those of social workers), while accepting the reality of a continuing role for other levels of care. It is in the context also of the need to provide an integrated network of complementary services to meet measured health needs in the population.

Health policy reflects the interaction of economic, political, social, demographic, historical, cultural and international factors. It is dynamic, and new challenges constantly confront policy-makers: examples are the high number of non-national doctors staffing Irish hospitals, particularly in rural areas; the rise in AIDS; increases in medical litigation; and changes in medical and nurse training. Over the last two decades health policy has tended to emphasise the role of curing and caring, involving a rapid development of the acute general hospital system and a significant reliance on high technology medicine. Even outside the hospital system, policy has been tied very closely to the medicine-centred model of health care. In this regard, one of the more significant developments in thinking about health care is the 'Health for All' programme developed under the aegis of the World Health Organisation (WHO), of which Ireland has been a member since 1955. The basis tenets of the programme include:

(1) the removal of inequalities in health;

(2) the emphasis on health promotion and prevention of disease;

(3) active community participation in developing and implementing strategies for health;

(4) the need for multi-sectoral co-operation in ensuring the prerequisites for health;

(5) an emphasis on primary health care;

(6) the need for international co-operation in tackling health problems which transcend national boundaries.

The spectacular development of high-technology medical interventions over the last three decades has reinforced the perception of hospitals as the preferred setting for health care. Current policy of the Department of Health is to redress this imbalance and progress is being made towards the development of comprehensive community-based services. This reorientation of emphasis demands a significant change in the perceptions of health by the population at large and the professionals who work in the area. This view of health emphasises physical, psychological and social well-being, rather than an absence of illness, as the determinant of a healthy person. Also central to health policy of the Department of Health is an emphasis on health promotion and prevention—to assist people in a practical way to remain healthy. The greatest potential for reducing coronary disease, cancer and other major killers lies in altering personal behaviour.

Strengthening community services before institutions can be run down is a difficult task, particularly in a period when limited new resources are available. The management of this double-spending transition period presents a challenge and an opportunity to develop appropriate policies for effective patient care.

REFERENCES

Towards Better Health Care: Management in the Health Boards, (McKinsey & Company Incorporated, 1970)

Restructuring the Department of Health: The Separation of Policy and Execution (Dublin: Stationery Office, 1973)

Proposals for Plan, 1984–87 (Dublin: National Planning Board, 1984)

Report of the Commission on Health Funding (Dublin: Stationery Office, 1989)

Zimmerman, Joseph F., 'Health Administration in Ireland: Aspects of Reorganisation', in *Administration* Vol. 29.2, 153–70

10

Appeals

Every day officials in government departments and public bodies make hundreds of discretionary decisions which deprive people of entitlements and benefits or impose on them restrictions. Inevitably, many of those adversely affected by these decisions feel that they have not been treated fairly. Frequently they complain that they have not been given reasons for a decision, that they have not been given a chance to provide their side of the story, that there has been unreasonable delay, or simply that a mistake has been made. In addition, there are occasions when the actions of public bodies appear to exceed their legal and constitutional rights.

Since public servants are not the best judges of their own conduct, it is clearly desirable that there should be independent systems of review under which the grievances of citizens against public bodies can be effectively examined and, if well founded, remedied. By this means it would be possible to ensure that the exercise of discretionary power is not abused, that natural justice obtains, that there are not wrong motives or irrelevant grounds, that decisions are not taken arbitrarily, unreasonably or erroneously, and that, in short, the activities of public bodies are controlled in the interests of the people.

A formalised system of complaints and redress is not as well developed in Ireland as in many European countries. The reason for this relative lack is that Ireland has followed the British tradition in which all executive powers are vested by parliament in individual ministers who are accountable to parliament for their actions and those of their officials. This concept is enshrined in the Ministers and Secretaries Act 1924, which makes ministerial responsibility central to the Irish form of democracy; and it means that, in Ireland as in Britain, the idea of political rather than legal protection for citizens who have a grievance against the administration is embedded in political tradition. As a result, the development of appeals bodies has been both limited and patchy; for example, Ireland did not get an Ombudsman until 1984. The High Court has, of course, always been available to complainants, but the situations in which it is employed to intervene in relations between the executive and the citizen are rare. This is largely because of its long delays and prohibitive costs, not to mention its reluctance to get involved in administrative decisions.

The need for adequate appellate institutions and procedures was stressed by the Public Services Organisation Review Group. In this connection, it also recommended that ministers should shed their executive functions, making them over to executive agencies, a number of which would be created in each department. These agencies would be responsible for day-to-day work, including detailed operations such as the payment of grants, issue of licences and award of contracts (i.e. the type of activities frequently involving controversial decisions). Successive governments have, however, proved extremely reluctant to adopt this recommendation, thereby exemplifying the preference of politicians for the established practice of seeking political remedies.

The idea was discussed again in 1985 during the preparation of the white paper *Serving the Country Better*, but the proposal was dropped by the government in response to the general desire that ministers should retain their existing responsibilities and that politicians should continue to be the main channel for constituents' complaints. In the event, the white paper facilitated the voluntary establishment of executive agencies; but although some (The Social Welfare Services office and the Air Navigation Services office) have been set up informally, no minister has legally adopted the system.

In Ireland there are a number of informal methods and systems of a more formal kind for obtaining the investigation and, if appropriate, redress of grievances. The informal methods include approaches to public representatives (who may air the grievance by means of a parliamentary question), to interest groups and trade unions, and even directly to the decision-making body concerned, as well as publicity in the press and on the radio. The formal systems include the courts (both domestic and European), legally established tribunals, and the Ombudsman.

PUBLIC REPRESENTATIVES

By far the most frequently used of the informal remedies is the approach to a politician, usually a TD, who then uses his influence with the minister or with others who are responsible for making decisions. Such approaches are encouraged by the politicians themselves, who do not generally regard themselves as legislators and are more at home in dealing with constituency issues. The Dáil itself has long been regarded as a watch-dog against government, and the handling by TDs of individual grievances could be regarded as a natural extension of this. Furthermore, because of the Irish system of multi-seat constituencies, where members of even the same party are in competition with each other for election, there are considerable benefits to be gained from services provided for constituents.

For these reasons, little interest has been shown in other forms of remedy: for example, only four deputies took part in the debate on the bill to establish the office of Ombudsman, and after its enactment four years elapsed before an appointment to the vacant office was made. At an earlier stage, in 1966, the then Minister for Finance, had stated: 'The basic reasons we do not need the Ombudsman is because we have so many unofficial but nevertheless effective ones.'

This preference for the use of representatives is shared by the general public. A survey of the factors influencing electors during the 1989 general election confirmed emphatically the relevance and importance of looking after constituency matters: 73 per cent of those polled considered that it mattered a lot, and 17 per cent considered that it mattered somewhat.

Extent of Influence of Factors on Voting Intentions					
	A lot	Some-what	Not really	Not at all	No opinion
	%	%	%	%	%
Look after Constituency needs	73	17	6	3	1
Perform well on national issues	57	27	9	4	3
Policies of the Party	42	26	21	9	2
Choosing a Taoiseach	26	27	28	17	2

Irish Times, 2 June 1990.

There are a number of ways in which this informal systems works. By far the most widely used is that which is known as 'representations', where a politician belonging to the government party or parties makes a request by letter on behalf of his constituent to the minister responsible. Those in the opposition parties who have previously held office write personally to the secretary of the department, while ordinary backbenchers write to him formally or to an official whom they have got to know. Letters to the minister are, in the first instance, acknowledged by the minister himself, with an additional copy of his reply for the politician to send to his constituent. The original letter is then sent from the minister's private office to the appropriate section of the department for preparation of a final reply. Normally this reply will be prepared by the official who either recommended or made the decision complained of. Thus, unless a minister takes a personal interest (which he usually does only when personally approached by the party member making the representations) and the decision is one of a discretionary nature, it is unlikely that it will be altered.

Officials are not impressed by representations, to which they are well accustomed. The matter may or may not be re-examined, depending on the issue, the nature of the examination already made, and on the political standing of the person making the representations. The reply, prepared for signature by the minister on his own personal headed paper may, however, contain a fuller restatement of the reasons for the original decision and generally includes a soothing last sentence to the effect that 'the minister regrets that he cannot be of more assistance on this occasion'. It is then sent back to the minister's private office, where it is scrutinised by his private secretary before presentation to the minister for his signature. Again, an extra copy of the reply is sent to the politician concerned. In the vast majority of cases this ends the correspondence.

A minister receives directly all the grievances and all the requests for favours from his own constituents, irrespective of whether they are members of his own party or not. If the subject-matter relates to the work of his own department, the procedure is as outlined above. If it does not, the letter is transmitted over the minister's signature to whichever of his colleagues has the responsibility, with a request for favourable consideration, and the constituent is informed accordingly. In due course a final reply is received from the investigating minister whose investigation has been the same as that referred to in the preceding paragraph. This reply is sent by the minister to his constituent, who thus has evidence of the high level at which his letter has been dealt with.

Occasionally politicians, especially those who have been in the Oireachtas for some time and may have got to know many of the senior officials, inquire on the telephone about constituency affairs. This practice is not common, however, since it does not produce any written matter to show the constituent that action has been taken on his behalf.

Officials generally regard this elaborate and expensive representations procedure with a degree of cynicism, since it very rarely has the effect of having administrative decisions reversed. They complain that it has detrimental effects on their work. Since ministers demand that priority be given to representations, official resources are diverted away from dealing with the issues which the representations are intended to ameliorate. Officials who should be engaged full-time on, for example, paying grants have to detach themselves to deal with representations about delays in the payment of the same grants. They also point out that the system distracts ministers and senior officials from the policy-making activities in which they should be more properly engaged. A further undesirable feature of the system is the creation of an impression among the public that everything can be fixed.

Another type of public representative, the local councillor, can play a role as intermediary between the citizen and the administration at local authority level. Councillors have a certain advantage over TDs in following up individual complaints because of their close involvement with the administrative process and their more ready access to local offices.

PARLIAMENTARY QUESTIONS

The procedures relating to the tabling and answering of parliamentary questions have been dealt with in Chapter 3. Questions may be divided into two broad categories: those which relate to policy matters, and those which relate to matters of day-to-day administration. It is those in the latter category with which we are concerned here, and specifically those where TDs seek to have grievances ventilated.

By far the most numerous of these are the questions relating to matters such as the non-payment, inadequate payment or delay in payment of grants and allowances. The TD conveys his question to the Dáil office, whence it is sent to the minister's office and thence to the appropriate section of the department. The main difference in the treatment of this type of complaint and that of the 'representations' is that the reply to the parliamentary question is normally seen and approved by the assistant secretary concerned before transmission to the minister's office for presentation to the Dáil. Copies of the replies to all parliamentary questions are normally seen also by the secretary of the department, but not necessarily for clearance by him. Only on very rare occasions does this procedure result in any alteration of the reply at the insistence of one of these senior officials. What the procedure does ensure is that the reply will be technically correct and will be in such terms as to protect the minister from criticism by way of supplementary questions (where the question is for oral reply) or from further questions on the same issue on a subsequent occasion. Replies must arrive in the minister's private office at least twenty-four hours before they are due for answer; this rule, however, is not always adhered to, especially if there is an amount of information to be collected for the reply.

The replies to all questions which he has to answer orally are examined by the minister himself before he goes to the Dáil to present them. In these cases he will have the benefit of an accompanying note giving the background to the question, together with sufficient information to enable him deal with supplementary questions. To change the nature of the reply, i.e. to approve some benefit already rejected, is normally within his prerogative. However, this prerogative is very rarely exercised, and the minister normally accepts the judgment of his officials.

The replies to written questions are generally seen by the senior officials only, and are rarely seen by the minister. Copies of the reply are provided by the minister's private secretary to the Dáil to be passed on to the TD concerned and for subsequent publication in the record of Dáil debates.

Parliamentary questions have little effect on the work of civil servants beyond the amount of time taken up in the administrative procedure which the careful preparation of replies and notes entails. There is always a sense of urgency, since the standing orders of the Dáil provide that three clear days' notice only need be given, i.e. that deputies are entitled to, and invariably receive, answers to their written questions (by far the most numerous) on such short notice. The officials preparing the replies to parliamentary questions are obliged under their own standing departmental regulations to drop all other work and attend to the parliamentary questions. Information about the problems of individual constituents can, of course, be obtained by deputies, either through a telephone call or a letter especially now that members of the Oireachtas have secretarial assistance. However, civil servants are aware that the main reasons for questions on constituency matters are, firstly, to allow politicians to represent themselves openly as advocates of the defenceless citizen against the powerful minister and soulless bureaucrat, and, secondly, to provide them with written material which they can send to their constituents and to their local newspapers as evidence that they are about their constituents' business. Questions are, nevertheless, an essential element of democracy.

The value of the parliamentary question as a means of resolving grievances, however, is questionable. Neither ministers nor civil servants are disposed to admit readily that they have been remiss in the exercise of the discretion vested in them, particularly having regard to the adversarial manner in which question time is conducted in the Dáil. Thus ministers tend to defend themselves against what they regard as attacks on them and their departments and to justify decisions rather than admit error, and civil servants tend to seek additional arguments to support the decisions taken, rather than seek compromise.

Furthermore, Dáil standing orders contain a number of restrictions which greatly reduce the efficacy of the parliamentary question as a way of having decisions altered. Questions may be asked only about matters for which a minister has direct responsibility; thus any questions raised on matters connected with the day-to-day work of local authorities, health boards and state-sponsored bodies are automatically rejected. Debates or statements at question time are prohibited, and votes are not taken on issues raised. Moreover, the Dáil has no sanctions: it cannot alter a decision or punish decision-makers. The only course still open to a deputy dissatisfied with a reply is to seek the permission of the Ceann Comhairle to raise the matter again on the adjournment. Thus, unless he is in a position to make a forceful and detailed case on the basis of information not hitherto disclosed, he is unlikely to succeed in having a decision altered.

One effect that the raising of grievances through parliamentary questions may have, however, is to ensure that similar cases are handled more sympathetically in the future. To this extent, the parliamentary question could be regarded as being better at preventing rather than remedying grievances.

MISCELLANEOUS INFORMAL REMEDIES

An informal, though very effective, means of redress is provided by the media, both newspapers and radio. Many newspapers and some radio programmes provide facilities whereby people may bring to attention instances of what they consider to be unfair treatment by public bodies. On occasion, the media follow up the complaints directly with the bodies concerned. Otherwise the publicity itself often results in the bodies re-examining the cases complained of.

Another informal means is through pressure groups or through trade unions, particularly in cases related to employment-linked social welfare and health entitlements. No matter how formal a relationship may appear to be, the reality is that the officers in pressure groups and unions normally have good personal relations with the officials with whom they deal on a daily basis, thus enabling matters in which either side is interested to be discussed informally.

Everyone may, of course, use the hierarchical method of appeal. They may make a written complaint about a matter of concern to them directly to the chief executive of the organisation concerned. In general, this method is used by the more articulate and well-informed section of the community. It is perhaps, as effective as any of the means described above.

THE IRISH COURTS

While the courts have no concern with the vast majority of the administrative decisions of public bodies, since it is not their function to entertain appeals against such decisions, they are, however, concerned to ensure that actions and decisions are within the law. The High Court is available to citizens in certain circumstances to contest decisions with which they are not satisfied. The area of judicial review is somewhat complex, and the remedies provided are frequently hedged about with restrictions as to the type of person eligible to apply and the type of body against whom the remedy will lie. It is sometimes difficult even for lawyers to determine which remedy is appropriate to the particular circumstances.

Generally speaking, individual citizens acting alone in their own interest do not seek the help of the courts. The technicality and complexity of the law, referred to above, can be a deterrent, as can the long delays involved, and the inaccessibility to citizens of the case law and precedents on which so many of the legal decisions depend. The uncertainty of the law, owing to the fluidity of judicial interpretation, is a further factor. But above all, perhaps, is the prohibitive cost of legal proceedings, which is well beyond the reach of the ordinary citizen; even if he wins his case, he may be left with substantial costs to pay.

Types of Appeal
There is an extensive literature on all aspects of appellate procedures conducted in the Irish courts. It is possible here only to indicate in broad terms the three most usual situations in which the courts will intervene to provide remedies.

Constitutional Rights Infringed. A citizen may resort to the courts if he considers that an act of the Oireachtas infringes his constitutional rights. An example of this type of case is that of a farmer (Brennan) in Co.Wexford who contested the constitutionality of the rating system as it applied to him. Under the Valuation Acts 1852–64, his farm was valued by reference to the price of certain crops in the years 1849–52. The amount of the valuation determined his liability for rates and his eligibility for certain kinds of state assistance. He pleaded that this method of valuation violated his personal and property rights under the Constitution. The court found in his favour in 1984, because the use of the 1852 valuation long after farming methods had changed was an infringement of his property rights in that he was paying more in rates than neighbours with better land. The fact that there was no other source of review of the valuation open to him was a further attack on his property rights.

Constitutional Justice Disregarded. The second type of situation is where a public body making a decision did not observe the principles of justice provided for each citizen by the Constitution, i.e. that the decision-maker must not be biased or be seen to be biased, that an opportunity be given to the person whose case is under review to know what evidence has been given against him so that he can give his side of the story, and that no body should be a judge in its own case. The requirement to follow fair procedures binds ministers and officials to act in good faith and to listen carefully to both sides of the case. Court decisions suggest that when a citizen has a legitimate expectation that, for example, his application for a discretionary benefit such as a licence or a permit will not be refused without a chance for him to put his case, then he is entitled to some kind of hearing. Where he already enjoys the benefit, the expectation that he should not be deprived of it arbitrarily and unheard by the decision-maker makes his case legally and morally stronger. An example of this type of case is that of E. P. Garvey, former Commissioner of the Garda Síochána, who was removed from office and who brought proceedings before the High Court. The removal was struck down because he had been given no reason for it and no opportunity to indicate why he should not be removed.

Ultra Vires. Cases under the third situation, i.e. where public bodies have gone beyond the powers conferred on them by statute, are by far the most numerous. The body, for example, might not have observed prescribed procedures, or it might have taken extraneous matters into account in arriving at its decision. The court has no concern with the vast majority of administrative decisions, since it assumes, reasonably, that when the legislature allocates the power to make such decisions to a public body, it does not intend that the power should be taken over by the court. On the other hand, the courts are concerned that decisions are taken within the law. Therefore, the courts are available to citizens who contest the legality of decisions taken in their cases, and a number of remedies are provided.

Types of Remedy

Apart from damages, what the aggrieved citizen wants from the courts in the case of administrative decisions which adversely affect him is relief by way of an order of the court under one or more of the following headings: (1) invalidating the administrative decision; (2) requiring the public body to desist from or discontinue some course of action; (3) commanding the fulfilment of a legal obligation. The difference between an appeal and a judicial order or review is that the first involves a new decision while the second does not. There are five different orders which may be sought to meet the needs broadly outlined; these are briefly discussed below.

(1) Certiorari. This type of order presupposes a duty to act judicially. A judicial act comprises an act done by any competent authority, such as a public body, upon consideration of facts and circumstances, which imposes liability or affects the rights of others. An order of *certiorari* may be sought by a citizen who seeks to have a decision made by a public body declared invalid because the body acted in excess of its legal authority. The excess may be due to the fact that the body had no legal authority to make the decision it did, because the procedures adopted by it in coming to its decision were vitiated by its failure to observe constitutional or natural justice, as already defined, or because there was an error on the face of the record. Such an error would arise where there was a misinterpretation of a statute or where there was a failure to follow a procedure laid down in a statute. A failure of the latter kind would arise, for example, if the statute said that the body making the decision should consist of two lawyers and a layman and if instead it consisted of two laymen and a lawyer, or if a local authority was empowered to purchase land compulsorily for housing and if instead it could be shown to have been purchased for the making of a road.

Certiorari is a discretionary remedy in the sense that even though the complainant may prove his case, he may, in the exercise of its discretion by the court, be refused the remedy he seeks. This discretion is exercised, not in the arbitrary, but rather in a judicial manner. If an order of *certiorari* is granted by the court, its effect is to quash the decision and to leave the body which took it free to consider the matter afresh. Such an order may not attract damages, however. A person who wishes to obtain damages for any loss occasioned must seek a different kind of order, a declaratory order with damages.

(2) Declaration. The court may be asked to declare the rights and duties of parties before it. In some respects a declaration is wider than *certiorari* in that its reach is not confined to situations where there is a duty to act judicially. It is widely availed of in cases such as the withholding of discretionary benefits and the revocation of licences. It is a defence against the unlawful exercise of administrative power. It entitles the aggrieved person to take the initiative where the alternative would be to await action on foot of the unlawful act of the public body and, at that stage, to dispute its lawfulness. A declaration, as its name implies, declares the true legal position in regard to the rights and duties of the parties. It does not quash the original decision as an order of *certiorari* does. Nevertheless, the effect may be the same, since a public authority is unlikely to ignore a judicial declaration of the law.

(3) Prohibition. The issue of this order restrains an administrative body, which has a duty to act judicially and whose decisions affect rights or impose liabilities, from embarking upon or continuing a given course of action which would be in excess of its jurisdiction. The order has, therefore, a close affinity with *certiorari*, and essentially the difference between them is one of timing. Prohibition issues to restrain the making of a decision in excess of jurisdiction; *certiorari* issues to quash such a decision where it has already been made.

Prohibition does not apply if a public body is acting administratively, and it must be said that the difference between acting judicially and acting administratively is not always clear. Where it is acting administratively, its proceedings may, however, be restrained by injunction.

(4) Injunction. This is a coercive order from the court to stop its recipient from taking some particular action against a person who can show virtual certainty of its taking place and that it will cause irreparable injury. An injunction may be interlocutory, requiring interim cessation of the action so as to maintain the status quo pending final determinaton of a case.

(5) Mandamus. This remedy exists to enforce the performance of its duty by a public authority where neglect in the performance is adversely affecting some person. The authority may be pleading that it is not under a legal obligation to perform a certain duty. Persons affected may test the matter in the courts by seeking an order of *mandamus*. This order may also be the appropriate remedy in the case of failure to implement a judicial decree of damages given against the state.

EUROPEAN COMMISSION FOR HUMAN RIGHTS
The promotion and development of human rights is one of the main tasks of the Council of Europe, of which Ireland is a member. The European Commission for Human Rights, which is under the auspices of the Council, examines complaints by individuals who consider that an entitlement under the European Convention for Human Rights and Fundamental Freedoms has been violated in their case. If the Commission finds merit in the complaint and does not succeed in arriving at a settlement between the complainant and the government body concerned, it may refer the case to the Court of Human Rights at Strasbourg.

EUROPEAN COURT OF JUSTICE
The task of the Court of Justice at Luxembourg is to ensure observance of the law in the interpretation and application of the treaties setting up the European Community and in implementing regulations issued by the Council of Ministers of the European Commission. The court may review the legality of acts of the Council or Commission and is competent to give judgment on the actions of a member state, the Council or the Commission on the grounds of lack of competence, of infringement of an essential legal requirement, of infringement of a treaty or of any legal rule relating to its application, or of misuse of power. A person may appeal any decision given against him or against other persons which is of direct and individual concern to him.

TRIBUNALS
A number of tribunals have been set up to which aggrieved people may bring their complaints about the discretionary decisions made by public bodies. The tribunals may be individual persons or groups of persons who have been designated by law to adjudicate in these situations. Some examples are those where an application for a social welfare allowance has been rejected or where the valuation placed on a property for rating purposes is regarded as excessive. In those cases an appeal lies to the Social Welfare Appeals Office and to the Valuation Tribunal respectively.

Appeals tribunals in Ireland cannot be said to constitute a formal system. They have been established by individual ministers on a more or less *ad hoc* basis over a number of years, and there are inconsistencies in their composition, their procedures and the areas in which they operate. As regards the latter point, there is, for instance, provision for an appeal against assessment to income tax but not against assessment to customs duty; yet both of these functions are under the same jurisdiction, that of the Revenue Commissioners. Their total number, including bodies set up to adjudicate on issues arising between parties in the private sector such as the Employment Appeals Tribunal or the Rights Commissioners (which do not concern us directly here), is about eighty. This number is a small fraction of those in the United Kingdom, where there are over 2,000, supervised by a General Council on Tribunals.

Features of tribunals which they have in common are (1) independence of the administration and the power to decide cases impartially as between the parties before them. This makes the tribunal form of remedy different from that of an internal administrative review of a decision, which may sometimes be offered by a public body and may be carried out by the official who made the decision in the first place. (2) binding decisions reached by a person or persons who are not engaged full-time on this work and who are not judges. The members may represent opposing interests with, perhaps, some neutrals and a chairman who is often a lawyer. (3) flexible procedures, generally less formal than those in the courts. Tribunals can formulate their own standards and depart from these if the situation so warrants. (4) a facility to acquire considerable expertise in a particular and generally limited area. (5) less rigid attitudes towards precedents. Other features are speed and the absence of the heavy legal costs entailed in court appearances, where counsel can spend a whole day explaining to a judge how a particular scheme is designated to operate.

The Devlin Report, as part of its proposal to establish executive agencies, recommended that tribunals with unlimited scope of appellate jurisdiction should be set up within every agency or for groups of agencies. There would thus be a right of appeal to a single, independent, fully trained person attached to the body by which the decision was given; in cases of particular complexity two experts in the matter under examination might be brought on to the tribunal. This recommendation has not been adopted.

Examples of Tribunals

In some instances the tribunal is one person only, for example, in the area of social welfare, where almost 20,000 cases are dealt with every year. The Social Welfare Act 1952, which set up the system of adjudication in that area, provides for the appointment of a number of deciding officers and appeals officers. A case is decided in the first instance by a deciding officer on the basis of the information before him, without an oral hearing. His decision may be appealed to an appeals officer, who operates under prescribed procedures. These include the power to take evidence on oath and to require persons to give evidence and produce documents. Appeals officers have power to award costs and expenses and the award must be paid by the minister. It has been established by the High Court (*McLoughlin v. Minister for Social Welfare* (1958 IR 5) that an appeals officer is independent of the minister in the exercise of his functions, which are judicial functions, and that it would be improper for the minister to give him instructions as to how he should decide a particular case, or for him to accept such instructions. Thus appeals officers are different from other civil servants, who are answerable to their ministers for actions taken in the ordinary course of administration, such actions being invariably taken in the name of the minister who accepts both legal and political responsibility for them.

The social welfare tribunals now operate under the recently established Social Welfare Appeals Office following the recommendation in the Report of the Commission on Social Welfare, which had noted a perception that the existing appeals procedure was not independent of the workings of the Department of Social Welfare. The commission recommended also that the reasons for the rejection of appeals be given and this is also now being done.

Another example of a one-person tribunal is the Minister for the Environment, who may be appealed to by an officer of a local authority against a decision in his case, e.g. suspension. Similarly, the Minister for Industry and Commerce may be appealed to by a person aggrieved by a decision of the Controller of Industrial and Commercial Property (the Patents Office) not to register a trade mark.

An example of a two-person tribunal is that of the Office of the Appeals Commissioners to which appeals against assessments to income tax may be made. The commissioners are full-time, appointed by the Minister for Finance; one of them is normally a lawyer or an accountant and the other a revenue official. The appeals are held orally and are attended by the inspector who made the assessment, the aggrieved taxpayer and (if he wishes) his professional adviser. In 1988 the commissioners heard over 36,000 appeals, and in 1989 over 12,000. (Because of the introduction of self-assessment it is possible that the number may drop further.)

The Valuation Tribunal, which was set up in 1988, has four members (three lawyers and a property valuer), who are part-time. This tribunal deals with appeals against the valuation placed by the Commissioner of Valuation on buildings and other fixed property as a basis for the levying of rates by local authorities. The tribunal determined about 900 appeals in the first three years of its operation.

Some tribunals have more than four members, An Bord Pleanála, which dealt with 3,060 appeals in 1990 against the grant of planning permissions in some cases and against the refusal of others, has six members, all full-time. The Levy Appeals Tribunal, set up by the Minister for Labour to determine appeals by employers against assessments to training levies imposed by FÁS, the Training and Employment Authority, has sixteen members. Four of those must be lawyers, the chairman and three deputy chairmen. The other twelve must be representatives of employer organisations and trade unions.

THE OMBUDSMAN

Ireland has been behind many European countries in adopting the institution of Ombudsman. The reason for being late into this field is the preference for political remedies noted above. The necessary act was passed in 1980, but the first Ombudsman was not appointed until 1984. Discussion on the creation of the office began in the mid-1960s and received a further impetus with the publication of the Devlin Report in 1969. It was not until 1975, however, that the matter began to be considered in the Oireachtas—both then and subsequently only as a result of the efforts of private members. These efforts eventually led to the introduction of a government bill which became the Ombudsman Act 1980. This act provided for the establishment of the Ombudsman's Office, the appointment to the post to be made by the President upon resolutions passed by the Dáil and Seanad. Under the act, the Ombudsman has the same remuneration as a judge of the High Court, holds office for a period of six years and may be reappointed for a second and subsequent terms.

The Ombudsman may act either on a complaint made to him or where he himself considers that an investigation would be warranted. He may investigate the actions of any officials in the organisations within his remit where it appears '(a) that the action has or may have adversely affected a person . . . and (b) that the action was or may have been taken without proper authority or on irrelevant grounds; the result of negligence or carelessness; based on erroneous or incomplete information; improperly discriminatory; based on undesirable administrative practice; or otherwise contrary to fair or sound administration'. In short, he is responsible for ensuring decent standards of behaviour in all areas of administration. In his own words, 'I see my role as being concerned with not only the legal aspects of the complaint but also with the question of equity and fair play.'

In general, complaints have to be made within twelve months of the action complained of taking place. In general also, complaints are not accepted for investigation unless the complainant has already taken up the matter unsuccessfully with the public body concerned and has already used whatever appeal facilities are open to him. The services are free, and no lawyers are required. The Ombudsman's staff investigate on the citizen's behalf, and all the latter needs to do is to set out his complaint in a letter. The organisations within the Ombudsman's remit are government departments and offices, local authorities, health boards, Telecom Éireann and An Post. There is provision for extending the list of organisations by ministerial order. All matters relating to public service personnel (e.g. their pay, promotion or transfer) are excluded from the Ombudsman's remit.

For the purpose of his investigations the Ombudsman must be provided with all documents which he considers relevant. The Official Secrets Act does not apply to the supply by civil servants of documents or information to the Ombudsman. He may also require persons to appear before him for examination. Investigations are conducted in private, but he must give an opportunity to all parties concerned to comment. Where he finds that the action complained of has had an adverse affect on the complainant, he can recommend to the organisation concerned (a) that the matter in relation to which the action in question was taken be reconsidered, (b) that measures be taken to remedy the adverse effects of the action, or (c) that the reason for taking the action is given. The Ombudsman is empowered to require the body concerned to notify him within a specific time of its response to his recommendations. He has not, however, the power to overturn decisions; his power of recommending is considered adequate.

There is provision for a ministerial veto on investigations. If a minister so requests in writing, the Ombudsman may not investigate an action specified in the request. The minister must provide the Ombudsman with a written statement setting out the reasons for his request. The purpose of the provision is to provide a means whereby the discretionary decisions of a minister can be exempted from the scrutiny of the Ombudsman. It was never intended that the provision would be widely used, and the Ombudsman can, if he feels the provision is being abused, refer to this in his annual report. In fact no minister has to date vetoed an investigation.

To facilitate the work of the Ombudsman in dealing with government departments, each department nominates an officer in the grade of principal to act as liaison officer with the Ombudsman's office. It is this officer's duty to ensure that written or oral inquiries are directed to the appropriate section for attention, that time limits applying to requests for information are met, and that relevant documents and files are made available for inspection as required. Much of the work of the office is done on an informal basis as a result of discussions between the investigators and the officials concerned in the various bodies. Where these discussions are not concluded to the satisfaction of the investigators, and where there is *prima facie* evidence of maladministration, the investigation moves to a more formal stage. The Ombudsman writes formally to the chief officer of the body concerned, enclosing a written summary of the complaint and requesting written observations thereon. Such inquiries are dealt with as a matter of priority, and replies are issued within two weeks of receipt. If a department does not accept that a complaint has been properly referred to it (i.e. if it is of the view that the matter is not one for the Ombudsman, or if it considers that the complaint is not appropriate to the department), the chief officer conveys the departmental view to the Ombudsman within seven days.

The Ombudsman's annual report presents statistics and detailed particulars of complaints dealt with during the year and gives typical examples, together with information on general issues arising from the work of the office. Some tables from the 1989 report are reproduced in Appendix K. The report must be laid before both Houses of the Oireachtas. The Ombudsman may also make such other reports with respect to his functions as he sees fit. In 1987 he reported to the Dáil and Seanad that reductions in the financial allocation to his office had resulted in the loss of a number of investigators. Subsequently, following a review of the situation, the staffing was restored to its present strength of approximately thirty.

REFERENCES

Doolan, Brian, *Constitutional Law and Constitutional Rights in Ireland* 2nd ed. (Dublin: Gill & Macmillan, 1988)

Komito, Lee, 'Voters, Politicians and Clientelism: a Dublin Survey' in *Administration* Vol. 37, No. 2

Curran, Dermot, 'An Ombudsman for Ireland' in *Seirbhís Phoiblí, Journal of the Department of Finance*, Vol. 1, No. 2

Roche, Richard, 'The Ombudsman Proposals: a Critique' in *Journal of Irish Business and Administrative Research*, Vol. 1 No. 1

Appendix K
Annual Report of the Ombudsman, 1989

COMPLAINTS RECEIVED

	Carried forward from 1988	Received in 1989	Total on hands for 1989	Resolved	Assistance provided	Discontinued	Withdrawn	Not upheld	Total completed	Carried forward to 1990
Civil Service										
Social Welfare	210	650	860	130	271	46	10	266	723	137
Revenue Commissioners	52	171	223	12	73	15	6	59	165	58
Environment	34	86	120	8	18	15	1	40	82	38
Agriculture	17	39	56	7	12	4	0	27	50	6
Education	17	27	44	5	1	4	0	22	32	12
Others	49	53	102	8	13	8	1	24	54	48
Total	379	1,026	1,405	170	388	92	18	438	1,106	299
Health Boards										
Eastern	56	107	163	17	39	12	1	36	105	58
Midland	8	13	21	5	3	1	1	3	13	8
Mid-Western	3	7	10	1	1	–	–	4	6	4
North-Eastern	7	11	18	2	2	–	1	3	8	10
North-Western	3	9	12	–	6	–	–	3	9	3
South-Eastern	12	20	32	6	1	2	1	12	22	10
Southern	–	32	32	4	8	4	–	10	26	6
Western	13	38	51	6	5	6	–	8	25	26
Total	102	237	339	41	65	25	4	79	214	125
Local Authorities										
Carlow	2	5	7	–	–	1	–	4	5	2
Cavan	–	2	2	1	–	–	–	1	2	–
Clare	2	7	9	4	1	–	–	4	9	–
Cork Corp.	2	21	23	3	4	3	–	8	18	5
Cork County	7	29	36	1	3	2	–	14	20	16
Donegal	3	7	10	–	1	1	–	2	4	6
Dublin Corp.	23	26	49	3	8	8	1	13	33	16
Dublin County Council	9	17	26	4	2	4	1	8	19	7
Dún Laoghaire Corporation	2	5	7	–	1	1	–	4	6	1
Galway Corp.	2	13	15	1	3	2	1	3	10	5
Galway County	3	14	17	1	3	3	–	6	13	4
Kerry	–	8	8	–	–	2	–	4	6	2
Kildare	4	11	15	1	4	–	1	3	9	6
Kilkenny	1	–	1	–	–	–	–	–	–	1
Laois	1	2	3	–	1	–	–	2	3	–
Leitrim	–	–	–	–	–	–	–	–	–	–
Limerick Corp.	1	7	8	4	1	–	–	3	8	–
Limerick County	1	2	3	–	–	–	–	2	2	1
Longford	3	4	7	3	1	1	–	–	5	2
Louth	–	6	6	–	3	–	–	3	6	–
Mayo	11	25	36	3	4	–	1	12	20	16
Meath	3	5	8	–	1	–	–	1	2	6
Monaghan	–	2	2	–	–	–	–	–	–	2
Offaly	1	7	8	–	–	–	1	4	5	3
Roscommon	3	3	6	–	3	–	1	2	6	-
Sligo	2	3	5	–	1	–	–	2	3	2
Tipperary Nr	3	2	5	–	1	–	–	2	3	2
Tipperary Sr	2	3	5	2	1	–	–	2	5	–
Waterford Corp.	1	3	4	1	–	–	–	1	2	2
Waterford County	2	2	4	2	–	–	–	–	2	2
Westmeath	2	7	9	–	–	–	–	4	4	5
Wexford	1	2	3	–	1	–	–	2	3	–
Wicklow	3	10	13	2	1	1	1	5	10	3
	100	260	360	36	49	29	8	121	243	117

11

The Impact of
the European Community

Ireland became a member of the European Economic Community on 1 January 1973, joining at the same time as Britain and Denmark. The European Community dates from 1951 when the European Coal and Steel Community was established under the Paris Treaty. The Rome Treaties of 1957 established the European Economic Community (EEC) and the European Atomic Energy Community (EURATOM). In 1967 the institutions serving the three Communities were merged and are termed 'The European Community' (EC). The EC, as a supranational organisation, represents a distinct approach to international relations that is of profound significance for the member states in the economic, legal, social and political areas.

In the 1980s several influences combined to focus attention on the need for revisions of the original treaties establishing the European Community. As a result of these developments, the Single European Act (SEA) was agreed at the Luxembourg meeting of the European Council of Ministers in December 1985 and came into effect on 1 July 1987. The legal and procedural bases to enable timely achievement of the Single European Market by 1992 were provided by the SEA. It is essentially an updating of the treaties which established the EC.

The SEA was intended to consolidate the achievements of the Community over the previous quarter of a century, including measures to improve the Community's decision-making procedures (by means of a majority on the Council of Ministers) to promote balanced and integrated economic development in the Community, and to bring European political co-operation within the treaty framework for the first time. It also enshrined in the Community's treaty base a number of new commitments, such as, for example, the fostering of economic and social cohesion between the member states. The SEA marked a subtle but important shift towards a federal system of government throughout the EC.

CONSTITUTIONAL IMPLICATIONS

Accession to the EC heralded a new era in the context of the work of government and the public service in Ireland. The shaping and execution of community policies is now an everyday part of that work.

The Constitution had not anticipated membership by Ireland of a supra-national organisation such as the European Community. It was clear during the negotiations prior to accession that several articles were incompatible with EC membership (e.g., Articles 5, 15.2, 28, 29.4.1 and 34–38). An amendment in the following terms was accordingly put before the people in a referendum on 10 May 1972:

> No provision of this Constitution invalidates laws enacted, acts done or measures adopted by the State necessitated by the obligations of membership of the Communities or prevents laws enacted, acts done or measures adopted by the Communities, or institutions thereof, from having the force of law in the State.

There was a relatively high turnout of 71 per cent, with a total of 83 per cent voting in favour of membership. Thus the government and public service was given a clear mandate by the people in the context of membership of the EC.

The European Communities Act 1972 provided that the treaties of the European Communities and the existing and future acts of their institutions were binding on the state and thus brought European law into the Irish legal system. Since 1973 the Rome Treaty, as amended, has become part of the Irish Constitution and the exclusive law-making power of the Oireachtas provided for in Article 15 has been removed. As Henchy J. said in *Doyle v. An Taoiseach* (1985 ILRM 135), Community Law 'has the paramount force and effect of constitutional provisions'.

This was exemplified by the Supreme Court's ruling in *Crotty v. An Taoiseach* and others (1986 no. 12036P) that the Single European Act could not be ratified by Ireland unless the Constitution was amended, since the SEA contained provisions which were in contravention of the Constitution. The necessary amendment was approved by the people on 26 May 1987 and allowed the state to ratify the Single European Act.

EUROPEAN COMMUNITY LAW

The law-making power of the EC is extensive and unique. The three founding treaties of the EC and the later Single European Act are the primary sources of EC law, laying down principles and rules that are binding on the member states. The legal acts of the EC are the secondary source of law. Community legal instruments have direct applicability in the member states, and in a conflict between national and EC law the latter predominates. Membership of the EC has qualified the exclusive role of the Irish courts, since the body ultimately responsible for the interpretation of the Treaty of Rome is the EC Court of Justice.

The EC Court of Justice ensures that Community law is applied uniformly in the same way in every member state and that the rule of law applies within the Community. The Court has laid down rules on how the body of European law relates to the national legal systems of the member states. It has assisted national courts in developing a standard approach to the interpretation of Community legislation. The Court has heard cases brought against the nationalism and protectionism of member states.

For instance, in 1977 the Court ruled that national fisheries conservation measures introduced by the Irish government were discriminatory in that they excluded fishermen from other member states from fishing in Irish waters. In June 1990 the Court held that the forty-eight-hour rule on cross-border shopping, introduced in the budget of 1987, was illegal. Under Article 177 of the Rome Treaty, the European Court can give a preliminary ruling on the proper interpretation of European law and send the case back to the national courts for a decision in that light.

The operation of the EC Court of Justice shows that Community law is 'like an incoming tide. It flows into the estuaries and up the rivers. It cannot be held back.' (Lord Denning (H.P.) in *Bulmer Ltd v. J. Bollinger SA* (1974) 1 ch. 401 at 418. Membership of the EC has in fact resulted in a diminution of national sovereignty by placing legal restrictions on what an Irish government can do in a wide range of social and economic areas. The obligation to implement Community law and the resulting impact on Irish law have been of crucial significance in the operation of government and public administration in Ireland.

For the purpose of carrying out their tasks under the treaties, the Commission and the Council have three legally binding instruments available. These are collectively described as Community secondary legislation and comprise regulations, directives and decisions.

Regulations are of general application, immediate effect, and binding in their entirety. They are directly applicable in all member states, requiring no implementing measures by the national authorities, and become part of Irish law as soon as they have been formally adopted by the Council or Commission. They are the most common type of secondary legislation and generate rights and obligations for every person in the Community.

Directives are Community Acts adopted by the Council or the Commission. They are binding on any member state to which they are addressed as to the objectives to be achieved but leave the choice of method of implementation to the member state. They indicate the reasons on which they are based, are communicated to the countries to which they are addressed, and state in the text the date on which they come into effect. They are normally used in the harmonisation of legal provisions where the end is not specific. Directives are addressed only to the governments of member states; they create rights but do not create obligations for individuals in a member state. Directives can be implemented domestically in either of two ways: either by primary legislation, which involves the passing of a bill by the Oireachtas; or by secondary legislation, which involves ministerial regulations. The majority of directives are implemented through this latter method.

Decisions are legally binding instruments designed to achieve administrative aims and may be directed to a member state, a corporation, or an individual. They are used to fill out the framework of regulations where necessary.

The volume of this body of secondary law is increasing at an accelerating rate: there were 44 statutory instruments in the period 1971–4; 146 in 1975–9; and 247 in 1980–86. It was this increasing volume of work which prompted the Joint Committee on the Secondary Legislation of the EC to comment that it doubted 'if the general public or even parliamentarians appreciate the extent to which Community law which governs activities in the fields of trade, industry, transport, agriculture and services, is continuously being incorporated into our legal system either directly or through the agency of statutory instruments made by a minister.'

THE POLITICAL IMPACT: INSTITUTIONAL INNOVATIONS

Most of the important EC issues come before the full cabinet, either formally or informally. In addition, from time to time special government sub-committees are formed to deal with EC affairs. Three ministers in particular are intensively involved in EC business (Finance, Foreign Affairs, and Agriculture and Food), and are obliged frequently and regularly to attend meetings at EC headquarters in Brussels. Other ministers, such as those for Industry and Commerce, Labour, Health, Environment, Social Welfare and the Marine, attend when their areas of responsibility are discussed. The government is therefore fully aware of all developments in the EC affecting Ireland. The members of the Oireachtas are advised of such developments by the obligation on the government to report on these matters and by the existence of a joint Oireachtas committee to monitor this area (see below). Many opportunities exist for them to discuss and debate EC policy issues. Such matters can be raised, and are raised, in both Houses of the Oireachtas, either in the form of special motions or on the adjournment. The annual debate on the estimate for the Departmental Foreign Affairs, the presentation of the statutory twice-yearly reports on developments in the European Community, reports on meetings of the European Council and Dáil question time all provide opportunities for debate and discussion.

It has, however, been pointed out that 'the political system has shown few signs of coming to terms with the new dimensions of Community affairs. The

Dáil and Seanad have not developed effective means of supervising the executive activities of government, and this weakness extends to the executive activities of the Community.' In particular, there are insufficient arrangements for strengthening the power of the Oireachtas in supervising Community law in Ireland. (Barrington and Cooney 1984: 174).

Furthermore, there is an absence of proper accountability in relation to EC decision-making generally. In March 1990 a proposal in the Dáil to establish a committee of both Houses of the Oireachtas on foreign affairs to oversee and to strengthen the accountability for foreign policy was defeated. Ireland is the only country in Europe which does not at the time of writing have a foreign affairs committee of its legislature. Nor has Ireland yet developed a means through which members of the European Parliament can report on developments in the EC, although contact at this level will be even more crucial and of greater importance as further integration of the Community takes place. However, the 1991 Review of the Programme for Government 1989– 1993 indicates that the Government will propose the establishment of a European Affairs Committee with members of the European Parliament having the right of audience at its meetings.

Further European integration will result in changed roles and institutional relationships for many parts of the machinery of government. With more and more decision-making occurring in Brussels, and with an ever-growing body of Community law coming into effect, the role of the civil service will increasingly be that of translating EC directives into national law. This highlights the importance of procedures for monitoring the activities of the Council of Ministers as the competence of the Community expands.

Co-ordination: European Communities Committee

This committee, which is the main co-ordinating body on EC matters in Ireland predates EC membership. Until 1987 it was chaired by the Department of Foreign Affairs and was composed of the assistant secretaries of the Departments of the Taoiseach, Foreign Affairs, Agriculture and Food, Finance, Labour, and Industry and Commerce. Other departments were represented when the agenda covered matters relating to their area of competence. It has now been replaced by a new committee which is chaired, at the time of writing, by the Minister of State at the Department of the Taoiseach with responsibility for the co-ordination of government policy and EC matters. The creation of a ministerial post for EC affairs is an indication of the importance of this area. (A previous Taoiseach, Dr FitzGerald, had proposed, but not implemented, the division of the Department of Foreign Affairs and the creation of a Minister for European Affairs and Development Co-operation as a separate ministry with full departmental structures).

Meetings of the committee are attended, as occasion affords, by Ireland's permanent representative to the Community so as to maintain close relations between COREPER (the Committee of Permanent Representatives of the Member States) and the domestic civil service. It provides a forum for the most senior officials to exchange views on an interdepartmental basis, to discuss broad policy issues, to prepare regular reports for the cabinet, and to recommend national priorities in relation to the EC.

This situation contrasts sharply with that in some other member states. France, for example, has a Secrétariat Général and Comité Interministériel (SGCI) a 150-strong team, which co-ordinates France's interministerial initiatives and has sole co-ordinating responsibility for all negotiations between Paris and Brussels.

Joint Oireachtas Committee on Secondary Legislation of the EC

In 1973 a joint committee was set up on a statutory basis in order to strengthen the degree of control of the Oireachtas over EC secondary legislation. Its terms of reference allow it to consider and report on Community laws at every stage in the policy-making process. It examines EC acts, regulations and other instruments, together with draft EC legislation and the domestic implementing measures, and reports on them to both Houses of the Oireachtas. It is also required by its order of reference to examine the question of dual membership of the Oireachtas and the European Parliament. Participation in committee proceedings is open to all members of each House, with the right to vote confined to committee membership. The committee may recommend that any ministerial regulation made under the European Communities Act 1972 should be annulled. If a resolution annulling any such regulation is passed by both Houses within one year, it ceases to have statutory effect. Joint committee reports can be debated in the Dáil.

The life of the joint committee is coterminous with that of the Oireachtas. Membership is composed of eighteen members of the Dáil and seven members of the Seanad. Originally it was intended that ten of the members of the European Parliament would be part of the committee, but owing to difficulties in attendance this was subsequently changed to an entitlement to attend and participate, though not to vote. The chairman of the committee is usually a member of the main opposition party. Committee proceedings are open to the press, and reports of meetings are published, although the committee has the right to go into private session.

Hussey (1989: 14–15) states that the joint committee 'provides a useful forum for members of the Oireachtas to interface with representatives of professional and vocational bodies concerned with EC affairs, thus ensuring a cross-fertilisation of views with the adoption of common approaches towards proposals.' She comments, however, that 'the resources allocated to the committee unfortunately fall far short of what is regarded as adequate. The staff of the joint committee has been significantly reduced due to public sector cutbacks.' This is all the more important at a time when Ireland is facing a vastly increased body of EC law, given the legislative programme up to 1992 and beyond. Hussey notes that practically all member states have parliamentary committees to oversee Community legislation and suggests that the procedures of the Irish committee are in urgent need of review.

Committee on the Internal Market and Structural Funds

Until recently EC matters have had a low priority in domestic Irish politics. However, as a result of decisions taken by the European Council in 1987, there has been a reform of the Community's structural funds (the European Agricultural Guidance and Guarantee Fund, the European Social Fund and the European Regional Development Fund), with an expected doubling of their appropriations by 1992. The internal allocation of these funds in the country has become an item on the political agenda and has received sustained interest from political parties, pressure groups and the media. So also have the proposed reforms in the Common Agricultural Policy.

As the issues of the structural funds and the Single European Market developed, the Taoiseach Mr Haughey, established a special committee under his own chairmanship known as the Committee of Ministers and Secretaries on the Internal Market and Structural Funds in 1989. The remit of this committee has since been extended to include an examination of more general EC matters. This reflects the currently changing situation in which even highly technical subjects that were once only domestic in scope become politically charged at the international level.

THE POLITICAL IMPACT: GOVERNMENT AND ADMINISTRATION

The Civil Service

Adaptation to the demands of EC membership has been perhaps the greatest challenge faced by the Irish civil service since the foundation of the state. Not alone has participation in the European Community increased the range and complexity of the issues facing Irish civil and public servants by the addition of a new dimension to national policy-making, but membership has greatly increased the workload of many sections of the public service. As more and more issues fall within the ambit of the EC, a wider range of civil and public service agencies are becoming involved. All government departments and state agencies have been affected to varying degrees by membership. In the civil service the impact has perhaps been greatest in the central departments of Finance, Taoiseach and Foreign Affairs. Of the line departments which have responsibility for policy formulation and execution in specific sectors, the impact has been greatest in the Department of Agriculture and Food, which has been predominantly concerned with administering the Common

Agricultural Policy, and in the Department of Industry and Commerce, which is involved in the completion of the internal market.

Irish officials adopt an active approach to winning resources from the Community and have considerable expertise in regard to the guidelines and procedures associated with the various funds. Laffan (1989: 49) comments that 'Irish policy-makers have managed to secure a high proportion of the funds. Ireland received the highest per capita transfers from the structural funds between 1978 and 1980.'

Ireland, as a net beneficiary of all Community policies, has consistently adopted a positive role towards the development of the EC. Ireland has tried to look at the totality of relationships involved in EC membership and to be part of the development of these relationships. FitzGerald (1975: 5) noted that 'European idealism and Irish national interest have tended to coincide in Ireland's case.' This emphasis on what is often termed the communautaire approach connotes strong support of the EC's institutions and processes and of their further development as the most effective safeguard of the interests of a smaller member state. Coombes (1983: 9) comments that 'If the art of Community diplomacy is to win friends and influence people by displaying an understanding and commitment beyond immediate self-interest, then Irish representatives have certainly outdone the Britons and Danes.'

The Irish Permanent Representation in Brussels (in effect, the Irish embassy to the EC) is the largest Irish overseas mission and perhaps the most important. It consists of about fifty officials, of whom twenty are of diplomatic status. Their task is to act as a channel of communication from the Commission and the Council and to advise the government and departments about the strategies of other member states. The Permanent Representation services the meetings of COREPER and of many working parties of the Council.

The relatively small size of the European Commission means that the civil and public service has the responsibility for the implementation in Ireland of directly applicable community legislation. The relatively small size of the civil service facilitates informal and loosely structured administrative arrangements for the co-ordination of EC business; this enables a less formal and less institutionalised approach which can respond quickly. The civil and public service also evaluates the impact of Community policy in Ireland across a broad range of economic and social spheres. The greater use of qualified majority voting has speeded up the progress of directives through the Council hierarchy, so that national officials have now less time to prepare a response to Commission proposals and to ensure that Irish organisations are aware of the implications of proposed legislation.

It is suggested by some commentators that the linguistic attainments of staff will need to be monitored and developed as international contacts are expanded. Staff will need to be briefed and re-briefed on the complexities of the European

Community's institutions, policies and powers. Once the drive is over to complete the Commission's 279-measure programme of legislation in time for 1993, much more attention will be paid to implementation, compliance and enforcement issues to ensure that there is a single European market established on the ground. In this area member states' records on implementation are deteriorating due to the sheer volume of these directives. Commission officials have, where they could, been working closely with national authorities, offering assistance in getting the necessary legislation drafted and enacted. That technique has worked well in Ireland where encouragement from Brussels has quickened the pace of legislation. Hence there will be continuing focus and pressure put upon the enforcement agencies by the Community institutions and by national governments who are accountable to the Commission for compliance measures.

Department of Finance

The Department of Finance played a central role in negotiating Ireland's entry into the EC, and since the beginning it has had a large involvement with EC matters. While its co-ordinating role was gradually taken over by the Department of Foreign Affairs in the late 1970s, it continues to occupy a unique and prominent position in that it must be consulted by all other Departments on proposals that have expenditure implications. However, it has not overriding authority among government departments, and although it can advise, support and persuade, it cannot order; disagreements between departments have to be resolved at cabinet level.

The Department of Finance has retained responsibility for the important major sources of funds, together with control of the central economic issues such as the Community budget, Ireland's financial contributions, the Regional Fund, the European Monetary System and monetary policy, economic co-ordination, Community sources of finance, and the financial aspects of agriculture policy. Preparations for the single market will include the harmonisation of indirect taxes. This will entail major changes in the tax system—reductions in indirect taxes and in tax on interest on bank deposits. The need to replace this revenue through aternative taxes creates thorny political problems.

The European Regional Development Fund was set up in 1975 with the task of contributing to the correction of the principal regional imbalances within the Community. This it did by part-funding the expenditure of these regions on economic infrastructure and industrial promotion. In accordance with the EC's policy of focusing on national economic development, Ireland was designated as one region under the European Regional Development Fund and the Department of Finance retains control of the disbursement of these funds. Central government, through the Department of Finance, constitutes the regional development authority. Officials of the European

Commission have served on steering committees with Irish civil servants to oversee programmes such as the road development programmes.

Ireland has participated in the European Monetary System since its inception in March 1979. Successive Irish governments have insisted that development towards closer political integration must be based on the growing community of interest in the economic and social areas and, in particular, on the promotion of economic convergence between the more and less prosperous regions. This concern has been a central focus of Irish policy and administrations towards the EC. With GNP per head in Ireland running at two-thirds of the EC average, community help for the poorer regions holds obvious attractions.

Department of Foreign Affairs
The primary function of the Department of Foreign Affairs is to advise the government on Ireland's external relations and to act as the channel of official communication with foreign governments and international organisations. The role of the Department of Foreign Affairs in relation to the EC is primarily one of co-ordination, and to an extent it can be regarded as a gatekeeper between Dublin and Brussels. It does not get involved in the details of domestic policy; rather it tries to ensure that domestic departments adequately service meetings in Brussels and that policy developments in one sector do not impinge on general policy priorites. It integrates European business, maintains the priorities established between the various depart-ments, and ensures that policy remains coherent. It also acts as facilitator in disagreements between other departments over areas of competence.

The department plays a key role in Irish policy on European issues (e.g. in the discussions leading to the SEA) and in the domestic impact of European policies. The 1974 Paris summit gave the Ministers for Foreign Affairs the task of providing impetus and co-ordination to the development of the EC. Scott (1983: 84) notes that 'Foreign Affairs, hitherto a marginal department, made a successful quantum jump, enlarging its competences, mediating between other departments, and revolutionising its structure and staffing. However, it is impor-tant to recall that Finance kept the vital economic issues and major sources of funds to itself, leaving Foreign Affairs in sole charge of the political side, an area of absorbing interest to only a handful of officials, politicians, journalists and enthusiasts, and subject always to intervention by the Taoiseach.'

Department of Agriculture and Food
This department operates and implements EC schemes and regulations for agriculture. The Common Agricultural Policy (CAP) continues to contribute to the development and modernisation of Irish agriculture, both at farm and processing level. It provides strong market support for those products on

which Irish agriculture is particularly dependent, and it ensures vital outlets for agricultural exports through unlimited access to the Community market and by granting financial support in the form of export refunds so that Irish exports to countries outside the Community remain competitive.

While overall responsibility for the management of the CAP rests with the Commission, each member state plays an important role in the execution of the CAP through what are known as 'intervention agencies'. Those are the agencies which buy certain agricultural products from farmers when market prices fall below a certain level. In Ireland the Department of Agriculture and Food is the intervention agency. EC agricultural spending is provided from the European Agriculture Guidance and Guarantee Fund (EAGGF). The Guarantee section is responsible for financing export refunds and intervention to regulate internal markets (storage etc.), while the Guidance section is responsible for the financing of projects to improve agricultural structures in the member states. With the Guarantee section of the EAGGF under threat of a severe cut, the department faces a challenge in maintaining the development of Irish agriculture. Agriculture provides almost 15 per cent of Ireland's jobs, so reform of the CAP poses particular dangers. While the need for reform is acknowledged, it is less clear what reform package would prove less damaging.

Nearly all of the staff in the department are involved in EC affairs in one way or another. In 1989 some 1,300 officials attended 920 meetings in Brussels on agriculture-related matters.

Department of Labour
The Department of Labour is involved in the formulation and implementation of Community social and employment policy measures. It also formulates and transmits to the European Commission all Irish applications for assistance and claims for payment from the European Social Fund towards the cost of training and job-creation programmes. The main organisations assisted by the European Social Fund are the Training and Employment Authority (FÁS), the Industrial Development Authority (IDA), Shannon Free Airport Development Company (SFADCO), Údarás na Gaeltachta, Bord Iascaigh Mhara (BIM), CERT (the Hotel Staff Training Body), the Electricity Supply Board (ESB), the Irish Management Institute (IMI), the National Rehabilitation Board (NRB) and the Departments of Labour, Education and Environment.

Ireland's entry into the EC provided the decisive catalyst for change in the area of the statutory protection against sex discrimination in employment. The Anti-Discrimination (Pay) Act 1974 and the Employment Equality Act 1977 were enacted in order to implement Ireland's obligations under Council directives.

Department of Industry and Commerce

The Department of Industry and Commerce has responsibility for industrial development policy, science and technology, the development of exports of industrial products, international trade agreements and trade regulation, company and patents law, regulation of insurance companies and friendly societies, control of mergers, distributive trade legislation, consumer protection, and weights and measures. These are areas which are very much influenced by membership of the EC.

The Department of Industry and Commerce also oversees the implementation of the single market programme across government departments. Since more than half of the country's industrial output is exported, the freeing of restrictions on trade should prove beneficial. In other areas such as company law, for instance, EC directives have revolutionised practices in Ireland and have been incorporated in the Companies Act 1990. Commercial policy and competition policy are areas in which the EC has also made significant progress, which has had a major impact in Ireland as reflected in the Competition Act 1991.

EUROPEAN POLITICAL CO-OPERATION (EPC)

In 1970 the member states agreed to establish EPC as a means of co-ordinating foreign policy between them, and Ireland has participated in this system ever since it joined the EC. The goals of this co-operation are threefold:

(1). To ensure a better mutual understanding of the major problems of international politics through regular information and consultation;

(2). To promote the harmonisation of views and the co-ordination of positions;

(3). To attempt to achieve a common approach to specific cases.

EPC has been heralded as the best model for future European co-operation because of its flexibility, informality and confidentiality. It has had a significant impact on the work of the Department of Foreign Affairs. Concrete developments which have taken place in this context are: the transmission of a substantial number of telex and fax communications per week; monthly meetings of the foreign ministers to exchange information and to develop common standpoints; almost weekly meetings of national diplomats to examine important problems in international politics; regular declarations concerning issues of international tension in the name of the Community; representations of member states as one at international conferences and in international organisations; and discussions on political co-operation between the heads of state and government of the EC in the European Council. The exchange of information and views, part of the normal diplomatic process, has developed a 'co-ordination reflex' which makes the foreign policies of the various EC member states more transparent and predictable. The EPC process has in fact facilitated the emergence of a distinctive 'European' outlook or, in the words of Dr Garret FitzGerald, 'a common European viewpoint on so many issues, a viewpoint clearly differentiated from that of the super-powers or other political blocs'.

Political co-operation between the member states was introduced formally in the Single European Act, although it had previously been conducted on an informal basis. A secretariat is now established. Meetings take place monthly at official level and quarterly at ministerial level.

Since accession to the European Community Ireland has participated more actively in international affairs than at any time since the foundation of the state. This process has resulted in an expansion in the scope and range of issues facing the Irish diplomatic service, and indeed the civil service generally. Ireland has to be in a position to staff, and during the period of its presidency to chair, working groups on a wide variety of issues affecting different geographical areas or policy sectors. This process has culminated in the growth of a system of specialist officers dealing with particular areas or sectors.

In the later half of 1990 the emphasis moved increasingly towards political union in the EC. This culminated in an inter-government conference in Rome in December 1990 which discussed a wide range of proposals: transformation of the European Commission into an executive with an independent president; conversion of the Council of Ministers into an upper legislative house; strengthening the powers of the European Parliament; passing more EC laws on majority rather than unanimous votes; bolstering the authority of the Court of Justice; and a binding structure to produce a common stance in foreign policy, security and defence. Each of these proposals would significantly alter the EC landscape for the Irish civil and public service, together with business and industry, creating unprecedented challenges for Ireland's public servants. So, too, would the greater involvement of Ireland with the Western European Union and with proposals for a European defence policy.

The EC's drive towards political union receives little attention in Ireland. But one aspect of political union that does stir emotions is movement towards a common defence policy. This would run counter to Ireland's traditional neutrality, a policy which has yet to be re-formulated in the context of the new Europe.

TRANSNATIONAL INTEREST GROUPS

Many new alliances have been forged under the auspices of the European Economic Interest Grouping (EEIG), the Community's legal instrument for promoting cross-border co-operation between business partners since it was introduced by regulation in 1985. This is a new legal formula, perhaps the first to be truly European and one which is also highly flexible. It is available to all economic agents interested in developing their activities on a

Community scale in co-operation with partners from other member states. It aims to stimulate transnational economic co-operation, economic growth and the integration of the companies of Community member countries.

The Irish social partners are affiliated to European agencies which represent similar bodies in other member states. The Confederation of Irish Industry (CII) and the Federation of Irish Employers (FIE) are members of the Union of Industries of the European Community (UNICE). The Confederation of the Food and Drink Industries of the EC (CIAA) represents the interests of its members at Community level. There is also a European trade union representative body, the European Trade Union Confederation, to which the Irish Congress of Trade Unions is affiliated; this European body is closely linked to national sectoral bodies. COPA (Comité des Organisations Professionelles Agricoles) is the umbrella body of farmers' organisations from all the member states and includes the Irish Farmers' Association as the Irish representative. COGECA (Comité Général de la Co-operation Agricole de la CEE) is the representative body for agricultural co-operatives at Community level, and the Irish Co-operative Organisation Society Ltd is its Irish member.

These transnational interest groups have considerable power. Hussey (1989: 16) notes 'the challenge from the huge increase in the number and skill of interest groups. Their influence has given rise to certain apprehensions. The governments of member states have to consider ways of managing interest groups and ensure that their parliaments are not excluded from or crowded out to the periphery of the policy process.' The public sector must take care to ensure that its interests are well understood, not alone in Dublin but also in the Community's institutions, otherwise its concerns risk being overlooked, and regulatory or legal straitjackets may be imposed which are inappropriate and burdensome.

PREPARATION FOR THE INTERNAL MARKET

The European Community's drive to achieve the free internal flow of goods, services, money and labour by the end of 1992 is aimed at achieving lower costs as a result of doing business in a broader, single market. By the end of 1992 all remaining barriers to trade among the twelve nations of the European Community are scheduled to fall, creating a single economic unit encompassing 337 million people. This drive to bring down barriers and compete fairly across national boundaries has had implications for the government and public service of each member state. In Ireland a broad range of central government and state agencies are involved in the creation of the internal market.

The structural funds were earmarked for expansion to promote economic development in the less prosperous member states. In August 1988 the Minister for Finance announced a new regional consultative planning structure for Ireland, which was used in the preparation of the 'National Development Plan, 1989–93', submitted to the European Commission in March 1989. Seven regions were drawn up as a basis for subnational programmes for the structural funds; they have no wider function than this.

In each region a working group was formed to devise the programme for that region. Each working group was chaired by an official of the Department of Finance and involved county and city managers. Alongside these seven working groups were seven *ad hoc* advisory groups, each under an elected chairman and including the members of the county councils, city councils and larger urban district councils and local representatives of the social partners. These representative bodies included the Confederation of Irish Industry, the Construction Industry Federation, Chambers of Commerce, the Irish Congress of Trade Unions, the Irish Farmers' Association, the Irish Creamery Milk Suppliers' Association, and a number of others.

The Advisory Groups accepted submissions from interested bodies and persons. The National Development Plan contains material based on assessments received by the central government from the regional groups. Not only were economic and social interests consulted at local level through the regional advisory groups, but they were also consulted at national level through the Central Review Committee of the Programme for National Recovery and more recently the Programme for Economic and Social Progress. Priorities identified at regional level were reflected in the plan, although there was criticism of the degree of actual local consultation involved.

The plans and programmes of investment are part of a European Community policy to promote economic and social cohesion and to reduce disparities between the prosperous and less prosperous regions of the EC prior to the completion of the internal market. The European Commission, as part of the process of reforming the structural funds, has stipulated that, where appropriate, regional and local authorities should be involved in consultations leading to the drafting of multiannual programmes based on a particular sector or region.

The National Development Plan, 1989–93, for the first time in such a plan, shows planned expenditure in each region and sets out the public service agencies involved in the implementation of the development programmes. The agencies involved are listed in Appendix L.

CONCLUSION

In 1946 Winston Churchill said: 'We must build a kind of United States of Europe. If at first all states of Europe are not willing to join the union, we must nevertheless proceed to assemble and combine those who will and those who can.' Ireland has accepted the invitation to move further along the path to union.

The range of areas included in the competence of the EC is increasing all the time. At the June 1990 summit meeting of EC leaders in Dublin the idea of an 'energy community' was put forward by the Dutch Prime Minister. Exploratory talks between the Soviet Union and the EC were held with a view to diversifying Western Europe's supply by strengthening its gas pipeline system with the Soviet Union. The two intergovernmental conferences held in December 1990 on political reform of the EC's institutions, and economic and monetary union have demonstrated the flexibility and evolutionary nature of the EC in broadening its competence in areas not mentioned in the original Treaty of Rome or in the Single European Act. The agreement between the EC and the seven countries of the European Free Trade Association on the creation of a European Economic Area is further evidence of this. At the same time the number of countries expressing an interest in membership of the EC is increasing. In October 1991, the European Commission President, Jacques Delors, argued that immediately the Maastricht Summit was over, the EC needed to fix a new political and institutional rendezvous to prepare a structure for 24 to 30 members. Turkey applied for membership in 1987; Austria in 1989; Malta and Cyprus in 1990 and Sweden in 1991. Switzerland, Hungary, Czechoslovakia, Finland and Poland have made it clear that they too might be interested in joining. Predicting where the Eastern limits of an enlarged community might eventually lie has become impossible in the wake of the disintegration of the Soviet Union.

The political consequences of European integration will be just as important as the economic. There will be more pooling of sovereignty and a strengthening of Community institutions and powers, as well as intensified intergovernmental and inter-agency co-operation. Functions such as environmental health, food safety and policing are likely to be subject to more centralised direction. Others, such as economic development and training, are likely to be more decentralised as a result of Community pressures.

Changes in perspective and in organisation will be essential for managerial success in the public sector. The worldwide trends of internationalisation, liberalisation and harmonisation will continue to require constant reappraisal and review of the role, the functions and the procedures of public sector organisations.

With the prospect of major developments in the fields of political, social, economic and monetary union in the context of an enlarged European Community, it is clear that the performance of the political system, the civil service and public service in general in managing the potential and challenges of a truly integrated common market will shape the process of economic and social development in Ireland as it faces into the next century.

REFERENCES

Joint Committee on the Secondary Legislation of the EC, *Fifty-fifth Report—Functions and Work of the Joint Committee* (Dublin: Stationery Office, 1977), *National Development Plan, 1989–93* (Dublin: Stationery Office, 1989)

Barrington, Ruth, and Cooney, John, *Inside the EEC: An Irish Guide* (Dublin: O'Brien Press, 1984)

Coombes, David ed., *Ireland and the European Communities: Ten Years of Membership* (Dublin: Gill & Macmillan, 1983)

FitzGerald, Garret, Address to the Royal Irish Academy (10 Nov. 1975)

Hussey, Gemma, 'The Impact of 1992 on the Political System' (*Seirbhís Phoiblí*, Vol. 10, no.1 (1989), 13–17)

Laffan, Brigid, '"While you're over there in Brussels, get us a grant." The Management of the Structural Funds in Ireland' (*Irish Political Studies*, 4 (1989) 43–57)

Scott, Dermot, 'Adapting the Machinery of Central Government' (Coombes, op. cit. (1983) 68–88)

Appendix L
Main Public Service Agencies Involved in Implementation of the National
Development Plan, 1989–93

Tasks	Main Departments	Other Public Bodies
Overall economic and social policy including sectoral and regional planning; budgetary policy	Finance	County Development Teams
Industrial Development	Industry and Commerce; Gaeltacht; Education	Industrial Development Authority (IDA): Shannon Free Airport Development Company (SFADCO); Údaras na Gaeltachta (the Gaeltacht Authority); An Bord Tráchtála (Irish Export Board); EOLAS (Science and Technology Agency); National Development Corporation (NADCorp)
Tourism	Tourism, Transport and Communications; Office of Public Works	Bord Fáilte (Irish Tourist Board); SFADCO: Central and Regional Fisheries Boards; National Heritage and Arts Councils.
Agricultural and rural development	Agriculture and Food	Teagasc (Agriculture and Food Development Authority)
Fisheries; aquaculture	Marine	Bord Iascaigh Mhara (Sea Fisheries Board)
Telecommunications and postal services	Communications	Telecom Éireann; An Post
Transport	Environment; Tourism, Transport and Communications; Marine	Local Authorities; National Roads Authority; CIE (state transport authority); Aer Rianta (national airports company); Harbour Authorities
Energy and national resources	Energy	Electricity Supply Board; Bord Gais Éireann (Gas Board); Bord na Móna (Peat Development Board); Coillte (Irish Forestry Board).
Sanitary and other local services	Environment	Local Authorities
Education; training; employment	Labour; Education	FÁS (Training and Employment Authority); CERT (Council for the Education, Recruitment and training of staff for the Hotel, Catering and Tourism Industries); second- and third-level educational institutions

Source: *National Development Plan*, 1989–93 (Dublin: Stationery Office, 1989), 86.

12

The Management of Government

CHARACTERISTICS OF PUBLIC ADMINISTRATION

In considering the efficiency and effectiveness with which public sector tasks are carried out, it is necessary in the first instance to identify the unique aspects of public administration—those features distinguishing it markedly from management in the private sector:

(1) The prime purpose of public administration is to serve the public, i.e. to seek the common good.

(2) The public service is not judged on a profit basis.

(3) The activities of public servants are fixed by law.

(4) Public authorities have coercive powers; hence there is a need to provide for consultation, objection and appeal.

(5) There is fragmentation of authority and accountability in the public sector.

(6) The limited discretion and freedom of action of public administration.

(7) Public administration is carried on in a 'glass bowl' in that there is a high degree of transparency, with the taxpayers entitled to know how their money is being spent.

(8) Public administration has a social responsibility and has to balance achievement of the common good with the demands of vested interests. It also has to balance present necessities with future desirabilities.

(9) The much greater number of varying viewpoints which must be considered in the governmental process.

(10) There is need for a high degree of consistency in the actions of public servants.

(11) The public administrator works for, with and under the direction of politicians; hence public administration operates in a 'political milieu'.

(12) Public administration must act to compress the various demands made made upon it, e.g. education and health.

(13) The way in which things are done often owes more to political factors than to bureaucratic rationality.

(14) The system causes more time to be devoted to short-term issues than to long-term planning.

(15) Public administration deals with a great diversity of matters, many of which are purely governmental and which the government cannot opt out of, e.g. defence, prisons, social services, taxation.

(16) The scale, complexity, integrative and allocative functions of a society-wide base of public service operations, e.g. health and education.

(17) The difficulty of measuring much of the work of the public service.

(18) The concept of public accountability.

(19) Differences in organisation form and in employment practices e.g. local authorities and State-sponsored bodies.

(20) In much of what the government does it is immune from competition.

(21) Public administration does not depend on clients or customers for financial support.

(22) The problem of identification with the unit of organisation or overall government business organisation.

(23) The often simultaneous performance of competing functions in public administration, e.g. taxation and social welfare.

(24) An organisation culture determined by socio-political aims (in contrast to the market orientation of the private sector).

(25) The dual hierarchy of administrative and technical staff in the public service.

To this list might be added other aspects of the public service such as the fragmentation of authority and accountability; the need for equity and treating all citizens equally. Public sector management is largely concerned with a network of several different quasi-autonomous organisations which interact with each other. Indeed public service management has been described as 'getting things done through other organisations'.

PUBLIC MANAGEMENT

Private sector management models cannot be simply and directly transferred into the public sector. Private companies are essentially profit-making organisations, whereas public sector bodies aim to provide a high quality of 'service' (a much less measurable concept than 'profit'). Such differences, arising from fundamental institutional and political factors, account for the lack of success in past attempts to introduce business management practices directly into government.

Nevertheless, public administrators must ensure that the work is carried out with maximum efficiency and effectiveness. In order to achieve this, a new approach, termed 'public management' has developed which seeks to apply a business sector management approach to traditional public administration and to its concerns with democracy, accountability, equity, consistency and equality. It involves, for example, specialised methods of measuring outputs and outcome, always a problem in the public sector; hence the use of techniques such as performance indicators and cost-benefit analysis.

Action within the public service is subject to public accountability, enforced through the electoral system. The political process is not a limited one: all members of the public have the right of expression, and no issue, however small, can be assumed to be of no concern. In connection with the multifarious nature of the work undertaken in public management, Chase and Reveal (1983: 15–16) have commented:

> What makes public management so hard—and so interesting—is that all these players act simultaneously, with a few clear lines of authority, constantly changing public mandates, and frequent turnover of people. Getting the garbage picked up, a child treated for lead poisoning, a subway to the station on time, or an elderly person a social security cheque may not seem Herculean tasks. But when they are multiplied hundreds of times over, and their execution occurs in the context of the manager's environment, the real challenge of government becomes clear. The tasks can be done, and done well, by public managers who master their world; but such tasks can easily elude managers who are befuddled by the politics around them, disconcerted by the mixed signals they hear, and their own agenda and purpose.

The public service, particularly the civil service, operates under numerous constraints and controls which are not present in the private sector. Constraints include: social, economic, financial, legislative, political, international and accountability factors, such as the system of parliamentary questions, motions in the Dáil or Seanad, or the proximity of elections. An important constraint is the perplexity and vagueness of the objectives which the civil service organisations have, many of them of a social or redistributive nature, some of them conflicting. There are motivational constraints also in that the manager in the civil service is deprived of many of the motivational incentives and sanctions normally associated with such a post, e.g. there is no power to hire or fire, to award bonuses or to promote. Controls include these factors together with the Constitution, the cabinet, the judiciary and legal system, the Department of Finance, the Comptroller and Auditor General, the Public Accounts Committee, and public opinion and pressure groups.

PUBLIC SERVICE REFORM
Reform of the public service is a topic which sporadically rises to the top of the political agenda, only to submerge again rapidly. High levels of public expenditure and tax resistance have generated public interest in reform and

greater cost-effectiveness. Reform of the public service is necessitated by the desirability of structures changing to accommodate the changing responsibilities and tasks which the state carries out and the high rate of change in society generally. The emphasis on management, accountability, decentralisation, performance measurement, information technology and the image of the public service as well as the need for a clear set of goals and tasks clearly point to the need for an overhaul of the existing system of public administration.

The Irish public service has undergone a significant programme of change since the establishment of the Department of the Public Service in 1973. These changes range from the public service embargo on recruitment in 1981 to the more recent decision to establish delegated administrative budgets, together with other measures to improve efficiency and effectiveness which are outlined in this chapter. Public service reform is all the more important in a situation in which the public service has at its disposal a diminishing resource base which necessitates that greater care be taken to ensure that the decisions taken are the best available. The increased need for consultation and co-ordination has highlighted the need for reform. Reform can enhance control and lead to better informed and more considered decisions in the context of improved organisational communications.

Factors which make reform difficult include the fact that it is often experimental, threatening to security, externally motivated, based on personal orders, initiated during a time of crisis or radical change, and the difficulty of people changing the way they have traditionally undertaken tasks. The bureaucratic character of the civil service manifests itself in reluctance to delegate and in consequent centralisation of decision-making functions, excessive record-keeping, reliance on precedent, inflexibility, and resistance to change. The key to minimising these bureaucratic tendencies lies in increasing efficiency, enlarging external relations, minimising hierarchical tendencies, encouraging lateral mobility, improving personnel management and generally increasing the flexibility and initiative of the service. Reform depends, therefore, on emphasising the positive aspects of change and overcoming accumulated cynicism due to past unsuccessful changes. It has to straddle the political, managerial, and accountability dimensions. Various Public Service Advisory Councils have noted that successful reform depends on the commitment of elected representatives and of public servants, particularly civil servants. The preoccupation with Northern Ireland and European Community affairs; the economic situation nationally; changes of ministers and governments; fear of change; union attitudes; staff shortages and embargoes; public and voter apathy are also constraints.

In Ireland there have been two major blueprints for the reform of the public service in recent times. The Devlin Report (1969) presented a comprehensive plan based on two underlying principles: greater emphasis on policy-making, and the need for greater integration of the public service. The recommendations can be summarised under the headings of: the establishment of a Department of the Public Service and of a Public Service Advisory Council, the introduction of a policy-making core to be called the Aireacht (the senior staff closest to the Aire—the minister), a unified staff structure in government departments, classifications of jobs, career development, improved personnel practices, administrative audits, and appellate procedures.

The white paper *Serving the Country Better* (1985) was an important landmark in the development of the civil service and set out a blueprint for the future, together with a series of practical steps and initiatives to bring about the best possible, most cost-efficient and courteous service for the public. The emphasis in the white paper was on the introduction in all departments of management systems based on corporate planning and emphasis on personal responsibility for results, costs and service. A change of emphasis from public administration towards public management was the central theme of the paper. The need for clear aims and objectives in all public services was underlined.

Little progress has been made in implementing these proposals. However, the introduction of administrative budgets will effectively decentralise the administration of all government departments and provide a longer and more planned approach to management in the civil service as is discussed below under the heading of public financial management. In 1984 the Committee on Top-Level Appointments in the Civil Service was set up to make appointments on a more open basis. The appointment of an Ombudsman in 1984 was also a significant development.

EFFICIENCY AND EFFECTIVENESS

Performance measurement in the public sector is both necessary and difficult. It is necessary because it provides information about the way public sector resources are used and it enables politicians and bureaucrats to improve public sector efficiency and effectiveness. Difficulties arise from lack of data, ambiguity of methods, technical problems and scarcity of criteria.

Without good performance measures, public sector managers will be unable to assess how their organisation's activities are controlling the economy, efficiency and effectiveness. *Economy* is a matter of ensuring that actual inputs do not exceed planned inputs and of planning to reduce the level of input wherever possible and politically acceptable. The legislative and financial framework of the public sector encourages a concern for economy. *Efficiency* is usually expressed in terms of the ratio of output to input. This ratio can be improved by the 'productivity' route (input constant, output increased) or the 'economising' route (output constant, input decreased). The public service has tended to favour the latter route. *Effectiveness* has been relatively neglected until recently. Indeed, it could be argued that a rather narrow and short-term concern with economy and efficiency has sometimes been in conflict with longer-term effectiveness in the delivery of public services. Effectiveness is primarily concerned with outcomes or the ability to achieve intended results or ultimate objectives. As Drucker (1977: 44) remarks, 'Efficiency is concerned with doing things right. Effectiveness is doing the right things.'

Performance measurement in the public sector is still at a relatively early stage in its development. Performance measurement systems are however being increasingly introduced and are giving real effect to the concept of accountability, as well as facilitating interdepartmental comparisons and the assessment of progress over time.

There is at the same time a widespread recognition of the difficulties in applying performance indicators and of the fact that the diversity of output makes it very difficult in many instances to measure and evaluate an agency's output. In the civil service it is difficult to identify clearly a department's main operational objectives. Often these are contradictory, not alone between but also within departments. The Devlin Report recommended the establishment of an Effectiveness Audit Unit to be responsible for a 'unified direction of the public service', and the carrying out of performance audits.

Effectiveness criteria constitute major elements in the annual review by the Department of Finance in spending programmes. The higher profile now given to value for money has had a twofold effect. Firstly, it has heightened public expectations and, as a result, has applied pressure for management to seek ways of getting the maximum possible value from public spending. Secondly, it has focused attention on key areas and accelerated the changes which management were seeking. These changes can best be defined as an increasing thrust towards emphasis on economy, efficiency, and effectiveness. The overall effect has been to produce a significant cultural and managerial change, which is leading to the development of better measures of performance and a shift in measurement from activity to outputs.

The announcement by the Taoiseach of the establishment of an Efficiency Audit Group for the civil service in his speech to the Irish Management Institute Conference in Killarney in April 1988 is a further development in this process. The purpose of this group is 'to examine the methods and practices of all government departments in turn to ensure cost-efficiency. This is a concept which we have imported from Australia, where it has been successfully implemented. A similar process is operated in the UK.' The group is chaired by a professor of economics and includes other persons from outside the public service as well as senior officials. The savings such an audit could realise are exemplified by the indication given by the Department of Agriculture and Food early in 1988 that some 500 staff could be saved over the following two years by appropriate changes in administration. The group is examining the working and practices of each government department with a view to recommending improved or alternative practices and methods which would reduce costs and improve efficiency. In conjunction with departmental managements, it is seeking to establish whether, by more efficient or alternative work practices, costs could be reduced or a better service could be provided at the same cost.

INFORMATION TECHNOLOGY

Public services depend for their efficient operation on the collection, storage, processing, communicating and updating of large masses of data on all the various diverse aspects of national life. The significant advances in information technology have revolutionised public administration.

The dependence on information technology (IT) has evolved from modest beginnings in the early 1960s to a situation where computers are in widespread use today throughout the public service. Advances in technology, which resulted in the convergence of computers, telecommunications and office systems into what is now known as IT, have brought computing into the office environment where emphasis can also be laid on improving personal productivity and effectiveness by utilising mechanical means for obtaining, storing, using and communicating data.

The information technology era is generally acknowledged to have started around 1980. The period before that date is generally known as the data processing (DP) era. In recent years the technology has been developing at an accelerated rate of innovation and change. Software, systems design and telecommunications facilities have increased simultaneously. The progressive integration and linking of computer systems and networks has made office automation a reality.

There are three broad applications of information technology in the public service. The first concerns automation, the traditional form of data processing. This focuses on the use of computers and software to automate existing manual tasks and procedures. Typical applications include tax collection, issuing of social welfare payments, the automation of medical records, payroll, and personnel administration systems. The second application involves information. This requires the expansion and distribution of knowledge, created by IT, throughout the organisation in order to change behaviour. Examples of this include personnel management, financial planning, operations costing systems, budgetary control and efficiency monitoring applications. The third application focuses on transforming. IT is used to change the way the organisation works and to improve efficiency, enterprise, excellence, effectiveness and economy. Passenger scheduling in the airlines, electricity demand forecasting, collaborative systems, teaching systems, local area networks, decision support systems, and voice recognition systems are examples of this use of IT.

The role of information systems in the public service is changing rapidly. The information revolution, driven by dramatic improvements in cost and performance of the available technology, is radically altering the work environment of many organisations—restructuring whole programmes, realigning the balance of power and leverage of organisations and enabling services to be delivered more effectively. This transformation of role requires strategies for information systems to become an integral part of public sector strategy formulation. There is a recognition that, in developing the information strategy for the public service, the whole process must be adapted to the needs of managers and staff at all levels, and indeed led by them, not by the information specialists.

There are three conditions which are essential for effective implementation of change through utilisation of technology and innovation: these are

(1) The technology must be tailored to the needs of the organisation. Careful prior analysis and identification of needs and objectives must exist in any implementation strategy.

(2) A structure for mobilising and motivating people to change and to innovate must be built into the strategy.

(3) Careful assessment and understanding of the supports for, and more particularly the constraints on, adoption of the technology or innovation are critical in determining the strategy.

For public service managers, the critical issue is clear-cut: how best to allocate resources to capitalise on existing strengths while meeting the real needs of a constantly changing environment. Information technology has facilitated a process of information gathering, planning and decision-making to control and take advantage of change, rather than being driven by it. It provides accurate up-to-date information to facilitate the planning of successful programmes. It has made policy-making better informed and has contributed to flexibility, responsiveness, selectivity and better understanding. The rapid spread of the new technology into every kind of public service organisation has given rise to a range of issues that public service managers are addressing: freedom of information; organisation; security; and training. Management issues related to ensuring the most cost-effective operations are also important, as are personnel issues and related issues involving motivation, training, the retention of skilled staff, employee health and safety. New opportunities for applying this technology are becoming apparent at all times, as is most apparent in information-based authorities where the whole structure is being altered by the technology, e.g. computer-aided design, health care systems, electronic funds transfer, knowledge-based systems, and high-capacity digital communications networks.

The legal aspects of information technology are becoming increasingly important. The Data Protection Act 1988 gives effect to the European convention on the rights of individual privacy with regard to automated personal data. It distinguishes between data subjects, data controllers and data processors and provides for the appointment of an independent Data Protection Commissioner to supervise the operation of the legislation and to ensure that the code of conduct set out in it is scrupulously observed.

PERSONNEL MANAGEMENT

Personnel management is a crucial function of management, and one that may well determine the success or failure of an organisation. It is increasingly being recognised as one of management's toughest challenges, particularly in the public service in view of pay restraints, staff recruitment embargoes, voluntary redundancy, and natural wastage. Personnel management is particularly important in the Irish public service, which is very labour-intensive, employing over 196,000 people in over a thousand different grades. The fact that staff costs are such a high proportion of overall costs emphasises this and explains the efforts to reduce expenditure under this heading and to boost productivity. The emphasis has been placed on staff quality rather than on staff quantity—in recognition of the fact that management techniques are only as good as the people who use them.

The Department of Finance, in addition to its financial responsibilities, is responsible for the co-ordination of personnel and management policies across the whole public service. It has, however, no power to assume responsibility for activities within the service, or to enforce total co-ordination. It can issue guidelines, clarify objectives, enumerate resources and advise on implementation, but the active co-operation of individual departments and agencies is essential.

Of all the skills that managers require, perhaps the one that is most important is motivation. Speaking about motivation, in 1982 Mr Kevin Murphy, then Secretary of the Department of the Public Service, said:

> It has been said that today's civil service is much younger, more likely to see the civil service as a job which can be left if something better turns up, not particularly influenced by the ethics of public service and not particularly convinced that they should break their necks to achieve ministerial and governmental objectives, many of which they feel are not to the benefit of society or themselves.

These remarks are even more valid now than when they were made.

There are four broad strategies for improving motivation through the use of non-material incentives: increased use of participation in decision-making; using supervisory relationships effectively; improving the cohesiveness of working groups; and improving the content of jobs through job enrichment, job enlargement and job rotation. The suitability of these four resources depends, to a large extent, on the culture of a given organisation, which is an important determinant of their potential effectiveness. An example of a successful strategy to improve motivation is the Electricity Supply Board

'Bright Ideas' Programme, inaugurated in 1990. The total savings generated by this programme—a more sophisticated version of the staff suggestion scheme model—are estimated to be in the region of £11.5 million, a figure that far exceeded the most optimistic predictions.

Management and leadership are inextricably intertwined. Whereas management is something objective, leadership is subjective. Leadership is difficult to define, almost impossible to measure objectively, and cannot be taught in a lecture theatre. Yet it is always palpably there in every public sector organisation, reflecting the character and personality of the chief executive and his/her top management team.

Major changes are on the horizon for personnel policies in the Irish public service. Excellence in serving the public will require excellence in employee relationships. A performance-orientated culture is emerging and is driven by the increasing focus on privatisation and diversification in the public sector.

The trend is away from the multi-layered hierarchical organisation with well-defined job boundaries. Information technology is eroding some of the middle layers, leaving a flatter type of organisation in which there will be greater scope for employee participation in project teams which will have the flexibility to expand or contract to meet changing circumstances and targets. This will necessitate fewer constraints on flexibility to deploy staff and skill where needed. While such employee involvement will be difficult to implement, it will facilitate participation in target setting and more direct feedback on employee efforts. Employee commitment will be raised, and more fulfilling work will be available.

The rigid incremental pay systems which are based on relativities and have long been a feature of Irish industrial relations will tend to be replaced by reward packages that are individually tailored to meet specific organisational needs. The emphasis is now on reward mechanisms that differentiate between levels of performance. Here also the concept of 'permanent pensionable employment', traditionally associated with the public sector, will fall away. For example, at management level, top quality business experts will command a market-related reward package centred around fixed-term contracts which will emphasise achievement.

TRAINING AND DEVELOPMENT

Training and development are concerned with assessing what knowledge, skills, attitudes and expertise are required and continually ensuring that these are provided through appraisal and training both on and off the job.

The benefits of training in the public service are: more rapid development to full proficiency; increased productivity; improved quality of service, less wastage of time and materials; better utilisation of office equipment and technology; reduced unit costs; decreasing the amount of supervision; revealing the special talents of employees; increasing the versatility of employees; and, most importantly, improving motivation and morale. Training in the public service is aimed at staff groups at all levels of seniority and is a combination of on-the-job and off-the-job training on specific courses.

In the 1950s and 1960s the initial training programmes in the public service concentrated exclusively on traditional public administration subjects: public personnel management, organisation and methods (O & M) services, principles of organisation, government accounting and auditing, and so on. Although these subjects still make up a good portion of current training programmes, newer ones—such as information technology, policy analysis, industrial relations, organisation development, attitudinal and behavioural change, and information systems—are now being included. In addition, there is greater emphasis on management training for specific programmes and institutions (e.g. health service, local authorities and public enterprise). Training is increasingly oriented towards the application of information technology. Emphasis is on 'user skills' such as using keyboard and manuals, knowledge of computer conventions and limitations, assessing and manipulating data from a data base, using packages and on-line inquiry facilities, and dealing with faults and difficulties as they arise.

However, pressure on staff resources has led to a significant reduction of staff training throughout the public service. The past decade has been characterised both by significant developments in technology and by restrictions on resources. In the civil service the response has been to provide training on information technology for all grades, along with the establishment of learning groups within and among departments. Restrictions on resources have prompted a greater emphasis on communication between senior managers in order to assist in the development of a coherent, service-wide approach to common issues.

The amount of off-the-job training for civil service staff is low. Departments have had heavy pressures on them in the past decade with cutbacks in staffing levels and increased volumes of work which, they maintain, has made it more difficult to release much-needed staff to attend training courses. The Report of the Advisory Committee on Management Training (1988) found that while public service organisations spent more on management development than the average for all private sector companies, this was well below the average for large companies.

One of the difficulties with training and staff development is that the essentially long-term nature of the process may discourage investment. Furthermore, it is difficult in many cases to define and measure effective performance and to attribute improvements to the training cycle. Another difficulty is the concentration on post-entry and post-promotion training, to the neglect of in-service training and the training needs of lower-level staff in particular. Training is often seen as a luxury and an activity that has little or no effect. Public servants seldom demand training, unless they want a break from their daily routines, as the outcomes they expect from it are not of high value to them.

A flexible and dynamic public service requires a responsive and forward-looking training system. Training is clearly an integral part of the government's personnel management function; and policy and plans in training are therefore inseparable from policies governing other aspects of personnel management. Promotion, performance appraisal, staff deployment and career development should be closely linked with an effective training system. Although training alone is not a panacea for all the ills of the public service, it is an important instrument for improving organisational performance.

PUBLIC FINANCIAL MANAGEMENT

Evaluation

The evaluation of public financial management is largely a function of the way in which government works. Important factors in this context are:

(1) The structure of government is cellular and adversarial. Contrary to the description in management textbooks, there is not a solitary decision-maker with full authority over the conclusion of the evaluation.

(2) Attempts by one part of the public sector to accomplish its goals may make it more difficult for other public service agencies to achieve theirs.

(3) Government programmes are interactive, not static.

(4) Time is the scarcest resource in evaluation. The next scarcest resource is relevant facts. There is little time for basic research, and it is a question of mobilising what is already known.

(5) Owing to the interaction between different policy areas (such as social welfare and taxation), decisions can be made for reasons extraneous to the programmes most affected. Thus there is a danger of saying: 'Let's leave the administrative details until later.'

(6) Public policy issues tend not to be resolved at one attempt. Evaluation of public management is a continuous process, involving a systematic overall evaluation of the total range of services.

(7) Evaluation of policies focuses attention on the termination stage. In the public sector, terminations of programmes are quite rare.

Public policies often develop a life of their own with regard to the organisational factors and the clientèle groups which sustain them. It is often said that it is more difficult to terminate a scheme that has outlived its usefulness than to introduce a scheme that is demonstrably beneficial. There is, in addition, considerable reluctance to measure the effect of public expenditure programmes.

Financial Management Systems

The Irish system of public financial management puts considerable emphasis on accountability and parliamentary control over public expenditure. The formal system has, however, little to do with the appraisal of the efficiency and effectiveness of various public expenditure programmes. The budget is concerned with economic and social policy rather than with financial management, Dáil business focuses on the day-to-day administration of departments. The Comptroller and Auditor General, appointed under Article 33 of the Constitution, has two main statutory functions. The first, as Comptroller General of the Exchequer, is to ensure that no money is issued from the Central Fund by the Minister for Finance except for purposes approved by the Oireachtas. The second, as Auditor General, is to audit government accounts for accuracy and regularity. His reports are influential in helping to shape the recommendations of the Public Accounts Committee.

The Department of Finance has a central role in public financial management in Ireland. It has the statutory function to administer the public finances, to control the collection and expenditure of revenues, to supervise the purchases and disposal of commodities by departments, and to promote economic and social planning. It apprises the government of the full expenditure implications of policy proposals. Every submission to the government and every proposal for legislation includes details of estimated costs and how these should be financed. Submissions to the government must have been presented in advance to the Department of Finance so that that department may include its comments and advice to the government.

The Department of Finance is also empowered to review the structures and procedures adopted by other civil service departments and offices. It has responsibilities for personnel policy and organisational issues, a task formerly carried out by the Department of the Public Service, established in 1973 and subsumed into the Department of Finance in 1987. In addition, it has a responsibility to control, supervise, co-ordinate and advise all other government departments in financial matters. Instructions and advice are communicated to departments by official letters, minutes and circulars. These instructions are observed by departments because of the primacy of the Department of Finance in the administration of the public finances.

Each department is obliged to prepare and update on a regular basis its own plans for developing financial management within broad guidelines set by the Department of Finance. These guidelines are flexible and are continually being revised to take account of new situations. For example, the Department of Finance has issued detailed instructions in relation to 'letters of comfort', written assurances which expressly or by implication give a guarantee or undertaking not already authorised by legislation. The issue of such letters is not permitted under any circumstances, as they may be interpreted as imposing a liability on the Exchequer without Dáil approval.

In general, the main features of financial management include:

(1) an explicit and clear statement of departmental aims and objectives and specific results to be achieved;

(2) a top management system;

(3) a framework for delegation of responsibility for resources to line managers to enable them to manage their resources better;

(4) an effective budgetary control system;

(5) full costs of departmental operations, activities and programmes to be obtained;

(6) monitoring of performance against plans/targets;

(7) carrying out periodic in-depth evaluations of major departmental operations and programmes;

(8) proper appraisal of capital projects, including construction projects;

(9) good asset management;

(10) proper cash management;

(11) effective monitoring and control procedures vis-à-vis bodies under the aegis of departments;

(12) internal audit;

(13) effective use of modern technology, techniques and methods;

(14) prompt and effective implementation of findings of all reviews.

A number of deficiencies of Irish financial procedures have been noted; these include:

(1) the strong emphasis on inputs and paucity of information on outputs or impacts;

(2) the difficulty in introducing new services, compared with the relative ease in obtaining an increase in allocation for existing services;

(3) the obligation to surrender to the Exchequer the balance of any grants not spent at the end of the year. This creates an incentive for officials to spend their full allocation, whether or not this is in the national interest; hence also a continual tendency for public expenditure to drift upwards;

(4) the lack of uniformity of subhead classifications, making it difficult to isolate the annual cost of any service;

(5) the relative scarcity of unit cost data, of performance reporting systems and of planning targets and forecasts, making financial analysis difficult;

(6) the strains upon the system in recent years through having to cope with functions (e.g. the EC intervention scheme) not envisaged at its inception.

The focus in recent years has shifted from financial management to financial control. The Government's 1981 discussion document *A Better Way to Plan the Nation's Finances* suggested a more systematic analysis and evaluation of departments' programmes. The issue of the 'Comprehensive Public Expenditure Programmes' series which began in 1983 made available a broad range of material on public expenditure programmes. The publication by the Department of Finance of guidelines for financial management in 1984 has led to an improvement in standardising the treatment of financial matters within the civil service and in the review of all departmental activities. The most significant development in this regard was the announcement by the

Minister for Finance, Albert Reynolds, in the 1990 budget of his intention to fix administrative budgets on a three-year cycle, 'which would involve a real reduction in funding each year because of greater efficiency but which would allow greater managerial flexibility within those budgets'. The Department of Social Welfare, the Revenue Commissioners and the Department of Energy were targeted as the first three offices to change to the new system, as between them they represented almost one-third of the civil service. The scheme was extended to the entire civil service with effect from March 1991.

Under the new scheme, the heads of departments will have flexibility to strike a balance in the amount of their overall budget to be spent on the various components of their departments. One radical aspect of the new arrangement is that any savings made by a department can be used the following year in whatever area the head of department or line manager would think appropriate to the effective running of the department. Departmental heads will also have control of staffing up to and including higher executive officers level. For example, if the budget permits, a head of department could cut overtime and make a permanent appointment(s) instead. Pay increases will remain under the control of, and be paid separately by, the Department of Finance.

The emphasis is shifting towards control of the size of the original allocation to departments set in the first place, rather than the control of the spending of this. However, in order to ensure control of expenditure and adequate notice of deviations from target, departments are required to submit a monthly profile of expenditure to the Department of Finance for approval, showing how they propose to disburse their allocated funds over each spending area for the year. The sanction of the Department of Finance is also required before expenditure (whether new or additional) is incurred. The government is also examining ways of obtaining better value for money in the state-sponsored sector. Public enterprises have been subject to greater budgetary control, and corporate planning systems have also been introduced.

In a critical review in 1986 of past and current perceptions of financial management techniques, the then Secretary of the Department of Finance, Mr Maurice Doyle (now Governor of the Central Bank), referred to the persistent refusal of government departments 'to accept that they have any overriding responsibility to control, much less reduce, expenditure' and added that 'the consistent view taken over thirty-five years by managers, administrators and the so-called commercial state sector has been that it was the function of the Department of Finance to raise money and theirs to spend it.' He concluded: 'Government expenditure is not simply a management or an accounting process; it is the fiscal expression of governing and must, therefore, involve politicians.' It seems clear, therefore, that solutions to the basic problems of public finance depend largely on political will to achieve results rather than on the budget process or structures.

CONCLUSION

The public sector is distinctly different from the private sector. These differences can be explained, for the most part, by the levels of accountability which apply in the public sector. There are five such levels: political, public, legal, system, and market. In the private sector the market place provides the major element of accountability, and for this reason private sector management models cannot be transferred to the public sector without substantial adaptation.

While management practices in public service institutions are undergoing substantial changes in response to fundamental shifts in the work environment, they will have to continue to seek new levels of flexibility and selectivity and to learn to respond more quickly and effectively to diverse needs and clients. Previously the environment of the service was characterised by stability, continuity and predictability. In this context, standardised rules, centralised authority, machine-like organisations, predictable demand and given ends were very useful, particularly against a background of a steady supply of resources, and widespread consensus on the aims of the organisation. Slow adaptation, gradual evolution and emphasis on efficiency were perhaps an adequate method of survival. Now, however, the environment of the public service is characterised by constant change, pressures for the rationalisation of services, and funding constraints demanding cost-effective, efficient services and the need for choice between competing demands for limited resources.

For the reasons advanced in the preceding pages, and others which will no doubt continue to emerge, public management will be even more challenging in the years ahead.

REFERENCES

Report of Public Services Organisation Review Group, 1966–69 [Devlin Report] (Dublin: Stationery Office, 1969)

Serving the Country Better: A White Paper on the Public Service (Dublin: Stationery Office, 1985)

Chase, Gordon, and Reveal, Elizabeth C., *How to Manage in the Public Sector* (London: Addison–Wesley, 1983)

Drucker, Peter, *Managing for Results* (New York: Harper & Row, 1964)

Drucker, Peter: *Management* (London: 1977)

Blennerhasset, Evelyn: 'Senior Civil Servants and Information Technology: experience of pilot management development programme' (Dublin: Institute of Public Administration, 1987)

Managers for Ireland—The Case for the Development of Irish Managers (Dublin: Stationery Office, 1988)

Index

240   *Irish Government Today*